GREAT CAMP...

The Second Bull Run Campaign

GREAT CAMPAIGN SERIES

The Antietam Campagin
The Atlanta Campaign
The Chancellorsville Campaign
The First Air Campaign
The Gettysburg Campaign
Jackson's Valley Campaign
The Little Bighorn Campaign
MacArthur's New Guinea Campaign
The Midway Campaign
The Peninsula Campaign
The Petersburg Campaign
The Philadelphia Campaign
Rommel's North Africa Campaign
The Shiloh Campaign
The Vicksburg Campaign
The Waterloo Campaign

GREAT CAMPAIGNS

THE SECOND BULL RUN CAMPAIGN

July - August 1862

David G. Martin

DA CAPO PRESS
A Member of the Perseus Books Group

Cataloging-in-Publication data for this book is available from the Library of Congress.

First Da Capo Press paperback edition 2003
Originally published by Combined Publishing in 1997
ISBN 0-306-81332-7

Published by Da Capo Press
A Member of the Perseus Books Group
http://www.dacapopress.com

Da Capo Press books are available at special discounts for bulk purchases in the U.S. by corporations, institutions, and other organizations. For more information, please contact the Special Markets Department at the Perseus Books Group, 11 Cambridge Center, Cambridge, MA 02142, or call (800) 255–1514 or (617) 252–5298, or e-mail j.mccrary@perseusbooks.com.

1 2 3 4 5 6 7 8 9—07 06 05 04 03

Contents

Maps

Sidebars

Preface to the Series

*J*onathan Swift termed war "that mad game the world so loves to play." He had a point. Universally condemned, it has nevertheless been almost as universally practiced. For good or ill, war has played a significant role in the shaping of history. Indeed, there is hardly any human institution which has not in some fashion been influenced and molded by war, even as it helped shape and mold war in turn. Yet the study of war has been as remarkably neglected as its practice has been commonplace. With a few outstanding exceptions, the history of wars and of military operations has until quite recently been largely the province of the inspired patriot or the regimental polemicist. Only in our times have serious, detailed, and objective accounts come to be considered the norm in the treatment of military history and related matters.

Yet there still remains a gap in the literature, for there are two types of military history. One type is written from a very serious, hightly techinical, professional perspective and presupposes that the reader is deeply familiar with background, technology, and general situation. The other is perhaps less dry, but merely lightly reviews the events with the intention of informing and entertaining the layperson. The qualitative gap between the two is vast. Moreover, there are professionals in both the military and in academia whose credentials are limited to particular moments in the long, sad history of war, and there are interested readers who have a more than passing understanding of the field; and then there is the concerned citizen, interested in understanding the phenomenon in an age of unusual violence and unprecedented armaments. It is to bridge the gap betwen the two types of military history, and to reach the professional and the serious amateur and the concerned citizen alike, that this series, *The Great Campaigns of Military History*, is designed.

The individual volumes of *The Great Campaigns of Military History* are each devoted to an intensive examination of a particularly significant military operation. The focus is not on individual battles, but on campaigns, on the relationship between movements and battles and how they fit within the overall framework of the war in question. By making use of a series of innovative techniques for the presentation of information, *The Great Campaigns of Military History* can satisfy the exacting demands of the professional and the serious amateur, while making it possible for the concerned citizen to understand the events and the condtions under which they developed. This is accomplished in a number of ways. Each volume contains a substantial, straight-forward narrative account of the campaign under study. This is supported by an extensive series of modular "side-bars." Some are devoted to particular specific technical matters, such as weaponry, logistics, organization, or tactics. These modules each contain detailed analyses of their topic, and make considerable use of "hard" data, with many charts and tables. Other modules deal with less technical matters, such as strategic analyses, anecdotes, personalities, uniforms, and politics. Each volume contains several detailed maps, supplemented by a number of clear, accurate sketch-maps, which assist the reader in understanding the course of events under consideration, and there is an extensive set of illustrations which have been selected to assist the reader still further. Finally, each volume contains materials designed to help the reader who is interested in learning more. But this "bibliography" includes not merely a short list of books and articles related to the campaign in question. It also contains information on study groups devoted to the subject, on films which deal with it, on recordings of period music, on simulation games and skirmish clubs which attempt to recreate the tactics, on museums where one can have a first-hand look at equipment, and on tours of the battlefields. The particular contents of each volume will, of course, be determined by the topic in question, but each will provide an unusually rich and varied treatment of the subject. Each volume in *The Great Campaigns of Military History* is thus not merely an account of a particular military operation, but it is a unique reference to the theory and practice of war in the period in question.

The Great Campaigns of Military History is a unique contribution to the study of war and of military history, which will remain of interest and use for many years.

CHAPTER I

Spring 1862

The course of the Civil War changed drastically in May 1861 when the Confederate Congress decided to move their capital from Montgomery, Alabama, to Richmond, Virginia. Richmond was located some six hundred miles northeast of Montgomery, but was just over ninety miles due south of the Federal capital at Washington, D.C. The proximity of the two opposing capitals would act as a magnet to draw huge numbers of troops on both sides, as each government sought to defend its base of operations from the enemy's army's massed nearby. For this reasons, Virginia quickly became the cockpit of the war, and remained so until the very end.

The primary Federal strategy in Virginia from the very beginning was to advance and capture the Confederate capital at Richmond, and thereby deliver the knockout blow that they hoped would end the war promptly. The North's road to Richmond, however, had to cross a number of major waterways, each of which offered favorable defensive positions to the South's armies. As a result, Bull Run and the Rappahannock, Rapidan, Mattapony, North Anna and Chickahominy Rivers soon became as noted as the Potomac and the James. Because of the armies' slow march rates (ten miles was usually considered a good day's effort) and the constricted area of the Virginia theater between the mountains to the west and the ocean to the east, most of the fighting there consisted of set piece battles on well traveled terrain. Only occasionally were there wide open campaigns in Virginia itself, such as Jackson's spring 1862

McDowell's camps near Blackburn's Ford on Bull Run on 4 July 1862. McClellan had been counting on McDowell to join him for the final attack on Richmond, but McDowell was detained to cover Washington because of Jackson's successes in his spring 1862 Shenandoah Valley campaign.

Shenandoah Valley campaign, and the fall 1863 Bristoe campaign. Just once did a wide open campaign in Virginia lead to a major full scale battle within the state, and that was at Second Bull Run.

The first Northern "On to Richmond!" campaign in 1861 pretty much set the tone for the rest of the war. After the fall of Fort Sumter on 14 April 1861, President Lincoln sent out a call for 75,000 volunteers. By early July some 35,000 Union troops—the largest army yet assembled in the western hemisphere—were gathered at Washington under Brigadier General Irvin McDowell. At the same time, Confederate General P.G.T. Beauregard gathered some 20,000 men at Manassas and Centreville, located less than twenty miles from the advance Union posts outside Alexandria. McDowell was under a heavy pressure to attack before the ninety-day enlistments of many of his troops expired. He marched out of Alexandria on 16 July and took almost three full days to reach Centreville. After the Confederates withdrew to a position behind nearby Bull Run, McDowell set out to attack them on the morning of 21 July. The Union forces gained an initial advantage due to McDowell's flank attack on Beauregard's left, but the tide of battle was soon turned by a large number of Confederate reinforcements under General Joseph E. Johnston that had just arrived from Winchester. By the end of the day the defeated Yankees were streaming back to Washington, but the Confederates were too exhausted and disorganized to follow up their victory.

It was now clear to everyone in Washington that the war was not going to be decided quickly. Lincoln called for thousands of more men to be raised and forwarded to the capital in order to keep it out of enemy hands. To lead this enlarged army, Lincoln selected Major General George B. McClellan, a pre-war acquaintance who had been conducting a successful minor campaign in western Virginia. McClellan assumed command of the Union troops in Washington on 27 July and soon secured the city's defenses, so assuaging Lincoln's fears of an attack or siege by the enemy. McClellan then set about creating what he christened the *Army of the Potomac*, which would become the North's single largest and most famous field command in the war.

McClellan was a great organizer but was reluctant to take the field against an enemy army that he was convinced was at least as large as his own. He did not begin formulating serious campaign plans until the end of January 1862, after Lincoln threatened to take direct command of his army. His strategy was a novel one—to conduct an amphibious movement to Fort Monroe, located about 70 miles east of Richmond, and then advance against the Confederate capital from the east instead of moving directly against Johnston's army, then still encamped at Manassas.

McClellan began moving to the Peninsula on 17 March, taking with him some 121,500 men. He claimed that he was leaving 73,500 men to protect the capital as Lincoln had ordered, but the President was dismayed to learn that these numbers were padded in numerous ways, with only 26,700 actually in or near Washington. As a result, Lincoln ordered Major General Irvin McDowell's *I Corps* to stay behind at Manassas and not join McClellan's campaign. The loss of McDowell's 40,000 men would be a great blow to McClellan's campaign plans.

Major General George B. McClellan, commander of the Army of the Potomac, did not much care for Pope, particularly since their temperaments and politics were so different. His delay in pushing reinforcements to Pope, particularly during the last week of August, may have contributed to the extent of the Union defeat.

Instead of moving rapidly on Richmond once he reached Fort Monroe, McClellan allowed his command to become bogged down for a month in front of the Confederate defenses erected near Yorktown. This delay enabled Johnston to move his entire army to oppose McClellan. The Union commander, however, eventually forced Johnston to abandon Yorktown, and by May had approached almost to within sight of Richmond. McClellan then revived his hopes of having McDowell march to join him from Fredericksburg, provided that Nathaniel Banks could secure the upper Shenandoah Valley. McClellan's plans, though, were severely upset by Jackson in Stonewall's famous Shenandoah Valley campaign, which culminated in the twin Confederate victories at Cross Keys and Port Republic on 8-9 June 1862.

After completing his mission so ably, Jackson was called to Richmond on 17 June to help deal with McClellan. He left in his wake the defeated remains of three separate Union commands, Fremont's, Banks' and McDowell's. At long last Lincoln saw the error of his ways, the fact that the lack of a unified command structure in the Shenandoah Valley area had been one of the principal causes of Jackson's success. For this reason he decided on 26 June to unify these commands into one army, to be called the *Army of Virginia*.

What's in a Name

Many Civil War battles are known by more than one name. Often the Confederates would call a battle by the name of the closest town (Manassas, Sharpsburg, Murfreesboro), while the Federals would prefer to name the battle after a nearby river or stream (Bull Run, Antietam, Stones River). Other battles were sometimes called by the part of the field where the victorious side had the greatest success over its opponent (Pittsburg Landing/Shiloh, Pea Ridge/Elkhorn Tavern). For these and other reasons, each major action of the Second Bull Run campaign had an alternate name: Cedar Mountain/Slaughter Mountain; Groveton/Gainesville; 2nd Manassas/2nd Bull Run; Chantilly/Ox Hill. The battle of Fraser's Farm, fought on 30 June 1861 during the Seven Days Battle, was known by no less than seven alternate names.

Date	Battle Name (Union preference)	Alternate Name
21 July 1861	1st Bull Run	1st Manassas
7-8 Mar 1862	Pea Ridge	Elkhorn Tavern
6-7 April 1862	Pittsburg Landing	Shiloh
31 May-1 June 1862	Fair Oaks	Seven Pines
26 June 1862	Beaverdam Creek	Mechanicsville
27 June 1862	Gaines' Mill	1st Cold Harbor
30 June 1862	Frayser's Farm	Glendale, Nelson's Farm, Charles City Cross Roads, New Market Cross Road, Willis Church, White Oak Swamp, Turkey Bend
9 Aug 1862	Cedar Mountain	Slaughter Mountain
28 Aug 1862	Gainesville	Groveton
29-30 Aug 1862	2nd Bull Run	2nd Manassas
1 Sept 1862	Chantilly	Ox Hill
17 Sept 1862	Antietam	Sharpsburg
8 Oct 1862	Perryville	Chaplin Hills
31 Dec 1862 1 Jan 1863	Stones River	Murfreesboro
20 Feb 1864	Olustee	Ocean Pond
23-24 July 1864	Winchester	2nd Kernstown
19 Sept 1864	Opequon	3rd Winchester
6 April 1865	Sayler's Creek	Harper's Farm

Losing Union Commanders in Virginia

General/Army	Dates of Command	Won	Lost
Irvin McDowell *Northeastern Va.*	27 May 61 to 25 July 61		lst Bull Run
George B. McClellan *Potomac*	25 July 61 to 9 Nov 62	Antietam (draw)	Seven Days
John Pope *Virginia*	26 June 62 to 12 Sept 62		2nd Bull Run
Ambrose Burnside *Potomac*	9 Nov 62 to 26 Jan 63		Fredericksburg
Joseph Hooker *Potomac*	26 Jan 63 to 28 June 63		Chancellorsville
George Meade *Potomac*	28 June 63 to 27 June 65	Gettysburg	
U.S. Grant *Com in Chief*	12 Mar 64 to 4 Mar 69	Petersburg Richmond Appomattox	Wilderness Spotsylvania Cold Harbor

Union Commanders in Chief

Winfield Scott	1841 to 6 Nov 61
George B. McClellan	6 Nov 61 to 11 Mar 62
Office vacant	11 Mar 62 to 11 July 62
Henry W. Halleck	11 July 62 to 12 Mar 64
U.S. Grant	12 Mar 64 to 4 Mar 69

CHAPTER II

The Arrival of Pope

Once President Lincoln made his belated decision to created a united army out of the previously disjointed Union forces in northern Virginia, he faced a still more difficult choice on whom to select to command it. The three leaders of the new army's major component parts were all senior major generals, but each suffered stigmas from major defeats (Fremont and Banks in the recently completed Valley campaign, McDowell from First Bull Run). None of the senior commanders in McClellan's *Army of the Potomac* were really battle tested, and they were not available to be transferred, anyway, because McClellan was then entering the climax of his campaign at the gates of Richmond. A logical choice to command the newly created *Army of Virginia* would have been Major General Ambrose E. Burnside, who was then enjoying the fruits of his successful operation along the coast of North Carolina. Burnside had the necessary aura of success and was certainly available at the time, but Lincoln may have bypassed him because he was a Democrat; the administration already had its hands full with another strong willed Democrat general named McClellan. It is also possible that Lincoln was keeping Burnside available as a possible replacement for McClellan should the latter falter at Richmond; Burnside was indeed offered command of the *Army of the Potomac* around 25 July (which he declined).

The unavailability of any potential army commanders in the war's eastern theater forced Lincoln to look to the west. The best leader there was Major General U.S. Grant, who might have considered coming east because he was chafing under the shadow of his recently appointed superior, Major General Henry W. Halleck; Grant's dissatisfaction at the time was so great that he was privately considering resignation from the army. However, Grant's name was still under a cloud because of his drinking problem and the fact that he had allowed the Confederates to conduct a successful surprise attack on his *Army of the Tennessee* at Shiloh in April. The aftermath of Shiloh also stained the reputations of Grant's leading subordinates, including Major General William T. Sherman.

There were at the time two experienced army commanders in the west besides Grant. Major General Don Carlos Buell, commander of the *Army of the Ohio*, had been Grant's principal rival before the Shiloh campaign, and had arrived in the nick of time to save Grant's shattered command at Shiloh on the night of 6-7 April. Buell had also been subordinated to Halleck during the recently completed Corinth campaign. However, in the anticipated break up of Halleck's huge command, Buell was destined to return to the head of the *Department of the Ohio*, which was reconstituted on 12 July.

Halleck's third principal subordinate at Corinth was Major General John Pope, commander of the *Army of the Mississippi*. Pope had won national attention for his successful capture of Island No. 10 in the Mississippi on 10 March, and his reputation had not been sullied by Shiloh, where he had not been present. Just as significantly, he was a loyal Republican with well known views on abolition and aggressive prosecution of the war, which were quite agreeable to the administration. To cap things off, Pope was a personal friend of Lincoln's from before the war, and was even a relation to the President by marriage (one of Pope's second cousins had married Mary Todd Lincoln's oldest sister). Lincoln was certainly more inclined to give the *Army of Virginia* to Pope than he was to offer it to any other less known or less accomplished officer from the West.

Pope was summoned to Washington and arrived 22 June. He reported at once to Secretary of War Stanton, since Lincoln was out of town. Stanton outlined the military situation in Virginia, and explained that he and Lincoln intended to create a new army out of the three commands that had been unsuccessfully

Major General John Pope was a staunch Republican and a family friend of President Lincoln. He handled the initial stages of the 2nd Bull Run Campaign well enough, but lost control of events when Lee sent Jackson on a wide flank march deep into the Union rear. After the battle he was exiled to fight Indians in Minnesota.

opposing Jackson. This new army would then move towards Gordonsville in order to draw pressure away from McClellan's drive on Richmond.

Despite his later claims to reluctance, Pope promptly acceded to Stanton's offer after meeting with Stanton and Lincoln on 25 June. Pope's appointment, as well as the creation of the *Army of Virginia* itself, was announced in an executive order issued the next day. This same document announced that the objectives of Pope's army would be several: to protect Washington "from danger or insult;" to overcome Jackson's command; to "threaten the enemy in the direction of Charlottesville;" and to "render the most effective aid to relieve General McClellan and capture Richmond."

Pope's appointment was greeted with more enthusiasm by the Northern press than by the soldiers of his new command, to whom he was a total unknown. The *Philadelphia Public Ledger* praised Pope as a solid officer and offered the "reasonable presumption that the mistakes, blunders and defeats of the region are to be corrected." The *New York Tribune* waxed enthusiastic that Pope's aggressiveness would not allow his army to stand still on the banks of the Potomac. And the *New York Times* boldly predicted that Pope would soon "bag" Jackson and put an end to Stonewall's annoying command.

Pope's leading subordinates were much less excited about his appointment. All three of his corps commanders were his seniors in rank, so each justifiably felt slighted, as well as disappointed, that he had not received Pope's assignment. Major General John C. Fremont, who had been Pope's superior in Missouri in 1861, felt so strongly about the issue that he requested to be relieved rather than be demoted to corps command under an officer whom he considered to be inferior in character as well as rank. Fremont's request was granted on 28 June, and he would spend the rest of the war on the sidelines "awaiting orders." It should have been Pope's position to appoint Fremont's successor, but Stanton preempted him by appointing Brigadier General Rufus King as acting corps commander in Fremont's place. Two days later Stanton selected Major General Franz Sigel, one of Banks' division commanders, to command Fremont's corps. Pope certainly could not have been pleased by Stanton's usurpation of his command prerogatives, an act which did not bode well for his future relations with the administration. Pope was also well aware from his previous experiences with Sigel in Missouri that his new subordinate had more symbolic and political value than military skill.

McClellan was greatly surprised by the creation of the *Army of Virginia* and by Pope's appointment to command it, all the more so because he had not been consulted by the administration about either act. McClellan should have been relieved, though, to learn that a more organized effort was being made to give him support in north central Virginia. At that moment he needed all the aid he could get, for on 25 June, the day before Pope's appointment was announced, Lee's army in front of Richmond had begun a series of attacks on McClellan's command that were significantly altering the course of the campaign. For this reason, McClellan had no time to brood over Pope's appointment.

Pope, on his part, was in no rush to hurry to McClellan's aid. His first objective after he assumed command on 27 June was to begin to concentrate his army, which was strung out on a 60 mile front from Strasburg to Fredericksburg. On 28 June he directed Banks to move his 11,000 man *II Corps* from Middletown to Front Royal, where he would join the 13,000 men of Sigel's *I Corps*, which would be marching east from Strasburg. The two corps would be screened by Brigadier General John Hatch's 3000 man cavalry brigade at Front Royal. Pope apparently intended to move the two corps east of the Blue Ridge once they reached Front Royal, since the Shenandoah Valley then seemed to be clear of Rebels following Jackson's departure for Richmond. Pope also wished to move part if not all of McDowell's 18,000 man *III Corps* to occupy Warrenton instead of being stretched out at Fredericksburg and Manassas. Pressure from Stanton, though, prohibited him from ordering this move at the moment. The best he could do for the moment was to screen McDowell's front with Brigadier General George D. Bayard's 2000 man cavalry brigade.

Pope, oddly, did not elect to join his army at once after he assumed its command. Instead, he chose to direct the *Army of Virginia* from the War Department office on Pennsylvania Avenue in Washington. This act, of course, did not do anything to increase the confidence of his troops, who already had low morale for other reasons. McDowell's men were unhappy with their corps commander because of his reputation as a cold martinet, and Banks' and Sigel's troops were still smarting under the sting of the defeats that Jackson had just inflicted upon them.

Pope's primary concern during his first week in command seems to have been to monitor the progress of McClellan's campaign and not the supervision of his own army. Pope was well aware that the fierce nature of Lee's attacks during what is now called the Seven Days Battle, was changing the course of the war in Virginia, thereby rendering obsolete the list of objectives that he had received from Stanton and Lincoln on 26 June. Since he could not move his army down to Richmond quickly enough to aid McClellan, Pope felt that his best post was at the War Department, where he could closely follow the course of McClellan's battles. There he gave ready council to President Lincoln, who also was spending most of his time at the War

Department trying to interpret the contents of McClellan's frequent, long, and increasingly distressing telegrams.

Pope was particularly displeased when McClellan began shifting his line of withdrawal towards the James River rather than the York. He feared that such a movement would make it too difficult for him to move forward to support McClellan from the north, and that Lee's army, now interposed between the two Union armies, would be free to attack in either direction. When he stated his feelings to Lincoln, the President passed on the advice to McClellan, saying "General Pope thinks if you fall back it would be better towards the York River than toward the James." McClellan by then could have cared less what Pope felt, and without doubt began to resent Pope's unsolicited meddling all the more.

Pope restated his concerns in stronger terms when he was called to meet with Lincoln's cabinet on 28 June. When asked if he could move south to aid McClellan, he said that he would do as ordered, but was wary that the enemy might turn on him if McClellan were not given clear directions to attack at the same time that he advanced. He reportedly added that he had fears that McClellan might even sit idly by in such a situation and thereby allow the *Army of Virginia* to be "sacrificed."

Pope's rivalry with McClellan became even more intense after McClellan established his new base at Harrison's Landing on the James on 2 July. McClellan let it be known that he intended to stay where he was and that he would renew his attack on Richmond as soon as he received heavy reinforcements (including Burnside's *IX Corps* from North Carolina). He also felt that it was imperative for Pope to move south at once in order to open up a secondary front to the north of Richmond, so relieving some of Lee's pressure on the *Army of the Potomac*.

Pope was well aware of McClellan's desires as he penned his rival a lengthy letter on 4 July. After opening with the conciliatory note that "it is my earnest wish to cooperate in the heartiest and most energetic manner with you," Pope went on to explain the reasons that were preventing him from doing so. He had just taken command of his new army, whose troops were "much demoralized and broken down, and unfit for active service at the present." Pope needed time to get to know his men and get them ready for action. For now, his first object had to be to revive his troops, concentrate them, and arrange for "the security of the Valley of the Shenandoah and of the city of Washington."

Pope continued with an explanation of the disposition of the units under his command. He then explained that it had been his original intention "to aid you in any way in the immediate operations against Richmond" as soon as he was able. However, "the occurrences of the last few days have deranged this plan." Pope now felt that all he could manage to do successfully would be to guard Washington and the access to the Shenandoah Valley. He was honestly concerned that Lee would be able "to detach 50,000 men to march rapidly on Washington if it be uncovered by the movement of the forces under my command in either direction." In closing, he stated bluntly to McClellan, "Your position on James River places the whole of the enemy's force around Richmond between yourself and Washington. Were I to move with my command direct on Richmond, I must fight the whole force of the enemy before I could join you, and at so great a distance from you as to be beyond any assistance from your army."

Pope's reasoning was basically sound, even though it was very self serving. A move by sea to reinforce McClellan might indeed endanger Washington, or at least lose the Shenandoah, which had at last been reclaimed. A land march to aid McClellan would endanger his own command to attack by the enemy, since Lee would be able to leave a garrison to man Richmond's strong defenses and then march with the rest of his army against Pope.

This situation quickly developed into an impasse, as McClellan declined to renew his advance on Richmond until he was ready to do so, and Pope declined to do anything more than to march to Gordonsville and Charlottesville, "to cut off any force which may penetrate into the Valley of the Shenandoah from the direction of Richmond, and at the same time to concentrate my whole force with little delay in front of Washington in case of necessity." He would hold these positions "until some well-defined plan of operations and co-operation can be determined on."

It was not long before Pope developed what seemed to him to

be a quite reasonable solution to the impasse in Virginia. Since he could not move to aid McClellan without uncovering Washington, McClellan should be directed to abandon his position and return north to join up with Pope for a united advance upon Richmond from Fredericksburg or thereabouts. This is what Pope publicly suggested to the Congressional Committee on the Conduct of the War on 8 July. To his confidants, including Secretary of the Treasury Chase, Pope went a step farther and urged that McClellan should be relieved for "incompetency and indisposition to active movements." It is uncertain if Pope's goal now was simply to get rid of McClellan, or to try to get command of the *Army of the Potomac* for himself.

Lincoln and Stanton also felt the awkwardness of the military impasse in Virginia, and before long decided to resolve it by appointing a new superior over both Pope and McClellan. The office of general in chief had been vacant since Lincoln had relieved McClellan of the post in March. Appointment of a new head general might help to get the armies moving again. For this reason, Lincoln named Major General Henry W. Halleck as general in chief on 11 July. Halleck was well known as an able administrator, and he had done a good job of directing the war in the West during the previous nine months. However, his campaign to capture Corinth, Mississippi, had shown that he was as slow and cautious as McClellan in the field. Now that Corinth had been captured, Halleck could be safely recalled from the field to man a desk in Washington, where his talents could be better employed as the military advisor to the President, a post that Pope had been holding *de facto* for the previous two weeks. Halleck's slowness was at once shown by the fact that it took him 11 days to close up his office in St. Louis and come to Washington to assume his new post.

Halleck's appointment did not come as a surprise to Pope, who seems to have been lobbying for some time in favor of his former commander. Pope's enthusiasm for Halleck increased still more when the latter went to confer with McClellan at Harrison's Landing on 24-27 July and then returned with the conviction that the *Army of the Potomac* should be recalled from Richmond at once. It simply did not make sense, Halleck felt, to maintain two separate armies in Virginia. Since Pope could not be safely sent to aid McClellan without endangering Washington, there was no choice to recall McClellan. Lincoln and Stanton concurred, and appropriate orders were sent to McClellan on 4 August.

Pope hoped that Halleck's arrival in Washington would free him to take the field with his army. Active operations, though, would have to wait, since he received orders not to assume an offensive until McClellan's troops arrived, which would be mid-August at the earliest.

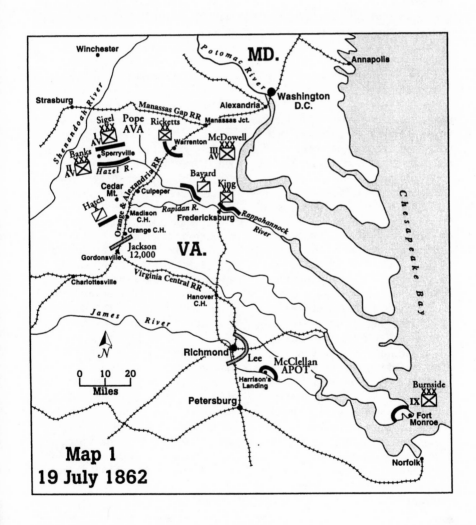

Map 1
19 July 1862

29

Pope

John Pope was born in Louisville, Kentucky, on 16 March 1822, and grew up in Kaskaskia, Illinois. His family was reasonably well to do, and his lineage stretched back to colonial times on both sides. The Pope family in America was descended from Nathaniel Pope, who came to Virginia in 1635; his daughter, Anna, married the great-grandfather of George Washington. On his mother's side, the general's ancestry extended back to the time of the Pilgrims.

Pope's father, also named Nathaniel, was an important early figure in Illinois. He was the state's first delegate to Congress, and then was named Illinois' first Federal district judge. A young lawyer named Abraham Lincoln often practiced in his court. Judge Pope was a strong abolitionist, and was a charter member of the Whig party. He passed all these beliefs on to his son.

Pope, who was stocky, bookish and ambitious like his father, was admitted to West Point in 1838 at the age of 16. He was a good but not brilliant student, and graduated 17th of the 56 members of the Class of 1842. Among his classmates were D.H. Hill, R.H. Anderson, Earl Van Dorn, and James Longstreet, all future Confederate lieutenant generals.

Upon graduation from West Point, Pope served first with the topographical engineers in Florida, where his commander was future Confederate general Joseph E. Johnston. After several additional rather boring assignments, he tried to pull strings to get transferred to a choicer post, only to find himself rebuked and transferred to the fringes of Maine. According to one report, he tried unsuccessfully to avoid this assignment by securing a note from his hometown doctor that he was suffering from secondary syphilis!

Pope was rescued from his exile in Maine by the outbreak of the Mexican War in 1846. He was attached to General Zachary Taylor's staff, and served there with another young lieutenant named George G. Meade (the future victor at Gettysburg). He was under fire for the first time at the battle of Monterey, where he earned a promotion to brevet first lieutenant; he was later raised to brevet captain for his valor at Buena Vista. His success helped feed his growing egotism, especially when the governor of Illinois presented him a sword after the war that had been voted by the state legislature.

Pope spent the next twelve years doing topographical duty at various locations that included Minnesota and New Mexico. In the 1850s he spent considerable time and energy experimenting with artesian wells. After being promoted to the rank of full captain, he was married in 1850 to Clara Horton, the daughter of an important Ohio congressman who had important connections in the emerging Republican party. Their first child, a daughter, was born in the family home in St. Louis in the spring of 1862, but died in July, soon after Pope was called to command the *Army of Virginia*. The couple later had four children, three sons and a daughter, all of whom reached adulthood.

During the secession crisis of 1860-1861, Pope did not hesitate to air his strong views that the government should act quickly and decisively to put down the rebellion. He even went so far as to write President-elect Lincoln with advice on how to deal with disloyal officers. Lincoln, who had known Pope's father reasonably well in the Illinois courts, was apparently impressed by the young officer's convictions, and in mid-February selected him to serve as one of the four army officers detailed to accompany Lincoln and his family on their train ride from Springfield to Washington. Pope used the occasion to get to know the new President on a personal basis, a connection that would prove most useful a year later.

Pope's elation at serving Lincoln so closely was soon quashed on 4 March, when he was unexpectedly notified that he was to appear at a court martial in Kentucky on charges of making remarks derogatory to President Buchanan! It seems that Pope had been very free in his criticism of the lame duck President during a speech in February, during which he chastised his commander-in-chief for letting the Southern states secede and seize so much Federal property. These sentiments, which were most agreeable to the audience to which they were expressed, had been reprinted in several newspapers and there caught the eye of some pro-Buchanan officers, who called Pope to task for his insubordination. This was not the first time that Pope's tongue got him into trouble, nor would it be the last. This episode, though, went away as suddenly as it appeared.

Soon after the court martial notice arrived, he received a special War Department order stating that it had been canceled at the request of the President. To this day it is not clear who pulled what strings in order to get Pope off the hook. It certainly did not hurt to have powerful friends in Washington who ranged from his father-in-law, Congressman Horton, to the President-elect.

Pope saw the opening of the Civil War as a great opportunity for carrying out his strong political views, and in the process secure quick personal advancement. At one point he requested to become Lincoln's Presidential aide and personal secretary. When this bid was not answered, he wrote again to the President to request a general's commission. Pope was serving as a Federal mustering officer in Chicago when he at last received his coveted appointment as a brigadier general of volunteers, dating from 17 May. Instead of thanking the President, Pope wrote to him at once to complain that he had not also received a promotion in Regular Army rank; he did not think it reasonable that the announced Regular Army promotions all went to Pennsylvanians, some of whom were inferior to him in seniority. One of these Pennsylvanians was his future rival, George B. McClellan.

Pope's boldness in the promotions arena was indeed quite amazing, since he had served only in the topographical engineers and had never commanded anyone in combat. He was fortunate to win assignment to command the *Department of Northern Missouri*, where one of his subordinates was an Illinois colonel named U.S. Grant; Pope's immediate superior at this post was Major General John C. Fremont, who a year later would ask to be relieved rather than serve under him in Virginia.

Some minor successes brought Pope a new job as a division commander in the *Army of Southwest Missouri*, and then the command of the *District of Central Missouri*. Luck and good timing then brought him an appointment on 23 February 1862 as commander of the newly formed *Army of the Mississippi*. His first assignment in this post was to take a force of 18,000 green troops and try to capture Island No. 10, a good sized Confederate fortification in the Mississippi River near the Tennessee-Kentucky border. Pope wisely chose to move first against Island No. 10's supply base at New Madrid, Missouri, which he captured on 14 March after an eleven day siege. He then focused his attention on nearby Island No. 10. The arrival of a supporting flotilla of gunboats on 15 March enabled him to begin reducing the Confederate fortifications. However, he was not able to isolate the enemy position until he built a canal near New Madrid in order to bring his transports, which were north of the Confederate fort, to its southern side. He was then able to ferry his troops across the Mississippi below Island No. 10 and invest the Confederate works from their landward side on 7 April. The Confederates saw how hopeless their position was, and surrendered almost immediately. Quite unbelievably, Pope had managed to capture almost 4000 Confederate troops and over 50 pieces of artillery at almost no loss to his own command.

Pope's unqualified success, even though it came over a much smaller opponent, brought him instant glory at the national level, particularly since it came at the same time as the bloody and closely fought battle at Shiloh. Pope, of course, was not one to turn from the limelight.

The next ten months were to be aggravating to him as he yearned for still more responsibility. Halleck decided to concentrate all the Union's major western armies at Pittsburg Landing for a great thrust against Corinth, Mississippi. Pope arrived there with his *Army of the Mississippi* on 22 April only to find himself assigned command of one wing of Halleck's force. Halleck's expedition started out eight days later, but took a full month to reach Corinth (which was only 20 miles away), largely because he stopped to entrench every night in order to avoid another Shiloh style surprise attack by the enemy. The Confederates, outnumbered by over two-to-one, evacuated Corinth on 29 May, and it was Pope's good fortune that two of his regiments were the first Union troops to enter the deserted city.

Pope won still more national acclaim for his role in the Corinth campaign, even though he personally had done little to merit such applause. The North was starved for heroes at the time, and Pope was more than pleased to play the role. This attention is what earned him his appointment to command the newly formed *Army of Virginia*, as noted in the text. But it also increased the haughtiness that made it difficult for him to work with so many of his eastern colleagues and subordinates.

Though Pope was relieved of his

command in Virginia just a few days after his defeat at Second Bull Run, much popular and political sentiment sympathized with him and began blaming McClellan for the loss of the campaign. Pope was a key figure at the military courts which investigated Generals Porter and McDowell for their roles in the battle. When Porter was convicted and McDowell was exonerated, Pope rightly felt that his own conduct had been cleared. Most recent scholarship, though, has not looked so favorably on his conduct of the campaign.

Pope's political connections made it seem like he lived a charmed life. Instead of being shelved for the rest of the war, as happened to his friend McDowell, Pope found himself merely exiled to command the *Department of the Northwest*, which he led from 16 September 1862 to 13 February 1865. The assignment was not really that disagreeable to him under the circumstances, since he was familiar with the area from his pre-war topographical work, and his wife and family were able to join him in Milwaukee. His position, though, was not a sinecure. There had been a major Indian uprising in Minnesota in August, and he needed to keep a firm control on the situation there. He did so successfully, and was rewarded with a promotion to the command of the *Military Division of the Missouri* in February 1865. Since this included Kansas and Missouri as well as the *Department of the Northwest*, Pope was able to move his headquarters from Milwaukee to his home town of St. Louis.

Pope went on extended leave for two years after the war ended, but was loth to give up the only real career he knew. As a strong willed Republican general, there was still plenty of work to be done. On 15 April 1867, he was appointed commanding general of one of the three military districts that the radical national Congress established to govern the conquered South. The political and legal controversies he encountered from his headquarters in Atlanta are too detailed to recount here. When the power of the Radicals began to wane, Pope found himself transferred in December 1869 to the *Department of the Great Lakes*, where affairs were tense because of Fenian activities along the border with Canada.

Pope had been in Detroit for only four months before he was again transferred to command the *Department of the Missouri*, which was really where he wanted to be, anyway. Since his new command included many of the government's western territories, his attention for the next two years was focused on assorted Indian problems and even several minor wars. Pope's long and devoted service to the army was at last fully rewarded in 1882 when he was promoted to the rank of major general in the regular army, along with a less strenuous post as commander of the *Department of the Pacific*. He retired from the army in 1886. His health deteriorated quickly, and he died on 23 September 1892 while on a visit to Sandusky, Ohio. He was buried in Bellefontaine Cemetery in St. Louis.

Pope's entire military career, particularly his management of the Second Bull Run Campaign, has long been a source of controversy. He wrote only one memoir to explain his actions, a lengthy article that appeared in the *Century Magazine* in 1887. His dislike for McClellan and Porter is readily evident there, and it is clear that he was interpreting many of the events of the campaign with too much hindsight. Some historians have treated Pope more sympathetically than others, notably John Codman Ropes and the recent biographers Wallace J. Schutz and Walter N. Trenerry. Most others, though, continue to view Pope as a braggart and a blowhard, an officer whose early luck in the war elevated him to a field command that was beyond his ability to handle.

Pope's Pomposity

During his sojourn in Washington from the time of his arrival on 22 June 1862 until he took the field on 6 August, Pope did more than simply spend all his time at his desk in the War Office. He thoroughly enjoyed making the rounds of all the parties and dinners that went on in the capital nightly, and was always ready to bend the ear of any congressman or public official (the higher ranking the better) who was willing to listen to his views on the war, the army, politics, slavery, or life in general.

Pope's unstructured schedule also gave him time to develop plans to instill new spirit into his officers and men. He felt that many of the troops in Virginia lacked aggressiveness and had developed an inferiority complex in the face of Jackson and Lee. This led him to be unduly harsh in rebuking his subordinates, acts that certainly did not help win him their loyalty and respect. For example, when Brigadier General Abraham Piatt reported a minor setback in a cavalry skirmish near Middletown on 15 July, Pope wrote him the next day, "Neither do I quite understand your calling an affair in which 2 men were wounded a 'sharp engagement'. I hope you will infuse a much bolder spirit in your men...I do not like the idea of an infantry regiment of this army retreating without more loss and better reasons than are set forth in your dispatch."

Pope's haughty attitude can also be seen in this excerpt from a proclamation that he issued on 14 July: "Let us understand each other. I have come to you from the West, where we have always seen the backs of our enemies; from an army whose business it has been to seek the adversary, and to beat him when he was found; whose policy has been attack and not defense. In but one instance has the enemy been able to place our Western armies in defensive attitude. I presume that I have been called here to pursue the same system and to lead you against the enemy. It is my purpose to do so, and that speedily. I am sure you long for an opportunity to win the distinction you are capable of achieving. That opportunity I shall endeavor to give you. Meantime I desire you to dismiss from your minds certain phrases, which I am sorry to find in so much vogue amongst you. I hear constantly of 'taking strong positions and holding them,' of 'lines of retreat,' and of 'bases of supplies.' Let us discard such ideas. The strongest position a soldier should desire to occupy is one from which he can most easily advance against the enemy. Let us study the probable lines of retreat of our opponents, and leave our own to take care of themselves. Let us look before us and not behind. Success and glory are in the advance, disaster and shame lurk in the rear. Let us act on this understanding, and it is safe to predict that your banners shall be inscribed with many a glorious deed and that your names will be dear to your countrymen forever."

This circular was obviously intended to bolster the spirit of his men, but it met with quite diverse reactions. To some of the men in the ranks, Pope's words spoke of an aggressiveness they long desired. Some of his officers, however, saw the proclamation as only so much bombast. For example, Colonel Rufus Dawes of the *6th Wisconsin*, who had initially welcomed Pope's appointment because he and his men felt that their corps commander, McDowell, was "incompetent, if not disloyal," wrote on 18 July, "General Pope's bombastic proclamation has not intended to increase confidence, indeed the effect is exactly the contrary."

Pope's address caused particular animosity in the *Army of the Potomac*. His eagerness to disdain such phrases as "lines of retreat," "bases of supply" and "taking strong positions and holding them," struck right at McClellan, who had often used these terms in conducting his

campaign against Richmond. *Army of the Potomac* troops were also offended by Pope's bragging about always seeing the backs of his enemies in the West, which was clearly a reference to McClellan's recent series of defeats before Richmond. If McClellan himself were not already hostile to Pope, the tone of this address surely would have turned him so. McClellan's good friend, Major General Fitz John Porter, felt that the proclamation made it clear to everyone what Pope's fellow officers had long known - that Pope was "an ass." Porter also predicted that Pope's proclamation "will make him ridiculous in the eyes of military men abroad as well as at home." This prediction was on the mark in many ways. Pope's strong wording and terminology, particularly his lack of concern for supply bases, could hardly have been more unfortunate, especially given the way the course of the Second Bull Run campaign would develop.

It should be noted that Pope's address did not bear the byline, "Headquarters in the Saddle," as is commonly believed. A popular story, then and now, relates that Lee, upon hearing this phrase, joked, "If so, his [Pope's] headquarters are where his hindquarters ought to be." One modern historian has traced the apparent source of this anecdote to a late July 1862 issue of the *Richmond Inquirer*. Pope took the time to deal with the issue directly in a rare bit of self effacement found in his 1887 *Century Magazine* monograph on the campaign: "A good deal of cheap wit has been expended upon a fanciful story that I published an order or wrote a letter or made a remark that my 'headquarters would be in the saddle.' It is an expression harmless and innocent enough, but it is even stated that it furnished General Lee with the basis for the only joke of his life. I think it due to army tradition, and to the comfort of those who have often repeated this ancient joke in the days long before the civil war, that these later wits should not be allowed with impunity to poach on this will-tilled manor. This venerable joke I first heard when a cadet at West Point, and it was then told of that gallant soldier and gentleman, General W.J. Worth, and I presume it could be easily traced back to the Crusades and beyond. Certainly I never used this expression or wrote or dictated it, nor does any such expression occur in any order of mine; and it has perhaps served its time and effected its purpose, it ought to be retired."

Some recent interpretations suggest that the wording and tone of Pope's controversial address were not offensive or even a surprise to Lincoln and Stanton, who may have approved it ahead of time or even helped to compose it. The same was probably true of an equally controversial set of orders that Pope issued during the third week of July.

The first of these, General Order No. 5, issued on 18 July, announced that Pope's men would "subsist upon the country" while in the field; this meant that provision would be taken at will from civilians, but in exchange for vouchers that could be cashed in by loyal citizens at the end of the war. Pope's purpose for this decision was to lessen his dependency on supply trains, as well as to deprive subsistence from the enemy. Most of his soldiers favored the order, which would in effect permit them to forage and appropriate foodstuffs at will, as long as appropriate vouchers were given in exchange for what was taken. In practice, however, the vouchers were not always taken care of. Pope also found that the order led to a decrease in discipline, since troops tended to leave camp whenever they could in order to go foraging. Confederate reaction to the order was understandably adverse. Farmers whose foodstuffs had been largely untouched by the Yankees during the first year of the war now found themselves quickly wiped out and left with little to live on. Nor could they even expect to redeem the vouchers they had received, since they did not intend to become citizens loyal to the Union for the rest of the war. Such hardship on civilians was certainly regrettable, but it was thought to be a necessary step as the Federal government began to take a harsher attitude towards the Confederates and the general prosecution of the war.

Two of Pope's other circulars, General Orders No. 7 (also issued on 18 July) and No. 11 (issued on 23 July) dealt with the problem of Confederate guerrillas behind Union lines. Pope had already shown during his tenure of command in Missouri that he would not hesitate to take unusual or even extralegal measures in order to ensure the security of his lines. General Order No. 7 directed that if any shots were fired at Union troops from a house, it would be burned and its occupants made prisoners. In addition, local civilians would be held responsible for acts of predation carried out by guerrillas. Whenever any such damage was done, the inhabitants for five miles around would be required to repair it, and also to pay for the time and subsistence of the Federal troops necessary to supervise the work. General Orders No. 11 authorized the arrest of all "disloyal male citizens" within reach of Union forces or behind Federal lines. Any of those arrested who would agree to take the oath of allegiance, would be permitted to go home, but if anyone violated his oath, "he shall be shot, and his property seized and applied to the public use." Those who refused to take the oath of allegiance would be deported "beyond the extreme pickets of the army." If they were found within Union lines again, they would be hanged as spies.

These last two orders were particularly hateful to the Confederates, to whom the concept of total war and all that it entailed were in violation of their Victorian sense of decency. Various Southern newspapers called Pope a barbarous enemy of humanity who should be shot on sight. Pope's orders were also quite offensive to Confederate General Robert E. Lee's sense of civility. On 28 July Lee called Pope a "miscreant" in a private letter to one of his daughters. Then on 2 August the Confederate commander wrote a letter to Union commander in chief Henry W. Halleck to object to the fact that Pope had directed "the murder of our peaceful citizens as spies if found quietly tilling their farms in his rear, even outside his lines." Lee was equally angry that one of Pope's officers had "seized innocent and peaceful inhabitants to be held as hostages to the end that

they may be murdered in cold blood if any of his soldiers are killed by some unknown persons whom he designated as 'bushwhackers'." In view of this situation, the Confederate government had no choice but to consider Pope and his officers to be "robbers and murderers" who were not entitled to the rights of prisoners of war if captured. In Lee's view, Pope was infamous and deserved to be defeated. The war had indeed taken on a personal nature for him.

These objections by the Confederates, of course, were of little concern to Pope, Stanton and Lincoln. In fact, Pope's orders were part of a wider war policy being formulated by Lincoln and some of his closest allies, who had developed a harsher attitude towards the Confederacy and now felt that sterner measures were needed to bring the war to a successful conclusion. In early July, the U.S. Senate passed the Confiscation Act, which authorized the seizure and use of all needed Confederate property, including slaves. It was also during July that Lincoln composed the Emancipation Proclamation, which he declined to issue until his troops won another victory; due to Pope's failure at Second Bull Run, Lincoln would not be able to release it until after the battle of Antietam in September.

Pope was not the only Federal field commander to proclaim a sterner policy towards the Confederate population at this time. On 3 July, U.S. Grant, commander of the *District of West Tennessee*, issued a general order authorizing the confiscation of private property "to remunerate the Government for all loss" in areas of guerrilla activity. In this policy he was encouraged by

Halleck, who directed Grant on 2 August to detain all active Confederate sympathizers and seize their property for public use. Grant was also instructed to "get all the supplies you can from the rebels in Mississippi," since "It is time that they should begin to feel the presence of war on our side." The nature of the war was surely changing on both sides.

One significant Union field commander, however, objected to the administration's change in attitude towards the prosecution of the war. On 7 July, George B. McClellan wrote Lincoln to say that war should not be made upon the Southern population. McClellan strongly felt that private property and the rights of citizens should be carefully guarded, even in the rebellious states. This opinion was clearly at variance with the administration's new policies, and helped deepen the widening schism between McClellan and the President.

Pope's stern new policies, then, were not entirely of his own creation, but had the full backing and encouragement of Lincoln and his closest advisers. In many sources, Pope has been vilified for his decision to carry the war to Virginia's civilians. Indeed, the strong tone of his general orders fits well to the negative persona generated by his pompous personality and subsequent loss of the Second Bull Run campaign. Nevertheless, any evaluation of Pope's military abilities and generalship should not be tainted by personal feelings about the changing nature of the war. Pope's proclamations in July 1862 were but one major step on the road to total war as practiced by Hunter, Sheridan and Sherman in 1864-1865.

Pope's Corps Commanders

Pope's three corps commanders during the Second Bull Run campaign were all senior generals who were not particularly well known for their fighting abilities. In fact, each suffered major defeats during other campaigns in the war, as a result of which they were all transferred to less important posts.

Franz Sigel (1824-1902), commander of the *I Corps* of the *Army of Virginia*, was probably the weakest of Pope's three corps commanders. He was born in Baden, Germany, and attended a military academy there. He then became a liberal revolutionary and played a leading role in the unsuccessful German revolution of 1848, after which he was forced to flee the country. He eventually reached New York, and then became a school teacher in St. Louis. When the Civil War broke out, Sigel helped recruit thousands of German Americans for the Union cause, and the tune "I Goes to Fight mit Sigel" soon became a popular camp song. He was quickly rewarded by the Lincoln administration with a commission as a brigadier general.

Sigel commanded a brigade at the battle of Wilson's Creek, and then played a key role as a division commander at Pea Ridge in March

1862, which was probably his best battle performance during the war. He was then promoted to major general and transferred east, where he commanded a division under Banks during Jackson's Valley campaign. Sigel was named to command Fremont's *I Corps* of the *Army of Virginia* when Fremont resigned rather than serve under Pope. He performed erratically during the Second Bull Run campaign, and lost Pope's confidence after the army withdrew from its line along the upper Rappahannock.

Sigel retained command of his corps after it was reassigned to be the *XI Corps* of the *Army of the Potomac*, but then found it necessary to retire briefly for health reasons. In March 1864 he was reassigned as commander of the *Department of West Virginia*, and soon lost the battle of New Market on 15 May. He was then relieved of duty on 8 July for "lack of aggression" in opposing Early's invasion of Maryland. He resigned from the army on 4 May 1865.

Sigel had an active postwar life in Baltimore and then New York as a publisher and lecturer. He also switched allegiance from the Republican party to the Democratic, after which he was appointed a Federal pension agent by President Cleveland.

Nathaniel P. Banks (1816-1894), commander of Pope's *II Corps*, was a political general who had no military experience before the war. From 1853 to 1861 he served as a Republican congressman and then Governor of Massachusetts. At the outbreak of the war he was President of the Illinois Central Railroad; one of this organization's vice presidents was George B. McClellan, and

Abraham Lincoln had been one of the firm's lawyers. These high connections brought Banks an early appointment as a major general when the war broke out.

Banks' first major assignment was as commander of the *Department of the Shenandoah*, whose troops later became McClellan's *V Corps* of the *Army of the Potomac* for a time. He was soundly outgeneraled by Jackson at the height of the 1862 Valley Campaign, and then lost to Jackson again at Cedar Mountain on 9 August 1862. His corps was so beaten up there that it was kept in the rear and so was not actively engaged in the remainder of the Second Bull Run campaign.

When Pope's army was discontinued in early September 1862, Banks found himself "kicked upstairs" to the command of the *Military District of Washington*; his old command meanwhile became the nucleus for the *XII Corps* of the *Army of the Potomac*. By the end of the year, he managed to get himself appointed to field command again, this time in the supposedly out of the way post as commander of the *Department of the Gulf*. In this role, he led the clumsy expedition that resulted in his greatest wartime triumph, the capture of Port Hudson, Louisiana, which surrendered to his forces on 8 July 1863 upon confirmation of Grant's capture of Vicksburg a few days earlier. Banks was then voted the official Thanks of Congress for helping to open up the Mississippi, but he soon dissipated his glory by his unsuccessful management of the spring 1864 Red River campaign.

Banks was relieved of field command after the Red River failure, but did not resign from the army until August 1865. He promptly returned to his career in politics, and served six terms in Congress before he had to retire in 1890 for medical reasons.

Pope's most experienced corps commander at the time of the Second Bull Run campaign was Major General Irvin McDowell (1818-1865), leader of the *Army of Virginia's III Corps.* McDowell graduated from West Point in 1838, and had a distinguished prewar career that included service in the Mexican War. When the Civil War began in 1861, he was promptly appointed a brigadier general, and through his connections with General Scott and Secretary of War Chase was named commander of the Union Army at Washington. He was pushed to fight the Confederate army at Bull Run before the enlistment of many of his men ran out, and developed a good battle plan. However, he was defeated by superior enemy numbers and the inexperience and weariness of his men.

Curiously, McDowell was not disgraced after the battle, but retained respect and was even promoted to the rank of major general. Given command of the *I Corps* of McClellan's *Army of the Potomac,* he then led the so-called *"Army of the Rappahannock"* during Jackson's Valley campaign. He was not directly engaged in any battles with Jackson, though several of his subordinates were. McDowell's troops then were reassigned to be the *I Corps* of Pope's *Army of Virginia.* McDowell served in effect as Pope's second in command during the Second Bull Run campaign, and shared in Pope's at times strange handling of the army. In particular, he did not communicate well with Porter on 29 August, and thereby contributed significantly to the latter's military demise.

McDowell was blamed along with Pope for the disaster at Second Bull Run, and was relieved of command five days after the battle. On 6 September, he requested a Court of Inquiry to investigate his role in the battle and try to clear his name. It met in Washington from 21 November 1861 to 23 February 1863, and lasted even longer than Fitz John Porter's more famous case, at which McDowell was a key witness. McDowell was formally charged with treason, drunkenness, and military incapacity, and was delighted to be exonerated on all counts. Even so, he was not reassigned to duty until July 1864, when he was sent far away to command the *Department of the Pacific.*

Strange to say, McDowell remained in the army after the war, and even rose to the rank of major general in the Regular Army. He commanded several important departments at various times until he retired in 1882.

It is interesting to note that none of the principal commanders in Pope's army who were "on loan" from McClellan's command had particularly distinguished careers after the battle, either. Major General Fitz John Porter, commander of the *V Corps, Army of the Potomac,* was court-martialed soon after the battle. Major General Samuel Heintzelman was relieved of command of his *III Corps, Army of the Potomac,* on 12 October in order to take on a desk job as commander of the *Military District of Washington.* Pope's most promising corps commander at the battle was probably Major General Jesse Reno of the *IX Corps*. Reno, who was ill during the fight at Chantilly, was killed in action while at the head of his troops in the fight at Fox's Gap just two weeks later.

This is not to say that there were no talented lower level Union commanders on the field. Major General Joseph Hooker, a division commander in Heintzelman's corps, would rise to command the *Army of the Potomac* during the Chancellors-ville campaign, and Brigadier General George G. Meade, commander of a brigade in the *Pennsylvania Reserves* division, would command the army at Gettysburg. Pope's subordinates at Second Bull Run also included quite a few future corps commanders, including Brigadier Generals John F. Reynolds, Robert Schenck, George Sykes, Alpheus Williams, John Gibbon, David Birney, Abner Doubleday, Dan Butterfield, and Colonel G.K. Warren.

CHAPTER III

Opening Moves

*D*espite his victory in the Seven Days Battle, Robert E. Lee was still in an awkward strategic situation at the beginning of July. He had succeeded at great cost in driving McClellan's command from the gates of Richmond, but the huge *Army of the Potomac* still posed a grave threat to the Confederate capital from its new base at Harrison's Landing, located on the James River some 20 miles southeast of Richmond. If McClellan renewed his offensive from there, Lee would certainly have his hands full trying to stop him. This situation was made perilous by the presence of Pope's newly formed *Army of Virginia* in the northern sector of the state. Lee in mid June had deliberately withdrawn Jackson's command from that area in order to deal with McClellan, and there were at the moment no troops positioned to stop Pope from trying to seize the Virginia Central Railroad, one of Richmond's primary supply arteries. There was also nothing to prevent Pope from marching south to support McClellan's drive on Richmond. If Pope approached the capital from the direction of Fredericksburg or Gordonsville, he would open up a second front and force Lee to divide his army in order to defend Richmond against the greatly superior Union forces.

Lee's immediate concern was to determine the intentions of the Union army gathered at Harrison's Landing, where McClellan had withdrawn after the battle of Malvern Hill on 1 July. It actually took Lee until the morning of 3 July to confirm the location of the Union army, and early the next morning he pushed his infantry forward to face the enemy yet again. By then the Union troops were strongly positioned and receiving bountiful supplies from the Federal boats that controlled the lower James River. Lee wisely chose not to try to attack McClellan's concentrated command, and spent the next three days vainly trying to interrupt the enemy's river traffic. When McClellan's troops refused to stir from their lines, Lee withdrew his army to the Richmond defenses on 8 July.

Each passing day gave Lee increasing confidence that McClellan was not going to renew his attack on the capital anytime soon. This respite gave him time to reorganize his army and consider the best way to deal with the combined threat posed by Pope's and McClellan's commands. McClellan's continued inactivity and news received on 12 July that Pope was concentrating at Culpeper, made it clear that somebody needed to be sent to face Pope. Fortunately for Lee, the defenses that he had constructed around Richmond made it possible for him to shift a considerable number of troops towards Pope's front and still have enough left to make a static defense of the capital should McClellan begin moving again.

It was not difficult for Lee to decide whom to send to face Pope. His only lieutenant who had a successful track record in independent command was "Stonewall" Jackson, who had just completed his highly successful Shenandoah Valley campaign the month before against many of the same troops and officers who now composed Pope's new command. Jackson's reputation was unsullied by his lackluster performance during the Sevens Days Battle, and he was perhaps more of a hero to Virginians at that time than was Lee himself. For these reasons, Jackson was an ideal choice for the assignment of watching Pope.

Jackson, however, was not initially sent out with a large command for the purpose of defeating Pope. Lee was painfully aware of the threat posed by McClellan's force at Harrison's Landing, and understood that the Federals might be deliberately enticing him to split up his army. For this reason he detached Jackson with just two divisions of some 14,000 men (his own and Ewell's divisions) on 13 July with orders to "proceed to Louisa Court House, and if practicable to Gordonsville, there to oppose the reported advance of the enemy from the direction of Orange Court House." Lee knew that he could recall Jackson if McClellan began moving towards Richmond, and that he could reinforce Stonewall if the situation warranted. For the moment he had no specific campaign plans, but would await developments. Lee's primary intention was to maintain all the initiative he could; he understood that remaining passive in the face of a numerically superior enemy would probably lead to defeat, particularly if the two Federal armies began to coordinate their movements against him.

Jackson moved his two divisions north across the South Anna River and by 17 July was encamped at Beaverdam on the Virginia Central Railroad, some 20 miles north of Richmond. The next day he marched a few miles farther west to Frederickshall, from which he sent out scouts to determine Pope's position. Once he learned that Pope's men were still no farther south than Culpeper, Jackson proceeded to Gordonsville on the 19th.

Jackson's occupation of Gordonsville on 19 July forestalled Pope's plans to destroy the railroad lines in that area. As already mentioned, Pope's original directive from Lincoln included instructions to threaten the enemy in the vicinity of Charlottesville (about 18 miles west of Gordonsville), and it was towards this end that he had moved to concentrate his command just to the east of the Blue Ridge Mountains. Pope anticipated little Confederate opposition in the area, and on 14 July ordered Banks to send his small brigade of cavalry under Brigadier General John Hatch on a raid against the railroad line at Gordonsville. From there Hatch was to push on to Charlottesville, damaging the railroad as much as he could, and if no resistance were met there, he was to move south to cut the James River canal some 50 miles west of Richmond. Pope's purpose was to cut off Confederate access to the upper Shenandoah Valley, and thereby curtail his own field of operations to a more manageable front.

Pope intended for Hatch to conduct a speedy cavalry raid, but Hatch misunderstood and took three critical days to prepare his expedition. He did not set out from Culpeper until 17 July, with his column encumbered by an infantry force and numerous wagons. Hatch's command then moved so slowly that it had scarcely reached Madison Court House, 15 miles northwest of

Gordonsville, when he learned that Jackson's infantry had just occupied his goal. Hatch did not proceed any farther, but meekly turned back towards Sperryville. Pope was justifiably furious at learning of Hatch's failure. Had Hatch moved promptly and quickly as ordered, he would have been able to accomplish most of his mission before Jackson's arrival.

Hatch made another attempt on 22 July to cut the railroad between Gordonsville and Charlottesville, but was unsuccessful and turned back again. This time he blamed the bad weather and the worn out condition of his horses. Pope by now had experienced quite enough of Hatch's cavalry skills, and on 27 July reassigned him to command an infantry brigade in King's division of McDowell's corps. Pope then selected one of his staff officers, Major John Buford, to serve as Hatch's replacement. This appointment was one of the best personnel moves that Pope would make, as events in August 9, and at the first day at Gettysburg, would prove. Buford was delighted to be able to take a field command (and the accompanying promotion to Brigadier General of Volunteers), though he was unable to join his troops until 3 August.

Pope also had other active cavalry commanders already in the field, including Colonel Judson Kilpatrick of the *2nd New York*. On 19-20 July Kilpatrick led a highly successful raid that destroyed a great amount of Confederate supplies as well as the depot at Beaverdam Station. (Kilpatrick also captured a relatively unknown Confederate captain named John S. Mosby. Little did the Yankees know when they paroled him a few days later, that Mosby would become one of the war's greatest partisan cavalry leaders.) This raid and other probes conducted under the able leadership of Brigadier General George D. Bayard, commander of McDowell's cavalry brigade, succeeded by 24 July at establishing the size and location of Jackson's command.

Despite the confirmation of Jackson's presence at Gordonsville, Pope was in no hurry to advance his much larger army and drive Stonewall back. He did not take the field himself until the very end of July, when he at last began to make preparations to concentrate much of his army in the area of Culpeper. Jackson all the while was chafing at the bit for a chance to strike out at

Major General A.P. Hill, commander of the famed "Light Division," fought well on both offense and defense in his first campaign under Jackson's command, even though he did not always get along well with Stonewall Jackson personally.

Pope's command. All he needed in order to assume the offensive, he wrote Lee, was a few more reinforcements. Lee, who had been warily watching McClellan's continuing inactivity, at length acceded to Jackson's request, and on 27 July informed Stonewall that he would be sending A.P. Hill's large division to him. Hill's 12,000 men would almost double the size of Jackson's command, and would enable Stonewall to meet part of Pope's army, provided that an isolated portion could be found and attacked. Lee, however, gave no specific instructions to Jackson other than the directive, "I want Pope to be suppressed." The tenor of Pope's recently promulgated general orders against civilians had enraged Lee, and the Confederate commander strongly felt that Pope was a "miscreant" who needed to be dealt with harshly.

Hill's troops began arriving at Gordonsville on 29 July, and Jackson at once began looking for an opportunity to strike at Pope, most of whose troops were still north of the Hazel River near Sperryville. For most of the next week Jackson shifted his men back and forth between Gordonsville, Liberty Mills and Barboursville, waiting for the right opportunity to make his move.

All of Jackson's attention, however, was not focused on Pope during the first week of August. Stonewall had strict rules about what he expected from his men, and did not hesitate to prosecute them or their officers when they failed to meet his expectations. Jackson became dissatisfied with the bad discipline and poor behavior of some of his cavalry during their regular skirmishes with Pope's forces, and decided to get rid of his recently appointed cavalry commander, Brigadier General Beverly H. Robertson. To do so, though, he needed Lee's permission, but Lee refused to fire Robertson. Jackson then turned his attention to conducting courts-martial for several officers who had incurred his displeasure during the spring's campaign. Most notable of these was Brigadier General Richard B. Garnett, whom Jackson accused of withdrawing the Stonewall Brigade without orders at the battle of Kernstown on 23 March. A court was assembled on 6 August at Ewell's headquarters at Liberty Mills, and soon grew quite heated. Ensuing events, however, would not permit the completion of the court martial. Garnett would be transferred to Pickett's division and would be killed at Gettysburg on 3 July 1863, his reputation still beclouded by Jackson's unresolved charges.

After a month of relative inactivity, the strategic situation in Virginia began to change radically during the first week of August. As already noted in the previous chapter, Union general in chief Henry W. Halleck visited McClellan at Harrison's Landing during the last week in July, and returned to Washington with the recommendation that McClellan's army be withdrawn from the James River to Aquia Creek, about 10 miles north of Fredericksburg. He also recommended that Burnside's *IX Corps*, which had been brought up to Fort Monroe from North Carolina in order to reinforce McClellan, should also be sent to Aquia Creek.

Pope's awareness that a final decision was being made concerning the fate of McClellan's army was a major factor controlling his inactivity at the end of July. When orders were at length issued on 4 August for McClellan to withdraw from Harrison's Landing, Pope was happy, since the arrival of McClellan's troops would make his front much more secure, even though the significant issue was still not resolved of who would command the combined armies. For the moment, Pope

McClellan made a belated reconnaissance to the Malvern Hill area at the beginning of August in an effort to persuade Halleck to let him keep his army near Richmond. Halleck, however, ordered him on 3 August to begin withdrawing from Harrison's Landing to Fort Monroe.

decided that it would be best to secure a line along the Rapidan River and its sources from the Blue Ridge to Fredericksburg. From there he could continue to conduct cavalry raids against the Virginia Central Railroad while he awaited the arrival of McClellan and Burnside at Aquia Creek.

Lee, of course, did not have a clear view of the Union change in strategy. He desired to send still more reinforcements to Jackson in order to help him deal with Pope, but stirrings in McClellan's camp made him anxious that something was afoot there. On 2 August McClellan sent a reinforced division (Hooker's) to occupy Malvern Hill, and there was considerable activity in that area for the next several days. It seemed to Lee that McClellan might at last be preparing to renew his attack on Richmond. This seemed all the more likely since news had just been received concerning Burnside's arrival at Fredericksburg, which in effect opened up a major new third front in Virginia. This situation caused Lee particular concern that Burnside might operate against Jackson's rear if Stonewall moved against Pope as had been planned. For this reason, Lee wrote Jackson on 7 August that he could spare no more reinforcements at the moment, and that Jackson would have to act on his best judgment about what to do next.

The Nascent Army of Northern Virginia

One of the first moves that Robert E. Lee took after assuming command of the Confederate troops defending Richmond on 30 May 1862 was to re-christen them the "Army of Northern Virginia," a title that clearly presented his opinion of his proper theater of operations. The units that formed the new army became famous in the fighting at Richmond and later operations, but their organizational structure would change markedly over the summer of 1862 as Lee quickly weeded out the older and more ineffective commanders and streamlined the army's structure.

Lee's army during the Seven Days Battle consisted of eleven divisions grouped into three separate "commands" (wings) led by Major Generals John B. Magruder, James Longstreet, and Thomas J. Jackson, plus Major General Theophilus Holmes' independent division. Experience showed that this was too unwieldy an organization, particularly when high command rested on undeserving shoulders. Quite understandably, Lee's first action after the successful conclusion of the Seven Days' Battle was to get rid of the generals whose performances had fallen short. He would then be free to reorganize his command under the more favored generals who remained.

The first of Lee's senior officers to leave was Major General John B. Magruder. He had shown himself to be not much of a fighter, and he was anxious to assume independent command in the Trans Mississippi Department, to which he had been provisionally assigned in late May. On 2 July, the day after the battle of Malvern Hill, Magruder applied for permission to leave Virginia, and Lee readily approved the next day. Magruder's large division was promptly broken up, with half assigned to Brigadier General D.R. Jones and the other half to Brigadier General Lafayette McLaws.

Major General Benjamin Huger was also under severe criticism for his lack of aggression in the recently completed campaign. Lee politely suggested that he take up a post in South Carolina, but then suddenly relieved Holmes of field command and assigned him a desk job as Inspector of Artillery and Ordnance. Huger does not appear to have objected, and the next year went to join Magruder in the Trans Mississippi Department. His division was turned over to Brigadier General R.H. Anderson.

Lee also was critical of the performance of 58 year old Major General Theophilus Holmes. Though Holmes' command technically belonged to the Department of North Carolina, he incurred Lee's displeasure enough to find himself transferred to the Department of the Trans Mississippi along with Magruder. His division was then assigned to Brigadier General John G. Walker.

The departure of Magruder, Huger and Holmes paved the way for Lee to reorganize his army into two wings, which was certainly a more efficient command structure than the three plus "commands" into which the army had previously been divided. Lee entrusted one wing to Jackson. This wing had at its nucleus the two divisions that Jackson had led so gloriously in his Spring 1862 Valley Campaign. These were Ewell's division, which was now increased to four brigades with the addition of Lawton's Georgia brigade from Jackson's old division, and Jackson's old division itself, now led by Brigadier General Charles Winder as the command's senior officer. Brigadier General William Whiting had also been serving under Jackson's command, but he and Stonewall had a major misunderstanding of some sort, so Lee detached Whiting's small division from Jackson's command. Lee also found it necessary to detach D.H. Hill and his strong division from Jackson's wing. D.H. Hill was a solid fighter, but he had a strong tongue and an uneven temperament, so much so that Lee found it necessary to assign him temporarily to North Carolina on 21 July. Hill's division was to remain in the defenses of Richmond for the moment, and so would not accompany the army to Second Bull Run. To compensate for the loss of Whiting's and D.H. Hill's commands, Jackson was assigned A.P. Hill's large division of six brigades. The fiery A.P. Hill did not get along at all well with Jackson's strange and dour ways during the Second Bull Run and Antietam campaigns, but this difficulty did not affect his fighting qualities.

Most of the troops not assigned to Jackson's wing were given to Longstreet's command. Major General James Longstreet had done a solid job in the Seven Days Battle, and had the important value of being a non-Virginian in an army in-creasingly dominated by Virginia officers. The transfer of A.P. Hill's large division to Jackson's wing left Longstreet with an overextended command structure consisting of six small divisions plus Brigadier General Nathan Evans' independent South Carolina brigade. The lack of any experienced division commanders brought Lee to break up Longstreet's former division of six brigades into two mini-divisions of three brigades each, commanded by Brigadier Generals James Kemper and Cadmus Wilcox. Longstreet's wing also included Brigadier General D.R. Jones' division of three brigades (formerly part of Magruder's division) and Brigadier General R.H. Anderson's division of three brigades (formerly Huger's). Lee also attached Brigadier General W.H.C. Whiting's division to Longstreet's command. To everyone's relief, the often disagreeable Whiting went on sick leave at the beginning of August, and command of his two brigade division devolved on Brigadier General John B. Hood.

Lee's decision to divide his army into two wings worked excellently during the Second Bull Run campaign, as did his selection of Jackson and Longstreet as wing commanders. Their temperaments balanced each other nicely, and the two would work together superbly in tandem through the heyday of the Army of Northern Virginia, from Second Bull Run through Antietam and Fredericksburg to the army's greatest triumph at Chancellorsville, where their partnership would be ended by Jackson's mortal wound. The only real tinkering that Lee still needed to do with the command structure he established just before the Second Bull Run campaign, was to decrease the number of small divisions in Longstreet's wing. This was done on the way to Antietam, when R.H. Anderson's and Wilcox's divisions were recombined under R.H. Anderson, and Kemper's and D.R. Jones' divisions were united under D.R. Jones. The addition of McLaws' division to Longstreet's wing and D.H. Hill's to Jackson's wing during the Antietam campaign would give Lee's Army of Northern Virginia the basic organization it would carry for the next nine months until Jackson's death necessitated a major restructuring of the army into three separate corps.

Lee's Chief Lieutenants

The fighting machine known to history as the Army of Northern Virginia took shape at Richmond during the Seven Days battle of June-July 1862 and rapidly reached peak efficiency in the next twelve months, when it fought four major battles (Second Bull Run, Antietam, Fredreicksburg, Chancellorsville) without a loss against a numerically superior foe. Much of Lee's success was due to the skills of his two leading lieutenants, James Longstreet and Thomas "Stonewall" Jackson, whose partnership reached an early and spectacular success during the Second Bull Run campaign.

Thomas Jonathan Jackson was born in western Virginia in 1824 to a relatively poor family. He had a particularly rough childhood during which his father died when he was 3 and his mother passed away when he was 7. To his good fortune, he was then raised by a kindly uncle, Cummins Jackson. After a brief and unsatisfactory stint as a constable, Thomas sought and gained admittance to West Point, from which he graduated in 1846, ranking 17th in a class of 59. He then went at once to the Mexican War, where his bravery as an artillery officer won him two battlefield promotions. After the war, he remained in the army until 1851, when he resigned in order to become a teacher at the Virginia Military Institute. In 1853 he married Elinor Junkin, daughter of the President of nearby Washington College. She died a year later after giving birth to a stillborn baby. In 1857 Jackson was married for a second time. His bride was Mary Anna Morrison, whose sister was married to future Confederate general Daniel Harvey Hill. Their first daughter died of typhoid fever in 1858 at the age of one month. A second daughter, Julia, was born in November 1862, and lived a full life.

At the beginning of the Civil War Jackson was appointed a colonel and led what would become the nucleus of the famous Stonewall Brigade. He acquired his nickname "Stonewall" at the battle of First Bull Run as a tribute to his defensive ability at the height of the battle. Jackson achieved perhaps his greatest fame during his Spring 1862 Shenandoah Valley campaign, when he marched his men with at times amazing speed and won all but one of his battles, in the process defeating or keeping in check Union forces that were three times the size of his own command. After the Valley Campaign was concluded, Jackson was brought to Richmond, where he and his tired troops did not perform as notably as before during the Seven Days battle. However, once they were rested and returned to the Virginia Piedmont, Jackson returned to his former form and literally marched circles around Pope's army during the Second Bull Run campaign. He also met great success with his capture of Harpers Ferry in September, and with his defensive work on the army's left at Antietam and on the right at Fredericksburg. Jackson's last great battle was at Chancellorsville, where his bold flank march against Hooker's much larger army won the day for the Confederates. At the very height of his success, though, Jackson was accidentally wounded by his own troops on the evening of 2 May 1863. He died eight days later of complications (pneumonia), and was buried in Lexington, probably mourned more than any other Confederate soldier who fell during the war.

James Longstreet's early life was similar in many ways to Jackson's, though he came from a more middle class family. Longstreet was born in 1821, three years before Stonewall, and as a South Carolinian was one of the few non-Virginians to attain high rank in Lee's army. Like Jackson, his father died when he was young, and he was raised by a favorite uncle, Augustus B. Longstreet, who was a well-to-do educator and writer. Longstreet graduated from West Point four years ahead of Jack-

son, ranking 54th in the 62 students in the Class of 1842. Like Jackson, he earned two promotions during the Mexican War, where he was wounded once (Jackson was unscathed). Longstreet then stayed in the army and served at various posts in the western plains until the Civil War broke out.

Longstreet's early fame in the Civil War was not as great as Jackson's. He also commanded a brigade at First Bull Run, but did not win the glory that Stonewall did. He then became a division commander during the early stages of the Peninsula campaign, when Jackson was conducting his famous Valley campaign. Longstreet's failure as a wing commander led to the Confederate defeat at Seven Pines, but he reestablished himself in that capacity by his reliable work during the Seven Days battle. When Lee reorganized his army after that campaign, Longstreet was given command of the army's right wing (later the First Corps), while Jackson was given the left wing (later the Second Corps).

Longstreet generally moved more slowly than Jackson, and usually favored defensive fighting over attacking. These characteristics can be clearly seen in the Second Bull Run campaign, where some historians are unjustly critical of his delay in counterattacking to support Jackson. Longstreet's mastery of defense can be seen in his performance at Antietam and Fredericksburg, while his ability to strike forcefully on the offensive was evident on the second day at Second Bull Run and the second day at Gettysburg.

Longstreet was not nearly as successful at independent command as Jackson was. He failed in his effort to recapture Suffolk, Virginia, in the spring of 1863 (when he missed being at Chancellorsville), and he likewise failed to retake Knoxville, Tennessee, that Fall. Longstreet's difference of opinion with Lee over the conduct of the Gettysburg campaign, where he favored the strategic offensive but the tactical defensive, as well as his opposition to the launching of Pickett's Charge, are well known. These differences may have led to his temporary transfer to the war's western theater in September 1863, where he aided substantially in the Confederate victory at Chickamauga. Lee welcomed him back to Virginia for the Spring 1864 campaign, when Longstreet became in effect the army's second in command. He was accidentally wounded by his own men during the battle of the Wilderness on 6 May 1864, at nearly the same location where Jackson had been mortally wounded almost exactly a year before. The wound put him out of action for almost six months. He returned to action in time to command a section of the Richmond defenses until the end of the war.

Longstreet's postwar career grew to be quite controversial. He chose to become a Republican (perhaps because he had been related to U.S. Grant by marriage), and accepted a number of political appointments from Grant and the following Republican presidents. Many Southerners could not forgive him for this, or for his criticism of Lee's conduct during the Gettysburg campaign; as a result, Longstreet began to be blamed personally for the loss at Gettysburg. He published his memoirs, *From Manassas to Appomattox*,

in 1896, eight years before his death in 1904.

Like Jackson, Longstreet married twice. In 1849 he was wed to Louise Garland, the daughter of his regimental commander; she was a cousin of Julia Dent, the wife of the future Federal commander, U.S. Grant. The couple had ten children, three of whom died during a cholera epidemic in Richmond in early 1863. Longstreet experienced more tragedy in 1889 when his uninsured house burned down, and then his wife died. The general astounded everyone when he married a second wife, Helen Dortch, in 1897—he was 85 at the time and she was only 34! She died in 1962, the last surviving widow of a Confederate general officer.

There is no doubt that Longstreet's performance during the war is colored by the length of his service and the controversies that attended his postwar career and writings. It is interesting to speculate what our view of him would be had he died in early 1864 instead of being wounded at the Wilderness, before he penned his controversial postwar writings. Similarly, it is hard to imagine what role Jackson might have played in the war if he had survived his wounding at Chancellorsville. His death at the height of his glory made him a martyr to the Southern cause, a role that surely would have changed had he lived to fight when the South had such depleted resources in 1864 and 1865. There is also no telling how he would have written about the war afterwards, had he lived through it and been able to write his memoirs.

CHAPTER IV

Cedar Mountain

*I*t was not until 29 July, a little over a month after he had taken command of his army, that Pope finally left his office in Washington in order to join his troops in the field. The position of his army had not changed much as it continued to guard a 60 mile front from the Blue Ridge to the Potomac River east of Fredericksburg. McDowell's corps, screened by Bayard's cavalry brigade, held the army's left wing, with King's division posted at Fredericksburg and Ricketts' division some 25 miles to the northwest at Warrenton. Most of Pope's weight was on his right flank, where he had moved Banks' and Sigel's corps to a position east of the Blue Ridge near Sperryville, about 30 miles north of Jackson's position at Gordonsville. Banks' front was screened by Buford's cavalry brigade, which had almost daily skirmishes with Jackson's mounted troops.

Pope's first action after taking to the field on 29 July was to hold a review of Ricketts' division at Waterloo Bridge, near Warrenton. He then joined Banks at the latter's headquarters near Little Washington. Here he developed a plan to concentrate his army near Culpeper, for the purpose of conducting a general advance to the line of Robertson's River. His plan was to take possession of Charlottesville and push Jackson back from Gordonsville. On 3 August he promised Halleck that he could accomplish this goal within 10 days if Jackson did not receive any more reinforcements from Richmond.

It seems odd, in retrospect, that Pope began his campaign just at the same time that McClellan was being pulled back from

Most of Banks' troops passed through the town of Culpeper on their way to fight at Cedar Mountain, located about 9 miles to the south-west.

Harrison's Landing. Pope, of course, did not at first know what was being done about McClellan, but Halleck and Lincoln surely did as they read Pope's daily telegraphic reports and approved his plans. They obviously felt that Pope had enough strength to deal with Jackson, but it might have been wiser to hold him back until McClellan's troops arrived at Aquia Creek. Perhaps the administration wanted to keep Jackson occupied so that he would not return to Richmond to help Lee attack McClellan while the latter was in the awkward process of withdrawing.

In preparation for his advance, Pope decided to establish a strong cavalry screen to the south of Culpeper. On 2 August he directed Buford to move his new command (the cavalry brigade assigned to Banks' corps) to Madison Court House, and from there send pickets and outposts out as far as Stanardsville and the Rapidan. He was to keep in constant contact with the enemy, and would have a provisional brigade of infantry in support along the Sperryville Road in case of need. At the same time,

Bayard was to assemble McDowell's cavalry and proceed to a point at least five miles south of Culpeper. He was to picket the Rapidan east of Buford's line, and would be supported by Crawford's infantry brigade at Culpeper.

The campaign got underway on 2 August when Brigadier General Samuel Crawford advanced two cavalry regiments (*1st New York* and *1st Vermont*) to Orange Court House. This probe was turned back by "Grumble" Jones' 7th Virginia Cavalry, but not before the Yankees captured some prisoners, who confirmed the news of Hill's arrival in Gordonsville.

Pope now moved his cavalry forward to an advanced position along the Rapidan. Once that line was secured, he began pushing his infantry forward. Ricketts' division, marching from Warrenton, reached Culpeper on 5 August, and Banks' troops began moving from Sperryville towards the Hazel River on the 6th, followed by Sigel's.

Pope's movements were promptly reported to Jackson by some of the numerous Confederate scouts and spies who were active behind the Union lines. From them Jackson learned that Pope's troops were greatly strung out in their line of march, and only a portion had yet reached Culpeper. This was just the news that Stonewall had been waiting to hear. On the afternoon of 7 August he abruptly halted the Garnett court martial and issued orders for his men to start moving north. His goal was to meet and defeat the Yankee vanguard before the rest of Pope's command could come up.

In order to succeed, Jackson had to push his men forward promptly and speedily. He had his troops under way by 1700 that day. Ewell's division moved up on the left to Liberty Mills on the Rapidan, and a few of his men apparently crossed to the north side of the river. Jackson's division, which was still under Jackson's personal command, left its encampment to the south and southeast of Liberty Mills and marched from 5 to 7 miles before bivouacking after dark just to the west of Orange. Hill's division, with Starke's Louisiana brigade attached, also marched north and encamped on the outskirts of Orange.

Jackson's plan was to cross the Rapidan early on 8 August and then continue north towards Culpeper, where he anticipated striking Pope's vanguard on the 9th. He sent out his marching

Major General Thomas J. Jackson's aggressiveness kept Pope continually off balance during the campaign, but cost his own troops heavy casualties at Cedar Mountain, Groveton, and 2nd Bull Run.

orders for the 8th sometime the night before. All troops were to be ready to march at dawn. Ewell would lead the way to Barnett's Ford, followed by Hill and then Jackson's division.

During the night, however, Jackson changed his mind and decided that it would be better for Ewell to move along the Rapidan from Liberty Mills to Barnett's Ford, rather than proceed to Barnett's via Orange. This route certainly made more sense, since Orange was already occupied Hill's and Jackson's divisions, which under Jackson's original orders would have had to sit and wait for Ewell to arrive and pass by before they could move out. Under the revised orders, Hill's and Jackson's divisions could march out at dawn and link up with Ewell at Barnett's. Ewell's separate line of advance would also make for less crowding on the road from Orange to Barnett's, and his activity along the Rapidan near Liberty Mills might deceive Pope's cavalry as to Jackson's intentions.

Jackson's revised plans were certainly an improvement, but they had one major hitch: Hill for some reason (probably a staff error) never received them, even though he was encamped very near Jackson's headquarters at Orange. At dawn on 8 August, Hill and his leading brigade were in Orange, ready and waiting for Ewell to come up so that they could fall into column behind him.

What happened next is difficult to untangle because of conflicting accounts by the principals involved. Jackson said that he soon noticed that Hill was not moving, so he rode to Hill's camp to find out why. There he met Hill, who stated that he was waiting for the division ahead of him to come up. Jackson made no comment, but instead left Hill where he was and sent orders for his old division, which had just reached the edge of town, to take the road ahead of Hill.

Meanwhile Hill (who never mentioned this brief meeting with Jackson) was still standing in Orange, waiting for Ewell to come up. After a while he saw an infantry column approach and then start passing his troops. Quite naturally, he assumed that this was Ewell's command, though in fact it was Jackson's division, which had just been sent on ahead by Jackson. It was not until more than a full brigade had passed that Hill found out the column's true identity. He was now in a quandary, since the only orders he had received directed him to march ahead of Jackson's division, not behind it. Hill decided that the best thing to do was to wait for all of Jackson's division to pass, and then fall in behind it. This decision was complicated when Hill saw a large wagon train come rumbling up behind Jackson's division. Since he understood that Jackson wanted each division to march with its own trains, Hill held his troops in place still longer as he waited for these wagons to pass him by also.

Once he finally began to move, Hill did not proceed far before his men were forced to halt because the wagons in front of them were not moving. Hill rode ahead to see what the problem was, and found a huge traffic jam. It seems that the main body of Ewell's force, which had been marching eastward along the southern bank of the Rapidan, had reached Barnett's Ford Road ahead of the rest of the army. As a result, the progress of Jackson's division was hindered because Ewell's trains were on the road ahead of him. Hill reported the situation to Jackson between 1600 and 1700, and soon afterwards received orders to return to Orange for the night. Since his lead brigade had managed to cover only a mile during the day and some of his rear troops had not moved at all, Hill simply bivouacked his men where they were.

Jackson's division also had a frustrating march during the day. Its lead elements had marched out quickly enough once they received their revised orders from Jackson. After passing through Orange, they had a clear road to Barnett's Ford, which the head of the column crossed at once. These troops then stopped for supper about a mile beyond the river, and for some reason waited for fresh rations to be brought up from their wagons, which were at the rear of the division's column. By this time, however, the tail end of the division's column had become entangled with Ewell's wagons, which were coming in from the southwest. As a result, some troops from Jackson's division did not clear Orange until noon. They managed to fight their way through the traffic jam at the ford and the joined the rest of their division, which was still halted at its meal stop a mile north of the ford.

Ewell's division was the only part of Jackson's command to cover a significant amount of ground on this confusing and very hot day (it was by one account 96 degrees at 1200 and still 86 degrees an hour after sunset). As already noted, Ewell had reached Liberty Mills on the Rapidan on the evening of 7 August. The next morning he sent part of his command across the ford there with instructions to march northeastward along the river in order to link up with the rest of the army somewhere along the Culpeper Road north of Barnett's Ford. This detachment made good time, and as a consequence reached Barnett's Ford well ahead of the rest of Jackson's men, most of whom had gotten off to a late start because of all the confusion in Orange already discussed. Ewell's men did not wait for the rest of the army, but proceeded north on the Culpeper Road. Just past Locust Dale they crossed Robertson's River and then Crooked Run. The day's intense heat forced the column to go into camp about 1400 at Crooked Run Church, after marching some 8 to 10 miles.

The remainder of Ewell's division had a tougher day's march. Ewell's orders were to proceed eastward with part of his division on the southern side of the Rapidan. Unfortunately for him, there were no direct roads in the area, and the men sent on

Brigadier General Charles Winder, commander of Jackson's old division at Cedar Mountain, was sick on the day of the battle but insisted on entering the fight. He was gravely wounded by a Union shell at the beginning of the battle and died that evening.

this route had to trek overland through the fields and woods as best they could. Ewell's wagons, which also took the southern route, had an even more circuitous march since they had to follow lanes and byways as best they could. When the wagons finally reached the Culpeper Road, they found that they had to share the roadway with the infantry and trains of Winder's division, so forming the traffic jam that totally blocked Hill's advance, as previously described.

Ewell's march north of the river was screened during the day by the cavalry of Robertson's Laurel Brigade. Robertson sent part of his command to the left to watch Buford's cavalry outposts near Madison Court House, and then deployed the bulk of his unit facing Bayard's troops on the road to Culpeper. The opposing sides clashed all day as Bayard's command was continually pushed back by Robertson's superior numbers.

Bayard's troopers, however, were far from passive during the day. Bayard felt that something was afoot when he learned of Ewell's advance to Liberty Mills on the evening of 7 August, so early on the 8th he sent Colonel Joseph Karge with 160 men of the *1st New Jersey Cavalry* on a roundabout probe in that direction. Karge's men came upon an enemy column of troops and succeeded at capturing a squad of 20 Confederate infantrymen, who confirmed that Ewell had crossed the Rapidan. During the afternoon, another squadron of the *1st New Jersey* saw the trains and troops of Winder's division in their camp at near Crooked Run Church in the vicinity of Cedar Mountain, and reported their findings to Pope.

All this activity by the Union cavalry caused great concern to Jackson, who was particularly worried about the security of his trains. For this reason, he decided to detach Lawton's large brigade and post it at the rear of Winder's division in order to guard his wagons. This assignment would prevent Lawton's men from participating in the coming battle, where their presence would be sorely missed.

Despite the successful advance of Ewell's division and Robertson's cavalry, 8 August had not been a good day for Jackson's vaunted foot cavalry. Jackson had succeeded in getting only half of his men across the Rapidan, and as a result his troops were almost as badly strung out as were Pope's. In addition, most of the Confederate troops were exhausted from the day's heat, which did not promise to let up on the morrow.

Blame for the poor day's march must be placed squarely on Jackson's shoulders. He should have directed Ewell to cross all of his troops at Liberty Mills and then proceed to Culpeper from there. This would have eliminated much of the congestion on the road from Orange to Barnett's Ford. Jackson also erred by not anticipating the bottle neck that would arise at Barnett's. There were other fords available for use, particularly the one at Peyton's Mill, two miles downstream from Barnett's. Jackson also should have held his trains back and given roadway priority to his infantry. Lastly, he failed to keep Hill accurately informed of his plans, either in writing or by direct meeting. Jackson had a bad habit of keeping his plans to himself and of telling his officers only as much as he felt they needed to know. This caused a particular problem with Hill, who was serving under Jackson for the first time. Jackson later put the blame for the day's snafus directly on Hill's shoulders, even though he himself was largely at a loss to explain why and when his plans went awry. The working relationship between the two generals certainly was not off to a good start.

Pope's troops also suffered under the blistering sun of Friday,

8 August, though their march was not nearly as confused as Jackson's. Brigadier General George H. Gordon noted that the roads were lined with troops who were exhausted from the heat or suffering from sunstroke, many of whom died. Pope had learned from his active cavalry outposts that Jackson's troops were crossing the Rapidan at Liberty Mills and points farther east. At first he was not sure whether Jackson's goal was Madison Court House or Culpeper. However, as the day progressed, it became evident that Jackson was heading northeast. Pope was not hesitant to confront Jackson, since he was certain that he outnumbered Stonewall's force, so he pushed Banks' corps forward to support Crawford's brigade and Bayard's cavalry, which had encamped behind Cedar Run, about four miles north of Ewell's advanced camp a Crooked Run Church. Banks' troops marched on the 8th from Hazel Run to Culpeper, about four miles north of Crawford's and Bayard's position.

Though he was committed to a concentration on Jackson's front south of Culpeper, Pope was still wary that the Confederates might make a move against Madison Court House. To guard against this possibility, he moved Ricketts' division of McDowell's corps to a position about three miles south of Culpeper, where the main road to Madison Court House branched off. From there Ricketts could support Crawford and Bayard if necessary, or he could march westward to guard the army's right flank.

On 8 August Pope ordered McDowell's other division, King's, to head west to Culpeper as soon as Gibbon's troops returned from a raid they were conducting against the Virginia Central Railroad. Pope, though, was aware that King would need at least two or three days to traverse the 30 miles between Fredericksburg and Culpeper. King's absence would lower Pope's available strength to about 40,000 men, provided that Sigel came up promptly. It seems that Sigel, who was encamped at Sperryville on the 7th, was having a slow time getting started on the 8th. Pope had ordered him to march to Culpeper, which was 17 miles to the southeast of Sperryville on a direct road. Sigel spent much of the day resupplying his men, and still had not broken camp at 1850 when he telegraphed Pope to clarify what route he should take to reach Culpeper. Pope replied in stern terms that Sigel was to take the direct road, and was to reach Culpeper by noon the next day. Some of Sigel's own staff officers had difficulty deciding if Sigel was deliberately malingering on the 8th or was just being "stupid," as one modern historian has put it. Whatever was Sigel's state of mind, his delayed advance greatly reduced Pope's strength at the anticipated point of contact with Jackson, so endangering the entire campaign.

This situation certainly did not please Pope, particularly since he had just received the following instructions from Halleck: "Do not advance, so as to expose yourself to any disaster, until we can get more troops upon the Rappahannock." Pope nevertheless did not recall the troops that he had posted south of Culpeper, nor did he at once advise Banks to act cautiously until Sigel arrived.

On the morning of 9 August Pope sent his chief of cavalry, Brigadier General Benjamin Roberts, to Banks with verbal orders "merely to keep the enemy in check by occupying a strong position in his front until the whole of the disposable forces under my command should be concentrated in the neighborhood." This, at least., is what Pope intended for Roberts to say. But it seems that Roberts spoke at length with Banks about Pope's plans, which included the intention of attacking once the army was concentrated. Banks had one of his staff officers write down what Roberts said, and at a Congressional hearing three years later produced a paper showing that his orders were "to move to the front immediately, assume command of all the forces in the front, deploy his skirmishers if the enemy advances, and attack him immediately as he approaches, and be reinforced from here."

Interpretation of these conflicting orders is crucial to understanding Pope's plans for the day, and also to attributing responsibility for the battle that followed. It is possible that both Pope and Banks altered their recollection of events afterwards in order to defend their actions. But what seems more likely is that Roberts (whose memory of the order in question differed from what Banks had written down) simply talked too much to Banks after telling him what Pope wanted him to do; he also communicated Pope's plans for later. Banks, who appears to

Major General Nathaniel P. Banks, commander of Pope's II Corps, was defeated by Jackson at Cedar Mountain on 9 August, and played only a minor role in the remainder of the 2nd Bull Run campaign.

have been itching for a fight, seems to have listened more carefully to Roberts' later words than to his original instructions. Whatever actually happened, the blame for this situation must rest with Pope, who should have sent clear written instructions to Banks.

Banks received his orders from Roberts around 1000 and then began moving his troops forward to support Crawford's and Bayard's line behind Cedar Run. As already noted, Crawford had moved to the support of Bayard the previous afternoon. He formed behind a branch of Cedar Run about a mile south of Colvin's Tavern. Bayard had been skirmishing sporadically with Confederate pickets all morning, and towards 1100 his men fell under the fire of some enemy cannons that had taken up a position on the northern slope of nearby Cedar Mountain. All indications were that heavy Confederate forces were heading their way, and Bayard and Crawford were both relieved to see Banks' troops begin arriving at 1200.

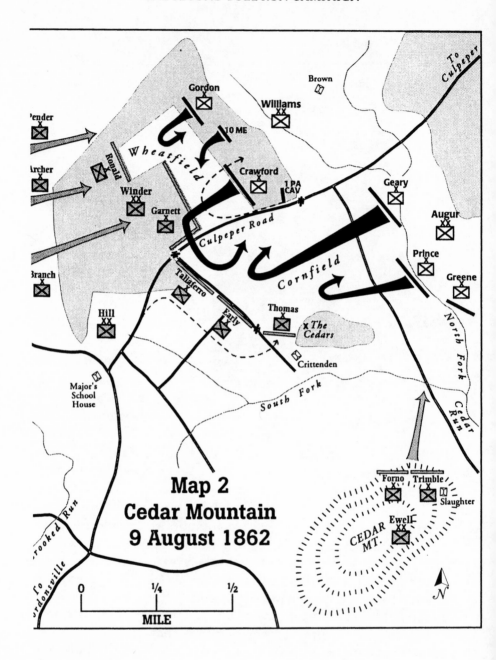

Map 2
Cedar Mountain
9 August 1862

Brigadier General A.S. Williams, commander of Banks' *1st Division* (to which Crawford belonged) arrived first with the balance of his command. He sent Gordon's brigade and a battery to some heights on Crawford's right, near which some of Bayard's cavalry were skirmishing with a few Confederate horsemen. At around 1400 Banks arrived with his *2nd Division*, commanded by Brigadier General Christopher C. Augur, and began posting these troops to the east of the Culpeper Road. There they relieved several of Crawford's regiments, permitting Crawford to reunite his command on the western side of the road, where he connected Augur's line with Gordon's. When his dispositions were completed at about 1500, Banks' line ran on a northwest to southeast angle for about three miles, with the Culpeper Road at its center. Banks' command numbered about 9000 men, including Bayard's cavalry, some of which were stationed at each flank of the infantry line.

Jackson, who was still disgusted about his lack of progress on the 8th, was not optimistic about his chances for success on 9 August. Early in the day he wrote to Lee from his headquarters near Locust Dale, "Today I do not expect much more than to close up and clear the country around the train of the enemy's cavalry. I fear that the expedition will, in consequence of my tardy movements, be productive of but little good." He had hoped when he started out two days earlier to be in possession of Culpeper by noon of the 9th, but this was now out of the question. His advance troops (Ewell's) were still five miles short of their goal, with their road now blocked by Federal cavalry and an undetermined force of infantry, and additional Union troops were now known to be in Culpeper.

Jackson's plan for the day, then, was simply to probe towards the Union forces near Cedar Mountain and see what was there. Around 0700 he sent Ewell orders to move forward and develop the troops on his front. While this movement was underway, Jackson continued to have concern for his left flank, in case Pope might attempt to make an advance through Madison Court House. For this reason, he directed Robertson to conduct a reconnaissance in that direction. Robertson dispatched "Grumble" Jones' 7th Virginia Cavalry, which rode all day and covered 25 miles "without incident or discovery of record."

The battle of Cedar Mountain, as seen from the Union lines. Cedar (Slaughter) Mountain is in the left background.

Ewell got his lead brigade, Early's, underway at about 0800. The day was already hot, above 80 degrees, and promised to be blistering again; temperatures outside of Washington D.C. would reach 98 degrees at 1400. Early's orders were to approach the Union cavalry camp known to be in his front. He was also to keep a cautious eye on the Federal troopers who had been active on the western side of the Culpeper Road. To this purpose Early detached one and one-half regiments, a quarter of his command, as he moved forward; these absent troops would also be sorely missed in the coming engagement.

Early reached Robertson's advanced cavalry line at midmorning and then halted for awhile to observe the position of the Union troops facing them. Late in the forenoon Early was ordered by Ewell to go forward and secure a crossroads in the Union front where the road from Madison Court House angled into the Culpeper Road from the northwest. As his troops formed in some woods near Major's School House, Early moved a couple cannons to the right to take position at the foot of Cedar Mountain. (Cedar Mountain was also called Slaughter Mountain, after the farm of a Reverend Philip Slaughter who lived there; the name "Cedar Mountain" has been preferred over the years because it is more euphonious.) These guns, joined by some of Robertson's, soon engaged the Federals and forced Bayard's cavalry to seek a more sheltered position. By now it was clear that Bayard was supported by a strong command of Union infantry, and that more Yankee troops were nearing the field.

Sometime before noon Jackson reached the front and conferred with Ewell. After reviewing the Union position, Jackson determined to attack it using a double envelopment movement. Early was to be sent up the Culpeper Road to occupy the enemy's attention, while Ewell took two brigades (Trimble's and Forno's) to the right, where they were to pass over the base of Cedar Mountain and then turn the Federal left. Early would be supported on his left by Winder's division as soon as it came up; Winder's line of advance would be to the left for the purpose of turning the Union right. (Brigadier General Charles S. Winder, commander of the Stonewall Brigade and senior officer in Jackson's division, had assumed command of the division that morning.) Jackson had confidence that his attack would succeed since his two front divisions, Ewell's and Winder's, easily outnumbered the Union troops he saw in their front, and he knew that Hill's troops were coming up behind Winder's to lend more weight to the attack if needed.

Jackson was in no hurry to attack, since it would take some time for Winder to come up and for Trimble to get into position. He sent orders for Early not to advance until he heard from Winder that everything was ready. Then, quite amazingly, he stretched out to take a nap on the porch of Ewell's headquarters. Ewell took the clue from his commander, and likewise stretched out under the shade of a tree. The heat of the noonday sun was apparently too much for almost everyone.

While he waited for Winder to come up, Early shifted his 1500 troops so as to avoid the view of some Union cavalry on the next ridge. Sometime after 1400 he finally heard that Winder had arrived, so he began moving forward towards his right. There he engaged and drove back a portion of the *1st Rhode Island Cavalry*. Upon halting, he saw a line of Federal cannons atop a ridge less than a mile away. Quickly he called for a battery to face them, and formed it in a grove of cedars on his right flank, supported by the 12th Georgia.

When Winder came up and began forming on Early's left, he, too, noticed the Federal artillery on the crest northeast of a branch of Cedar Run. By 1600 he posted Colonel T.S. Garnett's brigade on his extreme right front, poised to rush forward and try to capture the Federal guns. However, Garnett (not to be confused with Brigadier General Richard B. Garnett, who had previously been relieved by Jackson of command of the Stonewall Brigade) made a reconnaissance and found that the Union right extended much farther west than Winder had thought. Any attack on the Federal guns would have to move across the front of the enemy's right wing, which was too dangerous a venture to attempt.

When Ewell was apprised of this situation, he called off Garnett's attack and directed his artillery chief, Major Snowden Andrews, to bring up his best guns to a point along the Culpeper Road and engage the enemy. At about 1615 Andrews position four rifled guns and a Napoleon cannon as ordered and opened fire. Their shots provoked an instant and effective reply from Banks' guns. Early's cannons posted at the cedar grove joined the fray, and an active artillery duel followed for the next hour.

Eventually the Confederates began to get the better of the fight, but not without considerable loss. Among their casualties was Major Snowden Andrews, who was still recovering from a wound he had received during the Seven Days Battle. He was struck by a shell fragment that tore his abdomen open and spilled his entrails. Such wounds, or the peritonitis that followed, were almost always fatal. Andrews, however, refused to succomb, and he boldly asked a surgeon to sew him up. Amazingly, he did not develop peritonitis, but recovered enough to fight again at Second Winchester in June 1863, where he was again wounded. He survived this wound, too, and, equipped with a silver shield to cover his tender belly, lived on for another 40 years until he died in 1903.

The day's highest ranking casualty was to be Brigadier General Charles Winder, the newly appointed commander of Jackson's old division. Winder had been seriously ill for the past several days, but he let Jackson know that he would take to the field if a battle were imminent. Jackson let him rest until that morning, when he called the 33 year old general forward from his sick bed. Winder had to be carried to the field in an ambulance. After posting his infantry, Winder went to join Andrews' artillery and help direct their fire. At the height of the action, he turned to give an order and was struck by a shell that tore through his left arm and mangled his side terribly. He died a short while later.

Shortly after Winder was struck, the artillery duel reached a new crisis. Hill, whose division was just beginning to reach the field, was concerned by the ferocity of the ongoing artillery fight and directed his artillery chief, Lieutenant Colonel R.L. Walker, to bring forward his rifled guns to help. Walker had some difficulty advancing because of all the traffic on the Culpeper Road, but was eventually able to bring four guns forward and post them on Early's left front. His guns, though, were unsupported there, and Walker was totally unaware that he faced a strong line of Federal skirmishers less than 200 yards away. The Yankees at once attempted to seize Walker's guns, a movement that had good prospects for success because artillery fire against loosely deployed skirmishers was about as effective as trying to shoot flies with a gun. However, Early saw the Federal advance develop and ordered a portion of his left wing to charge with a yell. Early's sudden attack startled Walker's cannoneers as much as the Union skirmishers. The Yankees quickly withdrew as the Confederate guns redoubled their fire. Then, ominously, the cannons on both sides began to cease shooting in anticipation of the next stage of the battle.

Despite the confusion in Winder's division caused by the loss of their commander, Jackson was preparing to mount his attack as soon as Hill's division came up. Brigadier General William B. Taliaferro, Winder's successor as commander of Jackson's old division, had shifted his own brigade to the eastern side of the Culpeper Road in order to assist Early, and by 1730 Hill's infantry was starting to arrive. Hill placed his lead brigade, Thomas', on Early's right to help fill the gap between Early's line and the remainder of Ewell's troops on the northern slope of Cedar Mountain. (The new commander of William Taliaferro's brigade was his uncle, Colonel Alexander G. Taliaferro of the 23rd Virginia. For convenience, the brigade will simply be called "Taliaferro's").

Banks, however, was not about to sit still any longer. Since coming up in the early afternoon he had seen no action from the Confederates beyond skirmish and artillery fire.

At 1425 he reported to Pope that, "The enemy shows his cavalry (which is strong) ostentatiously. No infantry seen and not much artillery. Woods on left said to be full of troops. A visit to the front does not impress that the enemy intends immediate attack; he seems, however, to be taking positions."

Jackson's failure to press an attack during the afternoon persuaded Banks that the Confederates might be weaker than they appeared. At about 1700 he informed Pope that he was sending an infantry regiment forward on each of his wings to meet the Confederate skirmishers. It did not take long for this movement to develop into a general advance by his entire force. The reason why he ordered this attack is not clear. He may have felt that he had the authority to do so under the verbal orders he had received from Banks that morning, as already discussed, or he simply may have thought that he had a local tactical advantage that he could exploit successfully. Whatever were his reasons (he never filed a battle report to explain his actions), Banks would have done better to attack a few hours earlier, before Hill's men came up to double Jackson's strength.

Augur's troops on Banks' left advanced to the attack somewhat before Geary's division on the right. Augur's command consisted of just over 3000 men in 10 regiments, plus a battalion of U.S. regular infantry. He chose to leave Greene's brigade of two regiments behind on his far left in order to keep an eye on Ewell's two brigades posted on Cedar Mountain. His remaining troops (Geary's Ohio brigade and Prince's mixed brigade) would have only a slight numerical superiority over the two Confederate brigades (Taliaferro's and Early's) on his front. Since the Confederate line here was well bolstered by artillery, Augur's prospects for success were not great.

Augur's advance was screened by his battalion of *U.S. Regulars*, who were the same troops that had almost seized Walker's guns a short while earlier. These troops, a combined command from the *8th* and *12th* regiments, fought bravely all afternoon in a thick cornfield that offered them only a modicum of cover. Their bravery earned them the praise of officers on both sides, particularly the Confederate gunners in the cedar grove on Early's front. To commemorate their valor, the coat of arms of the present *21st U.S. Infantry* (whose lineage stems from the *12th* regiment of the Civil War era) features an eradicated cedar tree, so honoring the *12th's* bravery at the battle of Cedar Mountain on 9 August 1862.

The same cornfield that sheltered Augur's skirmishers made it difficult for his regiments to advance in battle line. The corn was dense and uncut, and temperatures there must have been unbearable with the heat close to 100 degrees. In addition, the corn was so high that the troops could not see where they were going. Their only advantage from the situation was that the corn also prevented the Confederates from zeroing in on the Yankee lines.

Geary's brigade, which advanced on the right of Augur's line, attacked in reasonably good order, even though it was headed into the teeth of Andrews' cannons and also suffered a flanking fire from Garnett's command to the north of the roadway. This fire felled Augur early in the fight, and soon Geary also fell, struck by two wounds. Nevertheless, Geary's four regiments continued to press their attack against Taliaferro's brigade.

Prince's brigade, on Geary's left, experienced difficulties of a different nature. His two front regiments (*3rd Maryland* and *111th Pennsylvania*) were unnerved when his rear line accidentally fired into them. Even so, Prince might have been able to handle Early's brigade and the Confederate cannons at the cedar grove, if Thomas' fresh brigade of Hill's division had not come up just then on Early's right. Thomas' men had already marched ten miles under the day's broiling sun when they were sent into action against Prince's right by Jackson himself. By then the cornfield between the two lines had become a veritable maelstrom.

Augur's far left brigade, Greene's, stood by and did not enter the fight as Geary's and Prince's attack lost its momentum after about half an hour of fighting. Ewell's two brigades on Cedar Mountain did not enter the fight, either, because they were out of musketry range. The only support Jackson's troops got from their far right was from six of Latimer's cannons posted on Cedar Mountain, which were able to lob shells into the rear of the Union lines.

Brigadier General A.S. Williams, commander of Banks' right division, began his attack about 15 minutes later than Augur. Williams had a force of 3700 men in two brigades of four regiments each. Crawford's brigade, on the left of the division line next to the Culpeper Road, faced most of Garnett's brigade across an intervening wheatfield about one-eighth mile wide. Gordon's brigade, on Crawford's right, was angled somewhat to the rear, and because of this had to follow Crawford's line into action.

Crawford began his attack shortly before 1800 with only three of his four regiments (*5th Connecticut, 28th New York* and *46th New York*), since his *10th Maine* had been detached to serve as artillery support. He was, though, supported on his right by six companies of the *3rd Wisconsin* of Gordon's brigade, which had been sent forward by one of William's' staff officers. The Confederates held their fire against Crawford's attack until the Yankees reached the center of the 300 foot wide field separating the two forces. They then let loose several crashing volleys that felled the colonel of the *28th New York* and seven color bearers in the *5th Connecticut*.

Crawford's troops staggered but recovered and rushed towards Garnett's line. Their impetus carried them over the rail fence at the edge of the field and into the Confederate position at the edge of the woods. A sharp hand to hand fight ensued, in which Crawford's men soon triumphed because they had more men at the point of impact. Crawford's success was not due directly to the force of his initial attack, which could and should have been repulsed by judicious use of Confederate reserves. The Union triumph was instead due primarily to the awkward handling of the Confederate troops in this sector. As already noted, W.B. Taliaferro had just moved his brigade to the right to support Early, so temporarily stripping away his reserves on Garnett's portion of the line. The 10th Virginia had been sent to aid Garnett's left, but it was stumbling through the woods and was not yet in position when Crawford's attack struck. At the same time, the right half of Garnett's command had shifted from Crawford's front and were at the moment firing south across the Culpeper Road against the right flank of Geary's command. These conditions left only two of Garnett's units, the 1st Virginia

Battalion and the 42nd Virginia, facing Crawford's troops when the Union attack struck.

The Stonewall Brigade had also been ordered to support Garnett's left, but it was not up yet either. It had been drawn up in an open field during the early part of the action, and began to suffer so badly from overshoots during the prebattle artillery duel that it was moved into the woods north of the Culpeper Road for protection. When the command was called forward at the start of the infantry battle, its troops tried to march forward through the woods in battle line, which was a slow and difficult process. The brigade's progress was not aided by the fact that its commander, Colonel Charles Ronald of the 4th Virginia, was new to his job that day because of Winder's elevation to division command. Ronald was slowly advancing his brigade in battle line when he received an order to deploy in column of regiments, which he did in spite of the woods. He had barely completed this change when he was ordered to go back into line formation again. These gyrations, and the difficulty of advancing through the woods, caused the Stonewall Brigade to come up too late to help Garnett.

The disorder on the Confederate left had been deepened by the mortal wounding of Brigadier General Winder during the artillery duel. Winder's replacement, W.B. Taliaferro, was not aware of Jackson's battle plans, and then focused too much of his attention on helping to repulse Augur's attack on the south side of the Culpeper Road. For this reason, there was nobody exercising effective overall command on Jackson's left when Crawford's attack struck.

All these factors helped Crawford punch a hole in the center of Jackson's line. The length of his line enabled him to outflank Garnett's left flank unit, the 1st Virginia Battalion, which was compelled to break even though it was a veteran command. Its retreat exposed the regiment to its right, the 42nd Virginia, which was also flanked and forced to yield. At the same time the 10th Virginia came up belatedly to support the left flank of the 1st, and found itself thrown back in confusion also. Ironically, the Stonewall Brigade was now close enough to move up to blunt Crawford's advance, but its commander had halted in the woods near the fighting in order to seek precise orders on where to attack. As a result, only one of his regiments, the 27th Virginia, made an initial counterattack. It, too, was overwhelmed and caught up in the throng of Confederate troops heading to the rear.

The momentum of Crawford's successful charge now carried his units into the back of Garnett's right wing. As previously noted, these units had turned to face south and fire across the Culpeper Road into Geary's attacking troops. Because of this maneuver, they had no protection against the unexpected onslaught of Crawford's troops into their rear. The Yankees let loose a volley into the back of the 21st Virginia from only 30 paces away, and then sent the unit reeling to the rear after a brief hand to hand fight. The 48th Virginia was overwhelmed in similar fashion. Crawford's men then charged across the Culpeper Road and slammed into A.G. Taliaferro's large 47th Alabama, a green unit that was fighting in its first battle. It and its equally raw sister regiment, the 48th Alabama, were quickly sent flying, and A.G. Taliaferro's entire line was unhinged just as Augur's attack was losing its steam. As Taliaferro's troops fell back, Early's line was exposed to attack, and it also began to unravel from the left.

It was now the crisis of the battle. Banks would have carried the field had Gordon's brigade moved up promptly to support Crawford. But the degree of Crawford's success was so great and so swift that Gordon's troops were left behind in the woods northeast of the field through which Crawford had initially charged. As a result, Crawford's exhausted and depleted regiments reached the crest of their attack near the cedar grove on Early's right, where they were at last stopped by the 12th Georgia and three of Thomas' regiments.

The tide of the battle now began to shift as A.P. Hill rushed up Branch's and then Archer's brigades to stabilize the Confederate line north of the Culpeper Road. Hill pushed forward with his troops, wearing his famous red battle shirt, and roundly cursed Jackson's men who were retreating through his troops while they were trying to form. Before long Jackson himself came up, and sharply admonished Hill that he was too late. Jackson, who had barely escaped being shot or captured just before Hill came up, then turned to help rally his own shattered troops. His famous blue eyes flashed brightly as he swung his sword in the air and called, out, "Jackson is with you...Rally, brave men, and press forward. Your general will lead you. Jackson will lead you. Follow me!... Remember Winder!" The effect of his bravery was electric on all the troops of both sides who saw him. Soon, though, he was persuaded by W.B. Taliaferro and others to retire and not expose himself so recklessly.

The bravery of Jackson and Hill and several other officers helped rally enough of W.B. Taliaferro's troops to open up a flanking fire on Crawford's regiments. At the same time Hill pushed Branch's brigade forward to the position formerly occupied by Garnett, so stabilizing the Confederate line north of the Culpeper Road. From there, Branch's men were able to throw a fire into the rear of Crawford's men, who by now were thoroughly fought out. Struck now by fire from three sides, the exhausted survivors of Crawford's command began to retire along the same route by which they had advanced. In the process they had to run a gauntlet of fire from Branch's fresh troops and also from Archer's, which were coming into position on Branch's left after a grueling forced march through the woods. Fortunately for Crawford's men, the 10th Maine now marched forward to give them cover as they tried to run back to safety. The 10th, as previously noted, had been detached to support the Union cannons early in the fight, and was only belatedly released by Banks to aid Crawford's attack. The 10th moved valiantly forward into a hail of Confederate fire, and lost 40 per cent of its men in just a few minutes before it, too, was forced to retire.

It was now about 1900, and Gordon's brigade at last came up to enter the fray. Gordon was supposed to have followed Crawford into action an hour earlier, but did not do so for reasons never adequately explained. His appearance now in the woods at the eastern edge of the field through which Crawford had initially charged came just in time to cover the retreat of the 10th Maine and the last of Crawford's troops. Had Gordon come up even half an hour earlier, when some of Ronald's regiments were the only organized Confederate troops north of the Culpeper Road, he could have helped Crawford's successful attackers sweep the field. But such was not to be.

The fighting north of the Culpeper Road was now entering its last stage. One of Banks' staff officers was concerned that the Confederates pursuing Crawford's troops might try to rush up and grab some of the Union cannons still posted in their original line. He spotted a four company battalion of the *1st Pennsylvania Cavalry* standing nearby and suggested to Banks that the unit be sent in a sacrificial charge in order to blunt the enemy's anticipated counterattack. Banks agreed, and sent Major Richard Falls and his 184 men to their date with destiny.

Falls' attack came just as the *10th Maine* was leaving the field. As the troopers began their charge with sabers drawn, the Confederates heard the ominous din of the galloping horses but could not see them because of the lay of the land and all the smoke covering the field. When the Yankee cavalrymen finally burst into view, there was a momentary silence at the spectacle as all the Confederate infantrymen in the area turned their weapons to bear on the unfortunate Pennsylvanians. The Yankees later claimed that they broke three lines of Confederate infantry in their charge, but in actuality they only managed to scatter Branch's skirmishers. The intense Confederate fire felled scores of Union riders and mounts, and forced the troopers to swing to the north and try to head for safety through the bloody field of Crawford's charge. Their retreat in front of Archer's freshly posted brigade was just as costly as their advance, though they did receive some covering fire from Gordon's troops. The *1st Pennsylvania's* dash to glory lasted less than 15 minutes and cost the unit about half of its men. It did nothing to alter the course of the battle.

The repulse of the *10th Maine* and the *1st Pennsylvania Cavalry* left only one organized Union command on the field, Gordon's three fresh regiments, now posted along the eastern edge of the wheatfield north of the Culpeper Road. Gordon at first conducted a limited counterattack against the Stonewall Brigade in order to support the cavalry's retreat, but he found that it was too difficult to tell friend from foe in the deepening twilight, so he withdrew all his troops out of the field and back to the protective cover of the woods. At one point Gordon was almost killed when he accidentally rode in front of part of Ronald's line. The Confederates on the other side of the field instinctively felt that they had a numerical advantage over Gordon's command, and at about 1915 began a counterattack. Archer's troops led the way, and were soon supported on their left by Pender's newly arrived brigade. Gordon's three regiments, outnumbered now by six to one, had no choice but to abandon the field to the Confederates and darkness.

Sunset also saw Jackson's troops dominant on the southern half of the field. Here the 14th Georgia, 13th Virginia and 31st Virginia had played key roles in driving Crawford back, whereupon they formed along the Culpeper Road to help repulse the *10th Maine* and *1st Pennsylvania Cavalry*. By then Augur's troops had also been played out and were withdrawing from the field. Their exit was speeded by Ewell's belated entry into the fight. Up until about 1800, Ewell's two brigades on Cedar Mountain had been only spectators of the battle. When he saw Augur's men move to the attack, Ewell sent his men forward. It took Trimble's brigade, which led the advance, an hour to reach the Union position. By then Augur was in retreat, so Trimble helped hasten the Yankees to the rear. By 1930 the Confederate column reached Greene's yet unengaged brigade at the left end of Banks' line and persuaded it, too, to leave the field. The last Union artillery then limbered up, and Banks' entire command was in retreat.

The battle, though, was still not over. Jackson was never one to rest after a victory. He was determined to pursue the defeated enemy and he wanted to take possession of Culpeper that night if he could, even though his troops were battered and exhausted and the temperature was still above 80 degrees. Jackson still had two brigades from Hill's division (Field's and Stafford's) that had not yet been engaged, plus some batteries and a little fresh cavalry. He conducted a brief moonlit reconnaissance and then sent his troops forward across the north fork of Cedar Run.

When Jackson's men emerged from the woods north of the run, they unexpectedly ran smack into s large body of fresh Yankee troops. This was Ricketts' division, which was at last approaching the field to cover Banks' retreat. Ricketts had spent most of the day holding a position immediately south of Culpeper, but was not ordered forward by Pope until he heard the noise of Banks' artillery fire at around 1700. For this reason

Knapp's Pennsylvania battery held the center of the Union battle line at Cedar Mountain. It was armed with six 10-pounder Parrott rifles, and lost eight men and fourteen horses in the engagement.

Ricketts was unable to arrive in time to aid Banks' attack. Ricketts was still forming his men on a line perpendicular to the Culpeper Road when Jackson's troops came up. The two sides sparred with each other awkwardly in the darkness, and quite an artillery fire fight developed when Confederate Captain Willie Pegram brought up his four guns on the Culpeper Road to test the Union position. The Yankees responded with a converging fire that turned Pegram's position into an "artillery hell" that killed twenty horses and a number of men. The fighting lasted until around 2300, when Pegram wisely withdrew. The battle of Cedar Mountain was at last over.

The two opposing armies faced each other for the next two days along Ricketts' front just north of the battlefield. Pope was reluctant to renew the fighting, despite the belated arrival of Sigel's corps. Likewise, Jackson decided not to press his temporary advantage, since his spies and cavalry scouts warned him of Sigel's approach even before Pope's *I Corps* arrived. On 11 August Pope asked and was granted the unusual request to go behind Jackson's lines and help bury the 450 Union dead left on the field, whose bodies had quickly bloated in the heat. All together Pope would report about 2400 losses in the battle, including 100 men lost by Ricketts in his night skirmish with Hill. Banks' command lost 28 per cent of its strength, including two generals wounded (Augur and Geary) and one captured (Prince). The Union losses were by far the heaviest in Crawford's brigade, which lost 867 men (about half its strength) as well as three of its battle flags. Jackson's command lost about 1400 men. Half of these came from Winder's division, since Garnett's and A.G. Taliaferro's brigades bore the brunt of the fighting.

Jackson at last withdrew from his advanced position on the night of 11 August and returned to Gordonsville. He had won the battle of Cedar Mountain, but had failed to inflict a decisive defeat on the enemy. Much of this was his own fault: he had not managed his advance to the field well, nor had he controlled the opening of the engagement well on the tactical level. Those who were on the field understood all too well how close the Confederates had come to being driven off the field before Hill arrived. Nevertheless, the victory served only to increase Stonewall's mystique. In typical Jackson fashion, he informed Lee of his triumph with the message, "God blessed our arms with another victory." Pope, on the other hand, was not discouraged by the defeat. Banks had managed to blunt Jackson's drive on Culpeper even without Sigel's aid, and the Confederates were eventually turned back to where they had started. Above all, Banks' men had fought well, even though they were not victorious. As one of Banks' lieutenants put it, "I am sorry I can't twist the facts into a glorious victory. It was a glorious defeat if such an adjective can be used with the noun."

George B. McClellan

Ironically, one of the most influential figures in the Second Bull Run campaign never appeared on the battlefield or fired a shot during the campaign. Major General George B. McClellan, commander of the North's mighty *Army of the Potomac*, was constantly on the periphery of the operation, and his movements and actions had as great an effect on the campaign as anyone other than Lee and Pope themselves.

McClellan, born in 1826, was a native of Philadelphia who grew up in well connected circles. He graduated second in the West Point Class of 1846, and, following distinguished service in the Mexican War, became noted as an engineer. The opening of the Civil War found him retired from the army and serving as president of the Ohio and Mississippi Railroad. He promptly offered his services to the government, and was named a major general of Ohio volunteers. McClellan's initial successes in a minor campaign in West Virginia at the beginning of the war won him national attention just when Lincoln was looking for new leadership in the dark days following the Union defeat at First Bull Run on 21 July 1861.

McClellan readily accepted command in Virginia, and used his administrative skills to create the formidable *Army of the Potomac*. However, he declined to take field command until he felt totally ready, despite constant proddings from Lincoln and his administration. McClellan also had a strong conflict with commander in chief Winfield Scott, whom he successfully manipulated to replace on 1 November.

The coming of winter gave McClellan an ample alibi to remain in camp, though Lincoln continued to press him to finalize his plans for the next campaign. At last the exasperated Lincoln threatened to take direct control of McClellan's army himself. This goaded McClellan into unfolding his plan, which consisted of a bold amphibious operation that would approach Richmond from the east. This maneuver, which finally began in mid March, went smoothly, though McClellan lost his strategic advantage when he permitted himself to be bogged down in an unnecessary siege of the Confederate works at Yorktown. He then began advancing ever so slowly towards Richmond, which he apparently also intended to besiege. His plan actually might have worked, but for two key factors. Jackson's successful Valley Campaign diverted a significant number of troops (notably McDowell's *I Corps*) that McClellan was depending on, and the wounding of Confederate General Joseph E. Johnston at the battle of Fair Oaks vaulted Robert E. Lee into command of the Confederate forces at Richmond. Lee promptly created the vaunted Army of Northern Virginia, and in a series of costly fights now called the Seven Days Battle (25 June - 1 July 1861), drove McClellan's army back from within sight of Richmond to Harrison's Landing on the James River.

McClellan fully intended to renew his campaign as soon as he rested his men and received significant reinforcements, particularly McDowell's *I Corps* and Burnside's *IX Corps*. His plan was not a particularly bad one, since his base was still quite close to Richmond; in fact, no Union army would approach the Confederate capital so closely for the next two years, and Richmond would end up being captured by Grant after the kind of long siege that McClellan had probably anticipated. Lincoln, however, was not patient enough to wait that long, nor could he endure McClellan's constant complaining and calls for supplies and reinforcements. On 3 August 1862, the President directed McClellan to withdraw from Richmond to Fort Monroe, and from there to transfer his command to Aquia Creek, near Fredericksburg.

Lee had also grown impatient with McClellan's delay, and was thinking of transferring the scene of action northward even before McClellan began withdrawing. In mid July he sent Jackson to defend Gordonsville from Pope's newly formed *Army of Virginia*. Then, when McClellan began his slow withdrawal from Richmond, Lee boldly decided to throw most of his army against Pope. The campaign of Second Bull Run was on.

Lee knew that he needed to defeat Pope in less than four weeks, before McClellan's troops began to arrive in sufficient numbers to tip the balance in the Union's favor. Halleck also understood the situation, and for this reason he ordered Pope to hold his line on the Rappahannock until McClellan could come up. Pope also understood what was occurring, and did not like the prospect of what would happen to his command once McClellan

arrived. Since McClellan was his senior as a general, there was a strong likelihood that Pope's army would be absorbed into McClellan's, and that Pope would find himself demoted or even out of a job. This situation set up a natural rivalry between Pope and McClellan that saw no ready solution. Pope responded to the competition by attempting to ingratiate himself more with Lincoln and Stanton, and by denigrating the *Army of the Potomac* for its failure to capture Richmond. McClellan replied in kind, and privately criticized McDowell, who was Pope's senior commander, as an inept inferior. This was certainly not a good command situation, and the question will always remain, whether McClellan deliberately sabotaged Pope's campaign in order to keep his own army.

McClellan was certainly in no rush to evacuate the Peninsula. His withdrawal from Harrison's Landing consumed two weeks and it was another week before he began dispatching troops from Fort Monroe. Porter's *V Corps* embarked on 20 August, Heintzelman's *III Corps* on the 21st, and Franklin's *VI Corps* on the 23rd and 24th. Sumner's *II Corps* left on the 26th, and half of the *IV Corps* on the 29th. McClellan left just one division behind to guard Fort Monroe, Peck's division of the *IV Corps*.

The transfer of McClellan's army began smoothly enough, as Porter's corps landed at Aquia Creek on 22 August and began marching westward to support Pope. Soon, however, unexpected logistical problems began to develop. There were simply not enough docking facilities at Aquia to handle so many arriving troops, so Heintzelman's corps and part of Franklin's had to be sent to Alexandria. The arrival of this many troops at Alexandria created a transportation problem that was further aggravated by the arrival of Cox's division from West Virginia. Railroad czar Colonel Herman Haupt had to hustle to find enough trains to forward all these troops to Pope's front and still keep Pope's supply trains running. In addition, the army had only so many sea transports available, and the troops formed at Fort Monroe had to wait for the boats sent north to make the return trip in order to pick them up.

This situation was all the more frustrating because Lee's campaign against Pope was reaching its climax. As affairs developed, only two of McClellan's corps, Porter's *V* and Heintzelman's *III*, reached Pope in time to aid in the fighting at Second Bull Run. Another two corps, Franklin's *VI* and Sumner's *II*, were close by and might have reached Pope in time had it not been for the transportation problems just described.

It should be noted, though, that McClellan played a significant role in delaying Pope's reinforcements at the critical moment. The disaster met by Taylor's *New Jersey Brigade* at Bull Run Bridge on 27 August convinced McClellan that it was folly to send his troops forward piecemeal to be gobbled up by the enemy as soon as they reached the front. Instead, he chose to hold his troops back until he could send them all forward en masse. This decision made all the more sense to him because the next troops to arrive at Alexandria, Franklin's *VI Corps*, did not have their cavalry or artillery with them. This logic brought

McClellan to advise Halleck on 27 August that "our policy now is to...mobilize a couple of corps as quickly as possible, but not to advance them until they can have their artillery and cavalry."

This decision was a critical one, coming as it did on the eve of the campaign's climactic battle. McClellan countermanded Franklin's orders to march to Gainesville, and held him back at Alexandria for two critical days until Sumner's corps could arrive and be formed. The presence of just one of these corps on the field with Pope might well have changed the course of the battle on the 30th. When McClellan finally did release Franklin and Sumner, they reached Centreville on 30 August, just a few hours too late to participate in the nearby battle on the other side of Bull Run. All they could do then was to serve as a rallying point for Pope's now defeated army.

The question remains, whether or not McClellan deliberately held back Franklin and Sumner so as to intentionally cause Pope's defeat. There is certainly no question that McClellan had a strong personal and professional dislike for John Pope. Pope was a loud braggart as far as McClellan was concerned, and he had no use for this kind of interloper from Illinois, even though he happened to be a staunch friend of Lincoln. (The fact that Pope was a strong Republican and McClellan was a conservative Democrat probably also played into the picture.) McClellan was certain that Pope would lead his command to defeat, as he confided to his wife before leaving the Peninsula: "They are committing a fatal error in withdrawing me from here, and the future will show it. I think the result of their machinations will be that Pope will be gladly thrashed within ten days, and that they will be very glad to turn over the redemption of their affairs to me."

McClellan, then, entered the campaign with an intense grudge about having to withdraw his army from Richmond. He was also certain that Pope would get himself defeated before the *Army of the Potomac* could be transferred north, so rendering the entire move a folly. But keeping command of his own army was utmost in his mind. It was not at all clear at the beginning of the campaign who would have control of operations once McClellan's troops were transferred north. The logical solution would have been for Halleck to come forward and lead the combined armies, as he had done in the west during the successful drive on Corinth after the battle of Shiloh. But Halleck was every bit as slow as McClellan in the field, and he at the moment had no interest in abandoning his desk in Washington. As a result, Halleck's (and Lincoln's) failure to clearly define Pope's and McClellan's roles in the campaign created a debilitating atmosphere of distrust and jealousy from the start.

McClellan keenly felt this awkwardness when he arrived at Aquia on 24 August. His orders from Halleck seemed to indicate that his role for the moment would be to forward his troops to Pope as fast as they arrived in northern Virginia. The logical question for McClellan, was what his job would be once there were no more troops left to send Pope. Would he then be a commander without an army? This possibility naturally made him reluctant to release the last of his units from his control.

This awkward command situation was not cleared up until the afternoon of 27 August. On that day, McClellan, who was then at Alexandria, petulantly repeated his complaint to Halleck that he could take no responsibility for what was happening in the field if he did not have authority over his own troops. Halleck, who was by now exasperated over the status of the campaign, wrote back that he was too overwhelmed with other duties to oversee Pope's operations directly: "I have no time for details. You will, therefore, as ranking general in the field, direct as you deem best." This authorization, though, had a significant condition: all McClellan's orders for Pope's commands had to be cleared first by Halleck.

McClellan should have been overjoyed to see his authority reinstated. But he could not avoid reverting to his old form. He declined to march to Pope's aid until he felt that Franklin's troops were fully prepared to move out, and they needed at least another full day to get ready. As a result, Franklin did not leave Alexandria until 0600 on 29 August. Franklin then advanced so slowly that he only covered 10 miles before encamping at Annandale; his next day's march would take him another 12 miles to Centreville. (How far a cry this pace was to Sedgwick's heroic 34 mile march to reach Gettysburg on 2 July 1863!) In addition, Sumner did not leave Arlington until 1430 on 30 August, despite the fact that everyone knew a desperate battle was being waged at Bull Run.

There is no question that McClellan shed no tears when Pope was beaten. This is exactly what he had been predicting all month; as late as 29 August he had suggested to Lincoln "to leave Pope to get out of his own scrape and at once use all our means to make the capital perfectly safe." Lincoln, of course, was enraged at the thought, and there were those in the administration, as well as Pope himself, who staunchly believed that McClellan and his allies had deliberately worked to sabotage the *Army of Virginia* and its campaign.

The implications of these accusations are mind numbing, since they would make McClellan guilty of treason. This certainly was not McClellan's intention. He simply declined to participate wholeheartedly in a campaign that he did not endorse, and he selfishly guarded his own personal interests by refusing to cooperate actively with a fellow officer whom he detested (Pope). In these actions, he was showing no personal traits that Lincoln had not been unaware of for the previous year. Lincoln also knew how slow and deliberate McClellan moved even under the best of conditions,

and nothing was going to change that. In spite of these shortcomings, Lincoln reinstated McClellan as army commander for yet another campaign, with quite predictable results. It was too bad that Lincoln was not a better judge of the character and military ability of both Pope and McClellan. The President simply felt that he had no better options at the time, much to the detriment of the country's armies in the field.

Despite the advantage of being gifted with Lee's campaign orders on 13 September, McClellan's superior army was only able to secure a draw at Antietam on 17 September, the bloodiest day of the war. McClellan's typical reluctance to resume the field after the battle led to his firing on 9 November. He would not hold military command again. Instead, McClellan turned his attention to politics, and he ran unsuccessfully against Lincoln as the Democratic candidate for President in 1864. His postwar enterprises included a term as Governor of New Jersey from 1878 to 1881. He died in 1885 and is buried in Riverview Cemetery in Trenton.

CHAPTER V

The Campaign Intensifies

On 12 August Lee sent congratulations to Jackson for his victory at Cedar Mountain, with the sincere hope that it was "but the precursor of others over our foe in that quarter which will entirely break up and scatter his army." Jackson's brief campaign, though, had failed to change the overall strategic situation. Pope's army was now united at Orange following the arrival of King's division on the 12th; Burnside's troops were still at Fredericksburg. What concerned Lee most was the status of McClellan's large army of about 85,000 men at Harrison's Landing. As previously mentioned, part of McClellan's force had made an advance to Malvern Hill on 2 August, which Lee feared to be a precursor of a renewed thrust against Richmond. However, these troops withdrew on 7 August, and by the 12th Lee had reliable information that McClellan's men were being loaded on transports and moved downstream from Richmond.

This was just the opening that Lee had been looking for. He knew that McClellan's troops would pose a new threat from wherever they landed, but it would take them at least two or three weeks to move and get reformed. This interval would give him a window in which to deal with Pope and Burnside. On 13 August Lee sent 10 brigades under Longstreet to join Jackson at Gordonsville. Another two brigades were sent to Hanover Junction to watch Burnside. The defense of the capital would be entrusted to Major General G.W. Smith, one of the army's senior officers, who had suffered a physical breakdown on 1 June. Smith was now ready to return to duty, and was an ideal choice

*Major General James Long-
street, commander of Lee's
right wing during the campaign, has been unjustly
blamed for unduly delaying
the massive counter-attack
that drove Pope's army
from the field of 2nd Bull
Run on 30 August.*

to command the defenses of Richmond while Lee went to meet Pope. Smith's immediate command would consist of D.H. Hill's old division (D.H. Hill had just been detached to command the Department of North Carolina) and Hampton's cavalry brigade. This force comprised some 7000 men, a force sufficient to shield Richmond until Lee could return, should McClellan surprise him and double back to attack the capital.

Longstreet's arrival in Gordonsville created an awkward command situation, since he was senior to Jackson. This problem, however, existed for only a short while, since Lee arrived at Gordonsville on 15 August to take charge of both generals. From them he learned that Pope had some 65,000 to 70,000 troops, including King's division and one division received from Burnside, concentrated in the Cedar Mountain area (Pope actually had only about 55,000 men). The Yankees were closely guarding all the crossings of the Rapidan River and Robertson's River on a 15 mile front from near Madison Court House to

Raccoon Ford, but they were vulnerable to a flanking movement on either end of their line. Longstreet favored a move around the Federal right, where the arm could enjoy the protection of the Blue Ridge Mountains, if needed. Lee, on the other hand, favored a march around Pope's left, for the purpose of forcing the enemy to fight by cutting off the Union supply line from Washington. The latter plan was determined upon, and Lee commenced drawing up orders for his troops to march to the east-northeast under cover of Clark's Mountain, and cross at Somerville and Raccoon Fords for the purpose of engaging the enemy. Jackson and Lee were anxious to begin the advance the next day in order to strike Pope on the 17th, but Longstreet demurred because he needed time to organize and provision his men. Lee assented, and set the army's departure for the night of the 16th, with plans to engage Pope on the 18th.

Lee's plans would have had a reasonable chance for success if they had not been upset by a strange set of circumstances. Part of his strategy called for Jeb Stuart to take Fitz Lee's brigade of cavalry and cut the railroad line at Rappahannock Station in order to prevent Pope from escaping in the direction of Washington. Stuart, who had been with Lee's brigade at Beaverdam Station, rode to army headquarters on 17 August to confirm his mission. He left orders for Fitz Lee to march that day to Raccoon Ford on the Rapidan, where he was to secure the crossing for Longstreet before setting off on his mission to Rappahannock Station. After conferring with R.E. Lee, Stuart departed for the village of Verdiersville on the Orange Plank Road, where he expected to meet Fitz Lee's troops during their march westward.

Plans began to go awry when Fitz Lee decided to take a different route to Raccoon Ford than Stuart had anticipated. Lee needed to supply his men with food and ammunition, so he detoured his march to go via Louisa Court House, where his supply train was then parked. He did not think that this would pose any problem, since Stuart had not given him a timetable for reaching Raccoon Ford. Fitz Lee did notify his uncle, R.E. Lee, however, that his horses were in bad shape and could not take the field on the 19th. This news forced R.E. Lee to reluctantly delay the army's advance until the 20th.

Stuart, meanwhile, had reached Verdiersville on the evening

of the 17th. He was surprised not to find Fitz Lee there already, and sent one of his staff officers to hurry him up. Stuart then took off his gear and went to sleep in the garden at the Rhodes house. At dawn the next morning he heard horsemen approaching from the east, whom he naturally assumed to be Lee's. He sent a messenger to direct Lee to him, and was surprised a few minutes later to hear pistol shots in that direction. The approaching column was not Lee's, but Federal cavalry! It seems that Pope had ordered a cavalry reconnaissance in the area, and as a result Buford sent out the *1st Michigan* and *5th New York*, both under the command of Colonel Thornton Broadhead, at noon on the 17th. The Union column crossed the Rapidan easily at Raccoon Ford, which Longstreet's infantry had left unguarded through an error by Brigadier General Robert Toombs, for which he was at once put under arrest. Broadhead then headed southeastward, and happened to be approaching Verdiersville just when Stuart was expecting Fitz Lee.

Stuart's headquarters was instantly in a turmoil. The general had no time to grab his gear. All he could do was to leap onto his horse, jump the garden fence, and ride frantically for safety. A short while later the entire party managed to reassemble nearby, and all were happy that nobody had been captured. Stuart, however, was displeased that he had been forced to abandon his cloak and sash, as well a fancy plumed hat that he had just won on a bet with his old friend, Union Brigadier General Samuel Crawford. The two had met during the truce after the fight at Cedar Mountain, and Stuart had bet that the northern newspapers would call the battle a Union victory. When they did, Crawford a few days later sent the hat through the lines to Stuart as his prize.

But Stuart lost something much more important than his hat that morning—his haversack, which contained R.E. Lee's orders for the raid to Rappahannock Station. Broadhead at once turned the papers over to Pope, who had already been fearing that Jackson might be reinforced and undertake the very turning movement that Lee was now planning. The contents of Stuart's pouch clearly informed him that Lee's entire army was on his front and headed for the Rapidan crossings.

Pope did not waste any time, and at 1330 on 18 August

92

Stuart's successful raid on Catlett's Station, shown here, on 22-23 August resulted in the capture of Pope's dispatch book, which gave Lee crucial information on Union dispositions.

informed Halleck of his predicament and the need to withdraw at once behind the Rappahannock. Halleck approved the move, and also directed Pope to "stand firm on that line until I can help you." McClellan's troops were on the way, and soon the two Union armies would be united on Lee's front.

That night Pope ordered his men to light their campfires and bed down at the usual hour in order to deceive the Confederates as to his intentions. Then at 2300 the Federals quietly left their camps and began marching to the northeast. This night march, of course, did not please all his men. Many of the *IX Corps* troops had just arrived that day, and they were disgusted to be heading back in the direction from which they had just come. One of

Reno's men observed, "We began to think that Pope was not a very smart general, or the enemy was particularly active and managed by better leaders."

Night marches are difficult undertakings at best, and so it was on the night of 18-19 August. Sigel's and McDowell's corps both needed to go through Culpeper, and it was not long before their immense wagon trains became entangled in a huge traffic jam. Had it been daylight, the wagoneers would have been able to avoid each other or make progress on the sides of the roads. As it was, the confused mass of vehicles stalled the progress of all the infantry stacked up on the roads south of Culpeper. The mess was not cleared up until midmorning the next day, when the infantry of the two corps were finally able to get moving.

Pope now directed his troops to withdraw on a wide front in order to use all the roads available and try to avoid any more traffic jams. Reno's division, which had managed to avoid all the confusion at Culpeper, marched by direct route though Stevensburg and crossed the Rappahannock at Kelly's Ford about 1600. Banks' corps had the shortest march route, straight up the main road from Culpeper to the bridge at Rappahannock Station (which had not been destroyed as Lee planned because of Fitz Lee's movements previously mentioned). Banks crossed the Rappahannock in the afternoon and formed to the south of the railroad. McDowell's corps was also heading for Rappahannock Station, but their late start and a difficult 20 mile march under the day's broiling sun left them a little short of their goal that night. Sigel's men took a more northerly course, which they fortunately had all to themselves. They crossed the Rappahannock that evening at the bridge at White Sulphur Springs, eight miles upriver from Rappahannock Station, and burned the bridge behind them

Thus Pope had his entire command safely behind the Rappahannock by noon on 20 August. Quite surprisingly, the Confederates did not pursue Pope's army closely. Lee did not learn of the Union withdrawal until mid day on the 19th, when some lookouts posted on Clark's Mountain saw the enemy's wagons heading to the northeast, as well as all the dust raised by Pope's marching troops. Lee and Longstreet climbed Clark's Mountain in order to have a look at the situation for themselves. After

Though the 2nd Bull Run Campaign was only Lee's second operation as commander of the Army of Northern Virginia, it was overall his best conducted offensive campaign of the war. This photograph was taken by Julian Vannerson in 1863.

viewing the depressing scene, Lee remarked to Longstreet, "General, we little thought that the enemy would turn his back to us this early in the campaign."

It was indeed a disappointing moment for the Confederates. Had Lee moved to attack Pope on 18 August as he originally intended, he would have caught the Yankees strung out in long columns in front of Culpeper. Even an advance early on the 19th would have enabled him to catch Pope's army on the move. As things developed, Lee discovered Pope's movement too late on the 19th to make it worth while to even try to catch the enemy. He let his men rest for the remainder of the day, and sent them orders to rest until the moon rose soon after midnight. Jackson, who was never one to waste time if he could help it, used the free afternoon to draw up his three divisions to witness the execution of three deserters.

20 August saw quite a bit of skirmishing between the oppos-

ing cavalry forces as the Confederate horsemen pushed forward towards Buford's troopers guarding Kelly's Ford and Bayard's command at Rappahannock Station. One of these clashes took place at Brandy Station, which would become famous the next June for being the site of the largest cavalry clash of the war. During the day Longstreet's wing headed for Kelly's Ford and Jackson marched towards Rappahannock Station. Longstreet reached his goal, but Jackson's men, slowed by the dust and the heat of the day, encamped between Stevensburg and Brandy Station, several miles short of their goal.

Lee drew all of his troops up to the Rappahannock on 21 August, only to discover how strongly Pope's forces were posted along their entire front. The river was crossable at only a few points (Kelly's Ford, Rappahannock Station, Beverly Ford and Freeman's Ford), and all of these were heavily defended by the enemy. The Confederate probes at Freeman's Ford developed into a lengthy artillery duel that Jackson terminated about 1500 when he decided to move farther north and make a try at the White Sulphur Springs Ford. Sigel, who was posted at Freeman's Ford, grew suspicious when the Confederate guns suddenly pulled back, and sent a strong reconnaissance party of three regiments under Brigadier General Henry Bohlen across the river to investigate.

Bohlen had the misfortune to run into Trimble's division, which Jackson had left as a rear guard. Trimble's troops, which were posted in the woods and so were unseen by the Federals, pounced on Bohlen's command and sent them flying. The Union retreat became a rout when Hood's division of Longstreet's corps, which had just come up to relieve Jackson's men near the ford, came up to join the fray. Bohlen was shot dead through the heart, and his panicked troops dove into the river to flounder across as best they could. In the process many were shot in the back or drowned in a sad scene reminiscent of the Union disaster at Ball's Bluff some ten months earlier.

While Sigel braced himself for a Confederate crossing at Freeman's Ford that never would develop, Jackson quietly marched his lead troops to the White Sulphur Springs Ford, five miles to the north. Stonewall was pleased to find the ford only lightly guarded by a few cavalrymen, and at about 1600 sent

Major General Franz Sigel, commander of McDowell's I Corps, lost his commander's confidence during the latter part of the 2nd Bull Run Campaign. He was a popular German officer who never fought in a winning battle after 1861.

part of Ewell's division over the river to secure the crossing. The 13th Georgia of Lawton's brigade, supported by two batteries, waded across the ford under the cover of a rainstorm and easily captured the few Union pickets posted there. At the same time, Ewell sent Early's brigade across an old dam a mile south of the ford, in order to outflank the Union position. Early had just finished his crossing when the heavens opened up. The river at once turned into a torrent, stranding all of Ewell's advance troops on the Union side of the river.

Pope had actually been anticipating such a move by Jackson. He knew that he did not have enough troops to defend the entire Rappahannock line and still maintain contact with Fredericksburg and Manassas, from which McClellan's reinforcements would be advancing. As a result, he developed a plan to hold Sigel's troops in place at Freeman's Ford and permit Jackson to cross the upper Rappahannock if Stonewall wished to do so. Once Jackson crossed the river, Pope planned to mass his troops, along with whatever reinforcements had arrived from McClellan, and then march quickly to smash Jackson's command near Warrenton.

Pope thought better of this plan, however, when he learned at about 2100 on 22 August that Jackson had actually secured a bridgehead at White Sulphur Springs. He now realized that a move north to meet Jackson would expose his rear to attack by Longstreet. At 2115 he telegraphed Halleck that he had but two good options: either to fall back with his entire command to Cedar Run, northeast of Warrenton, or to cross the Rappahannock with his entire force and assail Jackson's flank and rear. He personally favored the latter course of action, even though it would expose his flank to Longstreet and also leave the important railroad line to Catlett's Station unguarded. Even so, Halleck endorsed the attack on Jackson. He felt that Heintzelman's corps, which had just landed at Alexandria, and Porter's corps, which was at Aquia Creek, could be brought up quickly enough to support Pope's attack.

Pope's plans, however, were soon stymied by the same rain storm that stalled Jackson's advance. Before he could get his troops moving, Pope learned that the Rappahannock had risen so much that all its fords were impassable. As a result, it would be impossible to cross the river in order to strike Jackson's rear. On the other hand, Pope quickly understood that the Rappahannock's raging waters also isolated whatever troops Jackson had sent across before the storm. At 0700 on 23 August he boldly decided to march his entire command north to attack the Confederate bridge head at White Sulphur Springs, trusting that the swollen Rappahannock would for the moment prevent Longstreet from crossing to attack the Union rear.

Jackson was in fact fearing just such a maneuver by Pope. Since the rain continued to fall and the river continued to rise, he had little hope of crossing more troops to support Early and the 13th Georgia. The only thing that he could do was try to figure out a way to get his troops back to safety. His best option was to attempt to rebuild the bridge at the Springs which the Federals had destroyed on the 20th, so he set his engineers to work on the project early on the 23rd. In the meanwhile, Jackson brought up all the artillery he could to the river's west bank in order to support Early if the Federals attacked. The situation made the Confederate commanders extremely tense, so much so that Jackson and A.P. Hill both braved to cross the river in order to help Early draw up his defenses. Jackson was then reportedly so rude to Hill that the latter just turned around and returned to the western bank. As a last resort, Jackson directed his chief engineer to explain to Early how to march to Waterloo Bridge, five miles upstream, should the need arise.

The day's rains delayed Pope's advance so much that his vanguard, Milroy's brigade and a detachment of Buford's cavalry, did not arrive on Early' front until late in the day. By the time they deployed, it was too late to attack, so the Yankees decided to wait until morning. Meanwhile, Jackson's engineers at last completed rebuilding the bridge. Early was extremely eager to withdraw, and so was shocked when he received orders to hold his position. Instead of retiring his exposed bridge head, Jackson had decided to reinforce it! Soon after dark he sent the remainder of Lawton's brigade to support Early's line. Jackson's plan was to assess the situation in the morning and then retire only if the Federals were present in force. Early at once informed Ewell that there was already a large Union force on his front, and that his troops were hungry and completely exhausted. Ewell crossed the river to review the situation in person, and at last agreed with Early, He withdrew Lawton and Early shortly before dawn and so rescued them from what Early was certain would have been "inevitable destruction."

23 August also saw a flurry of activity at Rappahannock Station. Pope had decided to keep the important railroad bridge there intact in case he needed to recross to the western side of the river. In order to secure the bridge, he needed to maintain a strong bridgehead on the Confederate side of the river; it was manned by Hartsuff's brigade of Ricketts' division. Lee, on the other hand, was anxious to secure the bridge in order to prevent Pope from crossing and attacking the weakened Confederate front (which is just what Pope wanted to do before the rains came). For this purpose, Lee lined up almost 50 artillery pieces on the night of the 22nd in the proximity of the bridge. All these guns opened fire at 0600 the next morning, and at once provoked a Union response from across the river in what became one of the greatest artillery duels of the war. After about two hours of bombardment, Longstreet sent two infantry regiments forward to attack the Union bridge head. They were surprised when they reached the Union position and learned that Hartsuff's men had just withdrawn. The joyful Confederates then

Federal engineers and mechanics building a new bridge across the Rappahannock near Sulphur Springs. All the bridges along the waterway for miles were destroyed by both sides in order to prevent surprise attacks.

pushed forward to the bridge, only to be turned back by intense Federal cannon fire.

Longstreet did not know that the Yankees would have withdrawn even if he had not mounted his attack. McDowell, who commanded this sector of Pope's line, had received orders to pull out and move to face Jackson. McDowell was already in the process of withdrawing Hartsuff's troops before the Confederate infantry attacked. Once Hartsuff was safely withdrawn, McDowell ordered Brigadier General Zealous B. Tower, commander of his rear guard, to destroy the railroad bridge over the river. Tower first attempted to blast the bridge with a battery of cannons at short range. When this effort failed, he at length managed to set fire to the bridge. The burning structure collapsed into the river around 1200, so relieving both Pope and Lee of the concern that the other might cross the river there and make an attack.

While these important events were occurring at Rappahannock Station and White Sulphur Springs, something even more significant took place just a little farther to the north. On 22 August, Stuart had made an interesting proposal to Lee in an effort to break the stalemate existing along the Rappahannock. Stuart felt guilty over his failure to destroy Rappahannock Bridge a few days earlier as Lee had desired, so he offered to make amends by conducting a raid around Pope's right to Catlett's Station. He hoped that the destruction of the Orange and Alexandria Railroad bridge over Cedar Run would cut off Pope's supply line and so force the Yankees to withdraw from the Rappahannock.

Lee approved the expedition, and Stuart selected his best 1500 troopers for the raid. He left at 1000 on the 22nd and headed north through Jefferson to Waterloo Bridge, where he successfully crossed the Rappahannock without encountering any Union troops. He then rode on to Warrenton and Auburn Mills without opposition, and was nearing his objective at Catlett's Station when the heavens opened up in a thunderstorm. Stuart was debating whether he should turn back before the muddy roads and swollen streams should make his withdrawal too difficult, when he received a double dose of good news. His advance troops had succeeded, under cover of the rainstorm, in capturing the enemy pickets outside of Catlett's, and someone then brought in a captured Negro who claimed to know where Pope's nearby headquarters was.

This news sparked Stuart to continue his raid in spite of the weather. He sent the 1st and 11th Virginia regiments to deal with the Yankee garrison at Catlett's, while the 9th Virginia set out to try to capture Pope; another detachment was directed to burn the railroad bridge at Cedar Run, and the rest of his command was held in reserve. Stuart's raiders struck out of the darkness like lightning. The unsuspecting Union garrison at Catlett's was scattered in all directions, and lost prisoners by the score. When Stuart directed his troops there to withdraw at 0300 on the 25th, they brought with them 400 prisoners, 500 horses and mules, and a paychest full of several thousand dollars. The 9th Virginia disappointingly had not been able to find Pope, who was then absent from his headquarters, but they did bring back the Union

Virginia Negroes following Pope's soldiers in their retreat from Cedar Mountain. Union armies in the field were continually encumbered by Negro slaves seeking safety and protection from their former owners.

commander's dress uniform. Stuart playfully offered a couple days later to trade it back to Pope in exchange for the plumed hat that he had lost at Verdiersville, but the Union commander declined to reply. Stuart ended up sending Pope's uniform to Virginia's governor John Letcher, who displayed it for the rest of the war as a trophy in the Virginia State Library at the capitol in Richmond.

Stuart's raid failed to achieve its primary goal, the destruction of the Cedar Run bridge, because the structure's timbers were too wet from the rains to be set on fire. The raid, though, did succeed in a way no one had anticipated. Among the spoils that Stuart's troopers carried off from Pope's headquarters was Pope's dispatch book, which contained the Union commander's marching orders for the day, as well as other significant papers, including a copy of a note that Pope sent to Halleck on 20 August giving the exact strength of his command and the location of its major units. These documents also showed that McClellan's troops were going to march forward via Fredericksburg, and that Pope was apprehensive of being out-flanked on the upper Rappahannock. All of this information

Major General J.E.B. Stuart's small cavalry division of only two brigades performed admirably throughout the entire 2nd Bull Run campaign. His boldest maneuver, the raid on Catlett's Station on 22-23 August, was where he captured Pope's dress uniform—fair compensation for the plumed hat he lost at Verdiersville four days earlier.

Below: Mathew Brady's photographic wagon and workshop on the eve of the 2nd Bull Run campaign. Primitive cameras required long exposure times, thus no photographs were taken of troops in battle.

would prove most useful to Lee in planning the next stage of his campaign.

Stuart's raid also succeeded at helping to unnerve Pope, particularly since it came at the same time as Jackson's crossing at White Sulphur Springs. Pope tried to downplay the outcome of Stuart's raid as he headed north on 23 August to try to intercept Jackson's troops, but the ease and success with which the Confederate cavalry had operated in the Union rear was obviously a source of embarrassment to the Federals.

CHAPTER VI

Jackson on the Loose

S tuart's capture of Pope's dispatch book at Catlett's Station on 23 August made it clear to Lee that the Confederates had only a few days left in which to strike Pope before McClellan's reinforcements began to arrive in large enough numbers to change the balance of the campaign. So far Lee had held the initiative since he took the field from Richmond, and in less than one week he had succeeded in maneuvering Pope's *Army of Virginia* back from the Rapidan to the Rappahannock. But what Lee really wanted to do was to attack and overwhelm all or part of Pope's command, and at this he had been frustrated. The heavy rains that had stymied Jackson's advance across the Rappahannock at White Sulphur Springs on 22-23 August had slowed down both armies. Despite Stuart's successful raid, the opposing forces still faced each other across the river in a continuing stalemate. The only thing that had changed was that their center of gravity had shifted northward from Rappahannock Station to White Sulphur Springs. Pope, after failing to strike Jackson's bridgehead at the springs, had established his headquarters at Warrenton and was guarding the Rappahannock as far north as Waterloo Bridge. To him, it seemed that the tide of the campaign was about to swing back in his favor. Heintzelman's and Porter's corps of McClellan's army were within supporting distance at Alexandria and Kelly's Ford, respectively, and all Pope needed to do was to hold his position until these troops came up. Then the two united Federal armies could take the initiative against Lee.

Lee knew that he was at the crisis of the campaign. Everything so far had gone in his favor: McClellan had left the Richmond area, and the Yankees had been maneuvered out of central Virginia in time for the local farmers to begin their harvest. But he now needed to do something about Pope before McClellan's entire army arrived and the blue tide began to flow southward again.

Lee's response to the situation was not to become passive and surrender the initiative to Pope, but to continue to pressure the *Army of Virginia* in the hope that Pope might make a mistake upon which the Confederates might capitalize. Lee knew from the captured dispatches that Pope was concerned about his northern flank, which the Confederates had already been testing for several days. On 24 August Lee rode to Jackson's headquarters at Jeffersonton and proposed that Stonewall make a broad flanking movement around Pope's right and then march through Thoroughfare Gap in the Bull Run Mountains in order to strike Pope's supply base at Manassas Junction. This bold move would hopefully cause Pope to pull back from his line on the Rappahannock, so enabling Lee and Longstreet, who would be following Jackson's line of march a day or two behind, to strike the enemy at some vulnerable point.

The plan was indeed bold. If Jackson unexpectedly ran into part of McClellan's command coming from Washington, he would be delayed enough for the mission to be jeopardized. There was also the possibility that Pope might figure out what was happening and move to take advantage of Jackson's vulnerability. Lee was prepared for this eventuality, and apparently was ready to have Jackson withdraw to the comfortable and familiar environs of the lower Shenandoah Valley if necessary. From there he might "approach the Potomac and so cause apprehension in the Federal Government for the safety of the capital." A similar option was available if Pope chose to attack Longstreet's wing rather than Jackson's. In this case, Longstreet could be withdrawn into the protective Shenandoah Valley, and Jackson could be recalled. The recombined army could then operate towards the Potomac or withdraw towards Richmond, as the situation warranted. Lee's primary goal, then, was to try to push Pope back towards Washington and defeat him in the

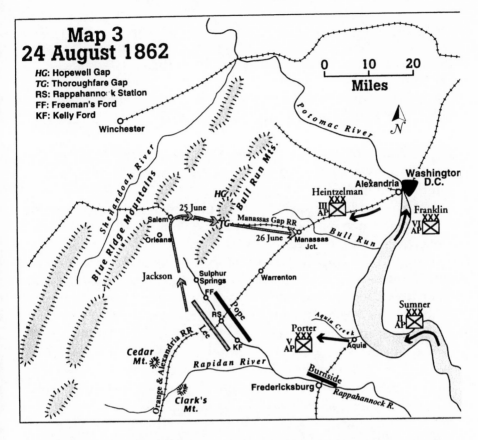

**Map 3
24 August 1862**

HG: Hopewell Gap
TG: Thoroughfare Gap
RS: Rappahannock Station
FF: Freeman's Ford
KF: Kelly Ford

0   10   20
Miles

Winchester

Potomac River

Washington D.C.

Alexandria

Heintzelman
III AP

Franklin
VI AP

Blue Ridge Mountains

Shenandoah River

Bull Run Mts.

25 June

Salem

Orleans

Manassas Gap RR

26 June

Manassas Jct.

Bull Run

Jackson

Sulphur Springs

Warrenton

FF

RS

Pope

Lee

Aquia Creek

Sumner
II AP

Porter
V AP

Aquia

KF

Cedar Mt.

Rapidan River

Orange & Alexandria RR

Clark's Mt.

Burnside

Fredericksburg

Rappahannock R.

process if possible. As Lee later admitted, "The disparity between the contending forces rendered the risks unavoidable." If Pope could not be attacked under favorable conditions or the plan went awry, Lee was apparently prepared to conduct a war of maneuver from the Shenandoah Valley in order to keep the Yankees off balance and away from Richmond.

Jackson was excited by the plan, and reportedly used his boot to trace some proposed movements in the dirt. Longstreet also approved the operation, so the necessary orders were issued later on the 24th. Longstreet was to relieve A.P. Hill's troops at Waterloo Bridge that evening so that they could pull back and prepare for their march.

The next morning, Jackson was to move out with about 27,000 men (Ewell's, Hill's and Taliaferro's divisions plus Stuart's cavalry) and "cross above Waterloo and move around the enemy's right, so as to strike the Orange and Alexandria

107

Railroad in his rear." Longstreet in the meantime was to divert Pope's attention "by threatening him in front and to follow Jackson as soon as the latter should be sufficiently advanced." Lee's most critical decision would be when and how to have Longstreet move. His decision of necessity would be based on the extent of Jackson's progress. In order to keep accurately informed of Jackson's advance, Lee assigned 25 specially selected troopers from the Black Horse Cavalry to serve as couriers between the two wings of the army. The fate of the campaign might well rest on their shoulders.

Jackson had his troops up at 0300 on 25 August to begin their march. Each man was issued 60 rounds of ammunition and three days' supply of cooked rations. Knapsacks were to be left behind, and all wagons were sent to the rear except for ambulances and the ordnance trains. Jackson meant business. Orders came down for "No straggling; every man must keep his place in ranks; in crossing streams officers are to see that no delay is occasioned by removing shoes or clothes."

The column was led out of camp by Captain James Boswell, Jackson's chief engineer, who was one of the few officers Jackson briefed about his plans. Ewell's division marched first, followed by Hill's and then Taliaferro's. Some 80 guns in 21 batteries accompanied the column, as did the 2nd Virginia Cavalry; Stuart was to join him en route. As they headed northwest from Jefferson to Amissville, Jackson's men at first thought that they might be returning to the Shenandoah Valley. For this reason they were slightly surprised when the column turned to the east and crossed the upper Rappahannock at Hinson's Mill Ford, which the Yankees had neglected to guard. So far, so good.

The ford caused a brief bottleneck, which was soon passed as the troops headed north to Orleans in Fauquier County. From there they continued north another five miles towards Salem, near which they encamped near dusk after a successful 15 mile march. Little did they know that Salem was the midpoint in their itinerary, being located on the Manassas Gap Railroad 15 miles to the northwest of Manassas Junction. Reportedly Jackson climbed a rock near Salem in order to watch his troops march by. The scene inspired them to begin cheering, which he directed them to stop because it might arouse the enemy. The troops responded by doffing their hats instead. Old Stonewall was visibly moved and remarked, "Who could not conquer with troops such as these?"

Pope, who had been managing his campaign reasonably well up to this point, lost control of events on the 25th. The day began as usual with an artillery fight against Longstreet's cannons posted across the river at Waterloo Bridge. By noon Pope received information from a number of sources that a large body of Confederates was marching northwest towards Amissville. Pope at once concluded that Jackson was headed for the Shenandoah Valley, and began preparing McDowell's corps to follow him. Then, in an apparent change of mind, he began shifting his remaining troops to the south, probably in order to get at Longstreet better. McDowell was to remain at Warrenton and Sigel was directed to march away from the river to Fayetteville, 6 miles south of Warrenton. Banks received orders to head even farther south, marching past the railroad at Bealeton in the direction of Kelly's Ford.

Late in the day, once Pope had more information that Jackson's advance was at Salem, he at last decided to send out a probe in that direction. Oddly, Pope did not send out a cavalry detachment towards Salem, but instead he ordered McDowell to cross at Sulphur Springs at dawn the next day and find out what Confederate troops were in that vicinity. Pope was still convinced, as he telegraphed Halleck, that Jackson was heading for Front Royal and that the troops at Salem were just a flank guard.

Pope's waffling on 25 August was just the sort of mistake that Lee was hoping for. During the day the Union commander broke up his defensive line on the Rappahannock and scattered his troops away from their concentration at Warrenton. At no time did Pope shift any units towards his most threatened point, Jackson's column at Salem. One reason for Pope's misinterpretation of the situation was that his cavalry, for once, had let him down. His three recently formed cavalry brigades, one attached to each corps of the *Army of Virginia*, had done an excellent job of scouting the enemy's movements since the beginning of the month. After three weeks in the field, however, the men and their mounts were beginning to wear out, particularly since

Fifty-seven-year-old Major General Samuel P. Heintzelman, one of Pope's corps commanders at 2nd Bull Run, was typical of the older, less inspired senior Federal officers who served in the Virginia theater during the first half of the war. He was "kicked upstairs" to various administrative posts after Chantilly.

there was a shortage of forage for some reason. Pope's movements were also restrained by a misperceived mandate from Halleck. Pope was acting under orders to hold the Rappahannock line until McClellan's reinforcements came up. This he single-mindedly continued to do, despite strong evidence that Jackson might be moving past his right wing north of Waterloo Bridge. He was also ignoring Halleck's injunction not to let the enemy cut him off from Alexandria.

Pope was not the only Federal commander who was flustered on the 25th. The arrival of McClellan's troops in northern Virginia caused a logistical nightmare that Halleck, who was supposed to be supervising the operation, was unable to manage. The problem became all the more acute when McClellan and some of his key officers began giving only passive cooperation to Pope and Halleck.

Halleck had originally intended for McClellan's troops to disembark at Aquia Creek, some 12 miles northeast of Fredericksburg, and march from there to join Pope. However, after Porter's corps began arriving at Aquia on 22 August, it became clear that the landing facilities there were inadequate and that part of the army would have to be forwarded to Alexandria. Heintzelman's corps accordingly began disembarking at Alexandria on the 22nd, followed by Franklin's corps and some of Sumner's; the rest of Sumner's was directed back to Aquia. The congestion at Alexandria was further increased when Cox's division arrived there from West Virginia on the 22nd.

This huge influx of troops at Alexandria required a large number of trains to transport themselves and their gear and supplies to Pope's army, then some 50 miles to the southeast. The problem was that Pope had garnered all the available train cars (over 200 of them) at Warrenton Junction for use in case he needed them. This situation provoked the assistant secretary of war to send Pope a harsh telegram stating, "If cars are not unloaded and returned to Alexandria reinforcements cannot be sent forward...You can use cars for either warehouses or transportation, but not both."

Pope promptly began releasing his trains, but their crews found only massive confusion when they reached Alexandria. There were so many demands for transport that Colonel Herman Haupt, superintendent of the army's military railroads, could not keep track of where all his trains were. His job became even more difficult when one of Cox's brigadiers, Samuel Sturgis, stopped a train outside of Alexandria and appropriated it for his own troops. Haupt then intercepted the train in person, armed with direct orders from Halleck that no subordinate officers were to interfere with Haupt's trains. Haupt bluntly told Sturgis that the latter's cavalier action would disorder the army's train schedules and delay all of Pope's reinforcements. Sturgis promptly replied, "I don't care for John Pope one pinch of owl dung!"

Lee's gamble, then, was beginning to pay off. Pope's misreading of the direction of Jackson's column gave Stonewall an open line of march to the Federal rear, and Haupt's problems with his trains would give Jackson an easier time at Manassas than he would have had otherwise. Jackson would also be aided by the fact that the transports carrying Sumner's corps were being delayed by a storm. In addition, Pope decided to keep his troops near Kelly's Ford stationary until he received specific orders from Halleck, who at the moment did not know where Pope's headquarters was. McClellan likewise was delaying the advance of some of his troops, since he claimed not to know where

Pope's army was. The Union command structure was beginning to break down again.

Jackson began his march early on the 26th, knowing that he had another full day's trek ahead of him into the heart of the enemy's territory. His men, as usual, had no idea where they were going, and as they entered Salem, many still believed that they might turn left to the Shenandoah Valley. Instead, they turned right to follow the Manassas Gap Railroad towards Gainesville. Their march proceeded smoothly, with only one major obstacle in their path — Thoroughfare Gap in the Bull Run Mountains. If the Yankees were holding the gap in force, Jackson would not be able to break through to accomplish his mission. Even if the gap were being held by a small number of Union troops, these would be able to at least inform Pope about Jackson's true position and direction of march. To preclude this possibility, Jackson rushed his cavalry eastward at first light. His troopers found no Federals in sight, much to Jackson's delight. Things continued to go smoothly as the day progressed. Stuart's cavalry, which had left its position on the Rappahannock at 0200, caught up with Jackson's column at midafternoon. At that time Jackson's advance still had not encountered any opposition.

Pope's relative inactivity to this point on 26 August is almost as difficult to understand as his confused marches on the 25th. He still assumed that Jackson was heading for Front Royal, and did not even bother to send any cavalry towards Salem to confirm his assumption. Instead, he held most of his force along the Rappahannock line all day, principally in the area of Waterloo Bridge and White Sulphur Springs. McDowell continued to conduct a lengthy artillery duel with Longstreet's cannons across the river, while Reynolds and Reno marched to his support in case he decided to cross and attack Longstreet. Banks still supported McDowell's left near Fayetteville, and Sigel insisted on maintaining a defensive posture at Warrenton out of apprehension for Jackson's intentions. Pope directed Porter to move his *V Corps* from Kelly's Ford to Bealeton, and held Heintzelman's corps in reserve at Warrenton Junction, pending further developments.

Pope's continued presence in strength along the Rappahannock made Lee feel more secure about Jackson's safety, but it also left him in a dilemma about when to move Longstreet's command. He had been alert to the possibility that Pope might withdraw from the Rappahannock because of Jackson's march, so enabling Longstreet to cross the river and attack Pope's retreating forces. As affairs developed, though, Pope did not retire and his position along the river was too strong to be attacked. In addition, as Longstreet pointed out, any attempt to aid Jackson by marching straight across the Rappahannock would run the risk of being delayed indefinitely by Union rearguards or defensive stands. Instead, Longstreet suggested, it would be better to follow Jackson's line of march, which would be safer and offer Lee more options. Lee agreed, and late in the afternoon sent orders for Longstreet to begin marching towards Salem. R.H. Anderson's division and S.D. Lee's artillery would take up Longstreet's position along the river in order to maintain a front against Pope and serve as a rear guard. If Pope moved more to the southeast, he could hopefully be checked by D.H. Hill's and McLaws' divisions, both of which were en route from Richmond.

Pope later claimed that he felt no concern for his rear at Manassas Junction because he had ordered Haupt to direct "one of the strongest divisions" there, and he had also ordered Kearny and Sturgis to post strong pickets along the railroad line. In addition, he expected Franklin's corps to arrive momentarily from Alexandria. However, there is no evidence that he really ordered Haupt to post a division at Manassas. Instead, all his messages were for Haupt to rush all the troops to Warrenton Junction, not Manassas. Lastly, if he expected the railroad line to be guarded by Kearny and Sturgis, he made no effort to confirm that this was being done. Nor did he double check the location of Franklin's command, which he in other sources said he did not expect at Bristoe until the 28th.

All this evidence strongly suggests that Pope was simply too inattentive to his rear, no matter how much he tried to cover up his tracks later. After all, he was the very one who had boasted on 14 July that he was going to discard ideas such as "lines of retreat" and "bases of supplies." As a result, the only troops guarding Pope's rear were three companies of infantry at Bristoe

THE SECOND BULL RUN CAMPAIGN

and three companies of infantry, a battery of artillery, and a green regiment of cavalry at Manassas. Jackson's raid would literally catch Pope with his pants down.

Jackson faced a key decision when his advance reached Gainesville at around 1400. His objective was the huge Union supply depot at Manassas Junction, but he was well aware that the area might be heavily fortified and full of Union troops. Instead, he thought that it would be wiser to first cut the railroad line at an easier site that would probably be less well defended. For this reason, he decided to strike first at Bristoe Station and then try to destroy the nearby bridge over Kettle Run if he could. He could then turn to deal more advantageously with Manassas Station, four miles to the northeast of Bristoe.

Jackson detailed Colonel T.T. Munford's 2nd Virginia Cavalry to lead the attack on Bristoe. Ewell's division would follow in support, headed by Forno's Louisiana brigade. Stuart's two newly arrived cavalry brigades (Fitz Lee's and Robertson's) were sent out to guard Jackson's right and watch for any signs of Pope's approach from the west.

It took almost two hours for the Confederate column to reach Bristoe. Munford, who arrived there first with his cavalry, cautiously approached the station and found that it was guarded by just one company of infantry and one of cavalry. He reported the good news to Jackson, who directed him to proceed and capture the post. Munford's ensuing charge totally surprised the Yankees, who had no reason to suspect that any Yankees were nearby. The Federal cavalrymen managed to mount up and scatter. Most escaped because Munford had only 100 men with him after making a few detachments en route, so he could not pursue them in every direction. The surprised Union infantrymen ran for the cover of a hotel and some other nearby buildings, from which they opened up an ineffective fire. Forno heard their firing and rushed up to help Munford deal with them, but Munford managed to secure their surrender before he arrived. Munford was pleased to report that he had killed or wounded 9 of the enemy and captured 43, including the lieutenant colonel of the *4th New York Cavalry*, at the cost of only three wounded.

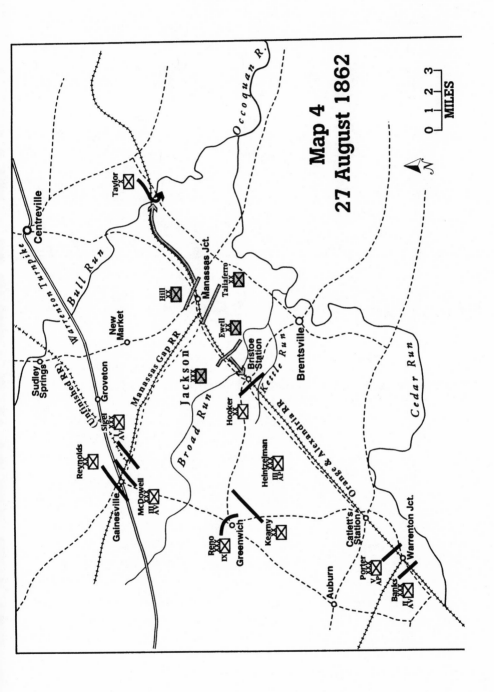

Map 4
27 August 1862

One of several locomotives destroyed by Jackson's troops at Manassas Junction on 26 and 27 August. Jackson's bold marches confused Pope and were the principal cause of the Confederate victory in the campaign.

Munford and Forno now set about disrupting the rail line to Warrenton Junction. They had seen a train go by heading northeast toward Mannasas Junction when they first reached Bristoe, so they posted some troops to wait and try to capture another. They would not have long to wait, since Colonel Haupt was then sending all of Pope's reserve trains back from Warrenton Junction to Alexandria, and these would give plenty of business to the Confederates this evening. The problem facing Jackson's men, however, was how actually to catch a Federal train. They soon saw one coming from the southwest, and some of the Confederates quickly placed a few rails across the tracks to stop it. The Union engineer refused to slow down and struck the pile of rails head on, scattering them all over. He then continued safely on his way. Before long, another train was seen approaching. This time, the Confederates had more time to cover the track with obstructions, including a bumper from the dead end of a nearby spur line. In case these did not do their job, a detachment of the 21st North Carolina drew up alongside the tracks in order to give the engine crew a volley. These preparations worked perfectly. The infantrymen fired when the train drew close, and then the engine hit the obstructions on the track. When all the dust finally settled, there were crumpled train cars all over the place. During all this confusion, the train's engineer somehow managed to blow a danger signal from his cab in order to give a warning to the next train coming up behind him. One of the Confederate soldiers who had been an engineer recognized the signal and promptly jumped into the cab and seized the throttle in order to blow an all-clear safety signal.

The Confederate derailers were still admiring their handiwork when the next train came up. Its engineer, who had heard the false all-clear signal, came on at full speed and smashed head on into the rear of the earlier train, throwing at least three cars into the air like toys. As one Southern officer put it, "the general effect was quite destructive." The wreckage of the two trains made the tracks impassable, and it would require some time and effort to get them cleared. The Confederates' only regret was that the train cars were empty transports and did not contain any foodstuffs for their hungry bellies.

Jackson's success to this point prompted him to go for still more game. He learned from the prisoners captured at Bristoe that the large Union supply depot at Manassas Junction, just a few miles down the road, was guarded by only a few hundred troops. Bountiful supplies and equipment were there for the taking. He had only to push some of his tired troops there before the Yankees became alarmed and summoned aid or started to burn everything. The Union troops posted there probably already knew of his raid from news brought by the engineer of the train that had broken through Munford's first flimsy rail barricade at Bristoe just a short while earlier. This meant that Jackson would need to act at once if he intended to capture the depot intact. He also needed to be wary of enemy troops coming up from the southwest. After the second and third trains had been wrecked at Bristoe, a fourth train had come up but had successfully backed away when its engineer saw all the fire and wreckage at the station. He would soon be alerting all the Union troops at Warrenton Station, and there was no telling how the Yankees would react after that.

Jackson was at first uncertain what troops he should send to

Manassas. Ewell's and Hill's men were closest, since they were at or near Bristoe, but most were exhausted from marching approximately 54 miles in just two days. Taliaferro's division was at the end of the column and so might be a little bit fresher, but it was significantly farther from the target. While Jackson was pondering the situation, Brigadier General Isaac Trimble came up and offered to take Manassas with his two favorite regiments, the 21st Georgia and 21st North Carolina, his "twin Twenty-firsts." Jackson assented, even though the two regiments combined had only 500 men. However, he thought better of the situation soon after Trimble departed at 2100, and sent Stuart with a portion of his cavalry to reinforce Trimble and "take command of the expedition."

The Federal commander at Manassas Junction, Captain Samuel Craig of the *105th Pennsylvania*, had in his charge only 115 men of his own regiment, plus eight guns of the *11th New York Battery* and a totally green cavalry regiment, the *12th Pennsylvania*. He was not particularly concerned when he heard from a passing engineer that there were some Confederate troops at Bristoe. Mosby's guerrillas had been active in the area for some time, so he naturally assumed that it was them or a cavalry raid. Even so, he decided to roust out 80 infantrymen and a few gun crews and post them abreast of the road to Bristoe. After sending out some pickets in that direction, he went back to bed.

Stuart's troopers reached the Federal pickets ahead of Trimble's infantry, and sent the Yankees flying back to Manassas. Stuart, though, decided not to press on at once for fear that the whole Union garrison might be alerted. This proved to be a wise decision. Captain Craig, who had been awakened by the disturbance, began to form his men, but when he saw no enemy approaching, he assumed it was a false alarm and ordered his men to stand down. Then he went back to bed again. Just after he retired, Trimble's infantry came crashing out of the darkness. The sleepy Federal troops were routed in less than five minutes after firing only a few shots. Trimble's men soon captured over 300 prisoners and six cannons, at a loss of just four casualties, two killed and two wounded.

The capture of Manassas Station also yielded a treasure trove of foodstuffs and supplies beyond the Confederates' wildest

The plundering of the bountiful Union supply depot at Manassas Junction on 27 August was never forgotten by Jackson's grateful troops, who burned everything they could not carry away with them.

dreams. Well over 100 boxcars were lined up on over a mile of sidings, all loaded with goods. Numerous warehouses were filled with everything from flour to the luxurious delights like oysters and pies that were sold by the sutlers. Even though it was dark, the Southerners at once realized their good fortune. Stuart's cavalrymen immediately began taking whatever they wanted. Trimble's infantry, on the other hand, were held back and received orders to guard the captured goods until Jackson decided what to do with them.

Jackson's immediate concern was to guard against a Federal counterattack. Now that he was squarely between Pope's army and Washington, he did not know which side he would be attacked from first, if not from both. At dawn on 28 August, he advanced Hill's and Taliaferro's divisions to support Trimble; Ewell's three remaining brigades and most of Stuart's cavalry

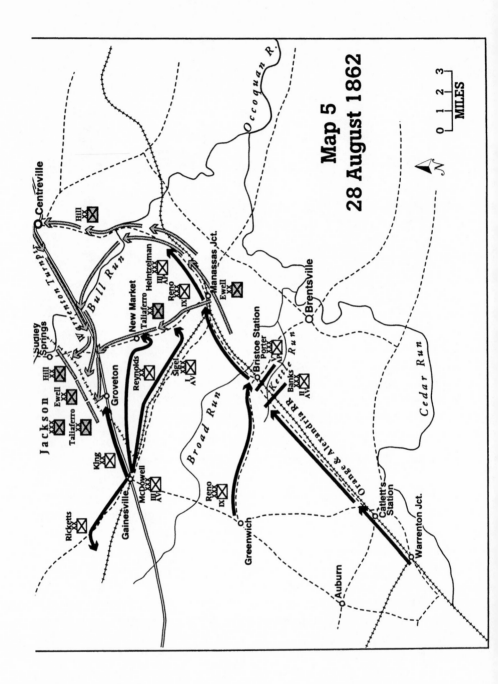

Map 5
28 August 1862

were left at Bristoe in order to watch out for Pope. The first new Confederate troops to reach Manassas Junction soon after dawn were the men of the Stonewall Brigade. These veterans were directed to march through the depot in order to guard against a Union approach from Centreville, but many of them could not resist attempting to dodge Trimble's thin guard line in order to plunder the commissary depot and its delicacies before continuing on their way. The hungry men of Hill's division likewise began helping themselves to all the Yankee victuals when they came up at around 0900.

Jackson himself was too preoccupied to put a personal watch on all the captured warehouses. He was up long before dawn to inspect the captured depot and survey the general situation. He saw no Yankees in sight, but did hear the booming of some cannons slightly to the east of the Junction. It seems that some Union artillerymen who had escaped capture the previous night had posted their two remaining cannons just to the west of Bull Run, where they had been joined by a big new regiment, the *2nd New York Heavy Artillery* (serving as infantry), which had just arrived in Centreville from Washington. The commander of the *2nd*, Colonel Gustav Waagner, had heard all the commotion at the Junction and marched across Mitchell's Ford in order to see what was going on. It was there that he linked up with the aforementioned cannoneers and then headed westwards until they met Fitz Lee's skirmishers, whereupon both sides opened fire. Jackson was immediately concerned by this firing and directed Hill to take his entire division to reinforce Lee. Soon after 0900, Hill had drawn up 9000 men and 28 cannons to the east of the Junction. Colonel Waagner was suitably impressed by the spectacle and promptly ordered a quick withdrawal.

At about the same time, a much stronger Federal force began moving towards Manassas Junction from the direction of Bull Run Bridge. Late the previous evening, Colonel Haupt, the energetic railroad czar, had been informed that a Confederate raiding party of uncertain magnitude had struck at Bristoe Station. Haupt soon proposed to Halleck that a brigade of infantry be sent forward to secure Bull Run Bridge, and from there guard a construction train that would be sent forward to repair whatever damage the enemy had done to the tracks between Bristoe and Manassas Junction. Neither Haupt nor Halleck really expected the Confederate troops to hang around Manassas very long, though they would probably do quite a bit of damage as long as they were there.

By midnight Haupt had located a brigade suitable for the task—Brigadier General George W. Taylor's *First New Jersey Brigade* of Franklin's corps. These troops were put on trains by dawn and sent west to Bull Run. Taylor had to detrain his men about a mile east of the of bridge because a wrecked train was blocking the track. He then marched to the bridge, but did not halt his entire command there as he had been ordered. Taylor, like Waagner, had heard about the Confederate occupation of Manassas Junction and assumed that it was just an enemy raiding party, so he began moving in that direction in order to drive it off. He left one of his regiments, the *4th New Jersey*, to guard the bridge and await the arrival of two Ohio regiments that were supposed to come up and support him, and then led his *lst, 2nd* and *3rd New Jersey* regiments forward into action.

Taylor's men were veterans of the Peninsula campaign, and calmly formed their battle lines as they approached Manassas Junction. Taylor saw only a few cavalrymen, who were proved to be Confederate when their cannons began shelling his lines. Jackson, who was present with Hill's infantry, calmly kept these troops out of view and directed them to hold their fire. Taylor was totally unaware that he was marching straight into the prepared battle line that Hill had drawn up to meet Waagner a short while earlier.

Jackson ordered Hill's cannons to open fire when the Yankees were less than 300 yards away. Their blasts tore great gaps in Taylor's line from his front and both flanks. Taylor desperately ordered a charge against the Confederates he saw in his front, only to run into a wall of infantry fire. Jackson knew what a fix the enemy was in, and boldly rode forward with a white flag in order to request their surrender. His only reply was a Federal musket ball that whizzed past his head.

Taylor was in no mood to surrender. Instead, he continued his fruitless attack for a few minutes longer, until he saw some Confederate cavalry move to cut off his retreat. He then ordered a withdrawal, which was conducted in fairly good order until

Bull Run, near the point where Brigadier General George W. Taylor's New Jersey brigade crossed just before being ambushed by much of Jackson's command on the morning of 27 August. Taylor was mortally wounded and his brigade lost over 330 men in less than half an hour of fighting.

the Yankees reached Bull Run Bridge, which created a bottleneck as all the troops pushed to get across. Then, when a Confederate battery came up to shell them, the Union retreat degenerated into a rout reminiscent of a similar situation at the close of the Battle of First Bull Run a year earlier. About 200 New Jerseyans were captured, General Taylor fell mortally wounded, and at least 150 of his men were killed or wounded. Still more men would have been lost if the *11th* and *12th Ohio* regiments had not rushed to the scene to cover their retreat. Hill's troops then took cover in some rifle pits that had been constructed nearly a year earlier, and the two sides maintained a heavy skrimish for the next several hours.

The rout of Taylor's command was to have repercussions crucial to the campaign beyond the destruction of one Union brigade. McClellan, who was then at Alexandria, was convinced that Taylor's command had been sacrificed because it was hastily rushed forward alone without cavalry or artillery support. That afternoon he suggested to Halleck that there was no purpose to push the rest of Franklin's corps forward without their supporting arms, particularly since he no longer knew Pope's exact position. A short while later, McClellan announced his new "policy" to "mobilize a couple of corps as soon as possible, but not to advance them until they can have their artillery and cavalry." As a result of this policy change, McClellan countermanded the orders that Franklin had received to march to Gainesville. He also directed Sumner's corps to remain at Alexandria until it was fully equipped and ready to advance. These orders were critical since they would prevent both Franklin and Sumner from arriving in time to help Pope at Second Bull Run. McClellan may have been right in choosing not to push these commands forward piecemeal, but he certainly could have taken a more aggressive stance than to hold back two entire corps outside of Alexandria. A move to advance as least as far as Annandale or Fairfax might have persuaded Jackson to abandon the Manassas area entirely, so changing the course of the campaign.

Meanwhile, Pope had slowly come to the realization that something was greatly amiss in his rear. At 2000 on the 26th he received a desperate telegram from Manassas stating that enemy cavalry had cut the railroad line there. Pope was certain that this was just a cavalry or guerrilla raid, and at 2020 ordered Heintzelman to send a regiment there from Warrenton Junction "to ascertain what has occurred." By 2100, though, reports began to filter in that something greater than a cavalry raid might be afoot. A variety of sources including a Confederate deserter, an "intelligent negro," and Buford's cavalry scouts, gave evidence that a strong Rebel force had been moving all day from Salem to White Plains. McDowell sent a report that the entire Confederate army seemed to be heading towards Thoroughfare Gap. A little while later, the army's line of communications to Bristoe Station and Washington was lost.

By midnight Pope understood that his right had been turned, and that there was probably more than just a cavalry detachment at Manassas. He now had three basic choices about what to do next. The safest option was to withdraw to the east to join Burnside's troops at Fredericksburg. Such a move, though, would leave Washington unshielded and would permit Lee to keep the initiative. A more risky option was to cross the Rappahannock and strike at the Confederate rear; this alternative had the same shortcomings as a withdrawal to Fredericksburg. Instead, Pope chose a third plan of action. He deduced that Lee's army was probably strung out over several counties, with its head at Manassas, its middle near Thoroughfare Gap, and its tail somewhere south of Salem. This column had to be vulnerable somewhere, so Pope decided to push his entire command northeastward towards Gainesville and Manassas in order to strike the Confederate lead elements, a move that would still offer cover to Washington. Pope's response to his predicament, in short, was to march towards Washington and "crush any force of the enemy that had passed through Thoroughfare Gap." It was actually a solid plan, one that threatened to trap Jackson's command between Pope's army and McClellan's troops, who were advancing from Alexandria.

To this purpose Pope sent out his marching orders early on 27 August. Sigel's and McDowell's corps, and Reynolds' division of *Pennsylvania Reserves*, were to march northeast from Warrenton to Gainesville, while Heintzelman's and Reno's corps would proceed northward from Warrenton Junction and Catlett's Station to Greenwich, located about four miles south of Gainesville. Porter would follow Heintzelman to Greenwich as soon as Banks came up to relieve him at Warrenton Junction; Banks was selected to serve as a reserve and guard the army's rear because his corps was still recovering from its defeat at Cedar Mountain. Pope confidently expected that once he reconcentrated his 65,000 men at Gainesville, he would be able to defeat the Confederates who were east of the Bull Run Mountains, especially if he received help from McClellan's troops at Alexandria.

This scenario was exactly what Lee had feared might happen. The previous day he had forfeited his chance to attack across the Rappahannock and strike Pope's rear when the Yankees withdrew, because he had shifted Longstreet's men too far to the north. Now all that he could do was to continue advancing Longstreet's wing along the line of march that Jackson had taken, so that the army's two wings could be reunited as soon as the situation would require. During the day, Longstreet's troops marched about 10-12 miles from their morning camp south of Orleans before bivouacking just east of White Plains, on the railroad line from Salem to Thoroughfare Gap. Their march was uneventful and without Union opposition.

Most of Pope's army also had a relatively uneventful march on 27 August, despite the fact that it was now the crisis of the campaign. McDowell's command safely reached Gainesville as ordered. Here it was unknowingly located exactly between the two wings of the Confederate army: Jackson's was about eight miles to the southeast and Longstreet's was about ten miles to the northwest. Most of Heintzelman's command reached their goal at Greenwich. Porter's corps, however, barely cleared Warrenton Junction, thereby considerably weakening the army's far right during its advance.

By far the most hazardous march by any Union troops that day was conducted by Hooker's division of Heintzelman's corps. Heintzelman had ordered Hooker to proceed to Bristoe and investigate the situation there before turning north to rejoin the corps near Greenwich. Hooker wisely sent his *72nd New York* ahead on a train to reconnoitered Bristoe. He did not like the report that the unit sent back: "Enemy in very heavy force. Do not deem it prudent to go on without further orders." Hooker, though, was one of the most aggressive commanders ever to lead a division in the *Army of the Potomac*, and at once began pushing his division up to support the *72nd New York* near Kettle Run.

Ewell, who had held command of the Confederate troops at Bristoe, had been alerted by the advance of the *72nd New York*, and in response formed his three brigades in battle line across the railroad. In order to avoid being surprised, he posted three regiments to picket Kettle Run, and sent one regiment to the right to watch for a possible Union advance from the direction of Greenwich.

By 1500 Hooker had formed Carr's brigade and pushed the Confederates back past Kettle Run bridge, which Ewell's men

The havoc wrought by Jackson's troops on the Federal supply depot at Manassas Junction was well documented by photographers soon afterwards.

managed to burn before they withdrew. He then continued to press forward, despite the fact that his men were exhausted from their ten mile march in the day's heat; they were also low on ammunition because they had never been properly resupplied after leaving the Peninsula. In addition, much of the division's artillery, and most of the officers' horses, had not yet arrived on their transports before the command marched to joined Pope's army.

Despite these disadvantages, the sharp fight that developed near Bristoe Station was waged on even terms for about an hour. By then, though, Ewell began to fear that his retreat route over Broad Run might be cut off. He was facing the unsavory prospect of having to retire without authorization from Jackson, which is exactly what had caused Dick Garnett to be relieved and put up before a court martial. To his great relief, orders finally came from Jackson to determine the enemy's strength and then retire, if necessary, towards Manassas. Ewell obviously welcomed the opportunity to pull back. He had his hands full, however, trying to extricate all his regiments safely. It took nearly an hour to pull his men back in successive lines of battle until they were safely formed behind Broad Run. The Federals by then were too exhausted to follow. Ewell's engineers burned the railroad bridge over the Run at about 1800, and the action drew to a close. Hooker's men had fought hard, losing more than 300 men, including half of the *72nd New York*. Ewell's losses amounted to less than 200 as he successfully shielded Jackson's rear from the Yankees. It is interesting to speculate how the "battle" of Kettle Run might have turned out if Hooker had more troops with him. Pope was still greatly underestimating the size and strength of the Confederate force at Manassas.

Jackson himself spent all day on 27 August at or near Manassas Junction. He first directed his surgeons to take what ambulances and medical supplies they wanted, and let his officers and cavalrymen appropriate horses as needed. In addition, the cannoneers of Carpenter's battery eagerly exchanged their four guns for four brand new shining cannons they found, complete with their caissons, limbers and accoutrements. Everything else was for the moment to be guarded by Trimble's infantrymen, at least as best they could against the depredations of the various covetous infantry units that passed by.

Jackson's initial plan was to issue some of the captured foodstuffs and supplies to his own men, and hold the rest for Longstreet's troops if they could come up before the Federals forced him to leave. During the morning he gave orders for the much needed goods to be issued to his needy men. The feasting that followed would be remembered for years by his grateful troops, most of whom were sorely lacking just about everything that was now available to them in bounty. J.F.J. Caldwell of Gregg's South Carolina brigade wrote later, "Fine whiskey and segars circulated freely, elegant lawn and linen handkerchiefs were applied to noses hitherto blown with the thumb and forefinger, and sumptuous underclothing was fitted over limbs sunburnt sore and vermin-splotched. Many a foot more worn and more worthy than those of the olden time pilgrims here received its grateful protection from the rocky soil. At the

Junction there was general jubilee. Hardtack and bacon, coffee and sugar, even soap, were distributed to us, and we were invited to help ourselves to anything in the storehouses, from a dose of calomel to a McClellan saddle."

John Worsham of the 21st Virginia wrote graphically of his reaction to such plenty after having had but little to eat for the previous several days: "Here are vast storehouses filled with everything to eat, and sutler's stores filled with all the delicacies, potted ham, lobster, tongue, candy, cakes, nuts, oranges, lemons, pickles, catsup, mustard, etc. It makes an old soldier's mouth water now, to think of the good things captured there. A guard was placed over everything in the early part of the day, rations were issued to the men, but not by weight and measure to each man. A package or two of each article was given to each company. These are some of the articles issued to F Company. The first thing brought us was a barrel of cakes, next a bag of hams. We secured a camp kettle, made a fire, and put a ham on to boil; and we had hardly gotten it underway before a barrel of sugar and coffee, the Yanks had it mixed, and a bag of beans were sent us. After a consultation, we decided to empty the ham out of the kettle, as we could take that along raw, and in its place put the beans on the fire, as they were something we were fond of and had not had for a long time. About the time they were commenced to get warm, a bag of potatoes was brought us; over the kettle goes, and the potatoes take the place of the beans. We now think our kettle is all right, as potatoes cook in a short time, but here comes a package of desiccated vegetables, and the kettle is again emptied, and the vegetables are placed on the fire, as soup is so good. We were also given a barrel of syrup. This was a liberal and varied bill of fare for our company, which was small then."

By midmorning, however, the pressure from Waagner's and Taylor's probes persuaded Jackson that he probably would not be able to hold the Junction until Lee could arrive. Instead, he began removing what he could, and then opened up all the warehouses to his eager troops. Hill's and Taliaferro's men soon found themselves in heaven as they began to gorge themselves silly. Jackson's only concern for the moment was that they would not get drunk on all the liquor stores. To prevent this, he

Federal troops entered Manassas Junction while the fires set by Jackson's retiring Confederates were still burning. A roundabout march route taken by two of Stonewall's divisions convinced Pope that Jackson had marched to Centreville instead of Sudley.

ordered all the liquor cases and bottles to be broken and emptied, except what his physicians needed for medical use. Even this did not totally achieve his purpose: some of his thirsty troops stooped to drink the liquid from the alcohol rivulets that were flowing near the warehouses.

Private Worsham describes his view of the orgy: "Our kettle of soup was left to take care of itself. Men who were starving a few hours before, and did not know when they would get another mouthful, were told to help themselves. Well, what do you think they did? Begin to eat. Oh, no. They discussed what they should eat, and what they should take with them, as orders were issued for us to take four days' rations with us. It was hard to decided what to take, some filled their haversacks with cakes, some with candy, others oranges, lemons, canned goods, etc. I know one who took nothing but French mustard, filled his haversack and was so greedy that he put one more bottle in his pocket. This was his four days' rations, and it turned out to be the best thing taken, because he traded it for meat and bread, and it lasted him until we reached Frederick City." Another soldier wrote, "To see a starving man eating lobster salad and drinking Rhine wine, barefoot and in tatters, was curious; the whole thing was indescribable."

CHAPTER VII

Groveton

*J*ackson's bold march to Manassas Station was certainly a fabulous success: he managed to seize his objective safely and capture the huge Union supply depot there, in the process disrupting Halleck's plans and forcing Pope to withdraw from his strong line along the upper Rappahannock. But by the afternoon of 27 August, Jackson realized that it was time to implement the second phase of his operation. The morning's fight against Taylor's brigade and then Ewell's lengthy engagement with Hooker at Kettle Run showed that the Confederate presence at Manassas was attracting strong enemy forces like a magnet. Longstreet's troops were still too far away to help, so Stonewall had no alternative but to move on. His choice of direction was quite limited. His cavalry scouts reported that strong Union forces were moving towards Centreville from the east and towards Gainesville, Greenwich and Bristoe Station from the west. Since he could not safely march to the south because of the Union forces at Aquia and Fredericksburg, Jackson's only secure line of withdrawal was to the north.

Jackson began sending his troops northward at about 2100. As they marched out, he ordered preparations to be made to set on fire all the captured supplies that had not yet been carried off from the Junction. All preparations were completed by midnight, when the torches were applied. The ensuing conflagration furnished quite a spectacle as all the Yankee warehouses and train cars burst into flames, and blasts from exploding ammunition boxes rent the air. The scene would never be forgotten by those who witnessed it.

Taliaferro's troops led the withdrawal, marching north from Manassas Junction at about 2100 via the Sudley Road. After they covered some six miles and crossed the Warrenton Road, they were allowed to go into camp before dawn at Matthew's Hill on the old First Bull Run battlefield, where they waited for the rest of Jackson's command to come up.

Taliaferro's men were to have a longer wait than Jackson had intended. Stonewall had a bad habit of not telling his plans to his subordinates, but instead informed them only as much as they needed to know in order to get started. In this case, he just told Hill and Ewell that he would send them guides to direct their march. Jackson's reticence to share his plans would almost lead his army to disaster this night.

Hill was ready to move out at midnight as directed. The appointed guide soon arrived, and began leading the division away from Manassas. Through some misunderstanding, the guide headed to the northeast towards Bull Run rather than northward on the Sudley Road as Jackson had wanted. The column crossed Bull Run at Blackburn's Ford and proceeded to Centreville, where it went into camp some six miles northeast from where they were supposed to be. Hill was quite lucky not to run into any large bodies of Union troops during his detour.

Hill's misdirected march in turn caused a grave problem for Ewell. During the night, Ewell had moved his three brigades slightly to the east of Manassas, in order to have some security in case the Federals made a night march in his direction from Hooker's front. Ewell's orders were to follow Hill's column, but he could not find any sign of it anywhere. Nor could he locate his own fourth brigade, Trimble's, which had been guarding Manassas Junction for the past two days. The guide whom Ewell received from Jackson was totally confused by the situation, and as a result Ewell had no idea where he was supposed to go. He certainly had no intention to stay in the exposed position where he was, so he started his men north. Quite by accident, he ended up taking the same road that Hill had traveled on towards Centreville. By the time he reached Blackburn's Ford, Ewell's vanguard caught up to Trimble, who had followed Hill. From

Trimble, Ewell learned that Hill had gone into camp five miles ahead at Centreville.

Sometime early in the morning, Jackson painfully realized that something had gone dreadfully wrong. Taliaferro's troops had reached the Warrenton Turnpike, and Hill should have been right behind. Instead, there was no sign of Hill or Ewell. Jackson promptly sent out some staff officers to locate his missing divisions and guide them to Taliaferro's camp. At length someone found Ewell near Blackburn's Ford, and give him orders to march to Groveton. Ewell started his men moving at dawn, led by Early's brigade and then Trimble's. The column had to move cross country on the north side of Bull Run for four miles until it at last struck the Warrenton Turnpike near the Stone Bridge, from where they had an easy march to Groveton. Forno's and Lawton's brigades came up even later. They had somehow lost contact with Early during the night and marched almost to Centreville before they were recalled to Groveton. Ewell's troops, too, were lucky not to be struck by Union forces during their confused withdrawal from Manassas.

Hill, who was not experiencing a very good working relationship with Jackson up until this point, had still more tribulation to endure on this strange march. He had reached Centreville at around dawn, and let his weary men have some sleep. After receiving Jackson's orders to march to Groveton, he moved out at about 0900 on the Warrenton Turnpike. He was near the Stone Bridge at around 1000 when he received fresh orders from Jackson to turn aside and head south to the Bull Run fords in order to intercept the enemy, who was "in full retreat." For some reason, Jackson's orders, which had been sent from the "battlefield of Manassas" at 0800, took two hours to reach Hill, who was less than five miles away.

These new orders show how eager Jackson was to start a fight on his own terms and not let Pope's army slip away to the safety of Washington's defenses. Early in the morning he had posted cavalry pickets from the 1st Virginia on the roads west and south of Groveton. They soon made a valuable capture: a scouting party from Sigel's corps rode into their lines and was gobbled up, as was a courier sent from McDowell to Sigel. The courier happened to be carrying a copy of McDowell's orders for Sigel and Reynolds to march on Manassas and attack the Confederate troops there. Jackson already had other intelligence suggesting that Pope was in retreat, and decided to try to take advantage of the situation by striking Sigel's troops as they advanced on Manassas. He hoped to inflict a quick defeat on the enemy, or at least slow Pope down enough to enable Longstreet to come up, whereupon the recombined Confederate army could take on Pope face to face. The last thing that Jackson wanted at the moment was for Pope's army to withdraw all the way to Washington and link up with McClellan's troops that were known to be at Alexandria.

Jackson's orders placed Hill in quite a quandary. His scouts and pickets had also been active, and had brought in two Union dispatches from Pope to McDowell. These indicated that Pope was not intending a retreat but was concentrating his entire force at Manassas. This meant that Hill would probably run into most of the Union army if he attempted to follow Jackson's 0800 orders. Hill understood that it would be much safer for him to disobey Jackson's orders and continue his march to Groveton, but he also knew that Jackson had arrested and court martialed his officers for less serious offenses than this. Even so, he did not hesitate to make his decision. As he wrote later, "I deemed it best to push on and join General Jackson." His decision proved to be the proper one. Jackson had misread the situation, and Hill had interpreted the Union movements more properly. Jackson as much as admitted his mistake by not taking Hill to task later for disobeying his 0800 order. Curiously, Stonewall made no mention of his error when he wrote his battle report, nor did he give praise to Hill for the latter's initiative. He stated simply that "Ewell's and Hill's divisions joined Jackson's on the 28th," so glossing over the night's misdirected marches and mistaken orders.

Hill's troops did not reach the rest of Jackson's command until sometime after noon. By then, Jackson had decided to temporarily take up a defensive position and await developments on his fast moving front. He knew now that Pope's troops were headed for Manassas, and he hoped that Longstreet, with whom he was still in regular contact, would come up soon enough to help him deal with the enemy. For the moment, he drew up his troops under the cover of a large woods north of the Warrenton Turnpike just northwest of the old Bull Run battle-field, and let them rest after their meandering all night marches. His position was secluded and well chosen. There were no Yankees known to be in his rear (to the north), so enabling him to retire to Thoroughfare or Aldie Gap if the need arose. More importantly, Longstreet's troops had a clear road to reinforce him once they passed through Thoroughfare Gap.

When he drew up his troops north of Groveton, Jackson was unaware how narrowly he had escaped Pope's plan to catch him at Manassas. As noted in the previous chapter, Pope had advanced his army in two wings on the 27th in order to strike whatever Confederate troops had crossed to the east of Thor-oughfare Gap. McDowell's wing, consisting of his own and Sigel's corps, marched up the Warrenton Turnpike and reached Gainesville after 2300. The head of Reno's command, followed by Kearny's division, was at Greenwich. Hooker's division, which was the only command sent directly towards Manassas, advanced from Kettle Run to Bristoe Station following Ewell's withdrawal to Manassas.

Pope himself spent most of the day at Warrenton Junction. When he heard of Hooker's fight at Kettle Run, he rode there at once to survey the situation. He was dismayed to see that Hooker's men were played out and also low on ammunition, with an average of only five rounds per man remaining. For this reason, Hooker was unable to advance beyond Bristoe that evening. More importantly, some prisoners captured by Hooker told Pope the size and identity of the Confederate force at Manassas: it was Jackson's command of about 25,000 men. Pope at last knew where Stonewall was, a riddle that he could and should have solved a day or two earlier.

Pope's initial reaction upon learning the size of the Confeder-ate force at Manassas was to send Porter orders to march at 0100 from Warrenton Junction so that he could reach Bristoe by daylight. Porter could then drive the enemy forces from Manas-sas "and clear the country between that place and Gainesville."

Pope revised his plans later in the evening, and decided to move his entire army towards Manassas in an attempt to trap Jackson. Kearny was directed to march "at the very earliest blush of dawn" from Greenwich to reinforce Hooker at Bristoe. From there, Heintzelman's reunited corps would march against Manassas from the southwest, supported by Reno's command, which would come up from Greenwich. Porter and Banks would also head for Bristoe from their camps at Warrenton Junction. Meanwhile, McDowell and Sigel would close the trap by marching on Manassas from the northwest, guiding their right on the Manassas Gap Railroad. Pope was confident that his 50,000 men in the area could defeat Jackson's command of half that size. He confidently asserted to McDowell, "If you will march promptly and rapidly at the earliest dawn of day upon Manassas Junction, we shall bag the whole crowd."

Pope's plan was well conceived, but it had several major flaws. Firstly, he had only one of his three cavalry brigades in position to do the screening and scouting essential to conducting an advance. This was Bayard's brigade, which was serving on the Warrenton Turnpike with McDowell's wing. Buford's brigade was operating on McDowell's left wing, and more will be heard of it shortly. The army's third cavalry brigade, Beardsley's, was being retained as a rear guard at Warrenton. These dispositions meant that there were no cavalrymen on Heintzelman's front at Bristoe to help determine the enemy's dispositions and movements.

Secondly, Pope made no allowance for the possible arrival of Longstreet to aid Jackson or otherwise interfere with his plans. Just as he had single-mindedly ignored all the prospects of where Jackson might be going when Stonewall's advance was seen near Salem on the 26th, so he now failed to consider what Lee and Longstreet might do while he was marching his entire command to Manassas. Pope had made no provisions for watching Longstreet other than to post Beardsley's brigade as a rear guard at Warrenton.. This was in spite of the fact that information continued to be brought in from several sources that a large Confederate column was near Salem. Pope later explained that he fully expected "to crush Jackson completely before Longstreet could have reached the scene of action." Even if he actually believed this, he should have made more provision to watch for Longstreet, just to be safe. His failure to do so would prove catastrophic, as soon will be seen.

Even if Pope had no concern for Longstreet's whereabouts, McDowell and Sigel certainly did. McDowell's corps was posted on the army's northern flank, closest to Longstreet's line of march. Buford's cavalry kept an alert eye on the Confederate advance, and even managed at one point to break into Longstreet's column between Salem and Thoroughfare Gap, in the process capturing several prisoners who betrayed the identity of the Confederate force. McDowell himself proceeded as far as Buckland Mills on 28 August, and stayed up late with Sigel debating what to do about Longstreet. Sigel, who was McDowell's junior and was currently in Pope's bad graces (Pope called him "utterly unreliable" after his evacuation of the Rappahannock line), offered what advice he could and then went to sleep. Finally, McDowell made up his mind at about 2330. He would send two of his divisions (King's and Ricketts') to Gainesville in compliance with Pope's orders of that morning to conduct an advance to that point. Meanwhile, he would take the rest of his impromptu wing to Haymarket, three miles northwest of Gainesville, in order to keep an eye on Longstreet. As historian John Hennessy has observed, McDowell's orders that night were some of the best issued by any Union officer during the campaign. His proposed position at Haymarket would enable him to face Longstreet or march to help deal with Jackson, as best the situation would demand.

McDowell had just sent out his marching orders to his troops when he received revised orders from Pope to march to Manassas at dawn. These instructions forced him to cancel the plans he had carefully reasoned out at 2230. He now sent out a new set of directions to his subordinates. Sigel was to march directly to Manassas with his right "resting on the Manassas Railroad." Reynolds was to form on Sigel's left and King was to form on Reynolds' left, extending his line as far as possible towards the Sudley Road. Since his units were already under orders to march out at 0200, McDowell altered their departure time slightly to 0245 rather than have them wait until dawn as Pope instructed.

Despite Pope's new set of instructions, McDowell was still sufficiently concerned about Longstreet's presence at Salem to assign one of his divisions, Ricketts', to stay behind at Gainesville and keep a watch towards the northwest. Ricketts was specifically instructed to be on the alert for any Confederate troops advancing through Thoroughfare Gap. If any appeared, he was to march to form on King's left and then join in the movement to Manassas. If the Confederates did attack or threaten from the direction of the Gap, Ricketts was to "form his division to the left and march to resist."

The third shortcoming of Pope's plan to trap Jackson was the fact that he did not consider the possibility that Jackson might not stay at Manassas until all the Union troops converged there in their march to catch him. Pope should have been alerted to this potentiality when he saw the fire of the burning warehouses that the Confederates torched after 2300 on the 27th. This should have signaled to him that Jackson was leaving the area. Nevertheless, Pope insisted on believing that Stonewall was still camped at Manassas, waiting to be pounced upon.

If Pope's men were going to have a chance to trap Jackson at Manassas, they needed to move quickly on 28 August. McDowell got the army's left wing off to a great start when he sent orders for his men to march at 0245. Since Manassas was about a three hour march away (eight miles or so), McDowell's troops had a good chance of reaching there by dawn. Pope's plan, though, began to go awry when Sigel did not begin moving until 0730. Sigel did not want to approach the enemy with his troops all strung out, so he waited for his divisions to close up on Gainesville before directing them to begin moving to Manassas. The lengthy delay, of course, backed up all of McDowell's troops lined up on the road beyond.

Sigel simply was not having a good day. He sent out several scouting parties to investigate the roads towards Manassas and Centreville, and one troop managed to get itself captured. So did a courier who was carrying McDowell's marching orders, as already has been mentioned. When he suggested to McDowell that perhaps they ought to leave a substantial force to guard the Warrenton Turnpike, McDowell was too frustrated to listen to him. By then Sigel's troops were floundering about the countryside as their commander tried to put their right "on the Manassas Railroad." To him this meant the Orange and Alexandria Railroad, not the Manassas Gap Railroad as Pope intended.

As a result of this misunderstanding, Sigel was about to head in the wrong direction!

McDowell, who was by now totally fed up with Sigel, gladly pushed his men forward once Sigel at last started moving at 0730. He did not clear Gainesville until 1000. About a mile past Gainesville, Reynolds' vanguard ran into some Confederate outposts from Taliaferro's division that were posted along the Warrenton Turnpike near the Brawner farm. The Confederate pickets fell back on the 42nd Virginia and two of Taliaferro's rifled guns opened up at the head of Reynolds' column; among the Yankees being shot at was McDowell himself, who had to hustle hastily to cover. Reynolds promptly brought up two batteries of his own and also sent forward a strong line of skirmishers from the *13th Pennsylvania Reserves*, A sharp skirmish followed, which soon persuaded the Confederates to withdraw towards Groveton rather than be overwhelmed.

McDowell did not quite know what to make of this short fight, other than the fact that it delayed his advance for about an hour. After a conference with his two division commanders, he decided that the Confederates whom Reynolds had faced were probably just a scouting party, since they withdrew out of sight after their brief confrontation. At 1300 he directed Reynolds to disengage and head south along Pageland Lane to Manassas. Little did he know that Jackson's entire command was only three miles to the east, near Groveton. Jackson, in fact, had started moving Taliaferro's entire division to the support of the 42nd Virginia at the Brawner farm, but it arrived too late to help. By the time that Taliaferro had his men in motion, the skirmish was over and there were no Federals in sight. Taliaferro's men then retired to the comforting shade of the woods north of the Brawner farm. Ewell's division, which had started to follow Taliaferro, stopped behind an old unfinished railroad line about three-quarters of a mile northwest of Groveton.

Pope, who had spent the night at Bristoe, was up at dawn and waited anxiously for the sounds of fighting in his front, where he expected Reno to begin engaging Jackson near Manassas at any moment. When there was no sign of Reno's advance by 0700, and Kearny's advance had not yet reached Bristoe, Pope began to grow quite testy. He was also annoyed that Porter was

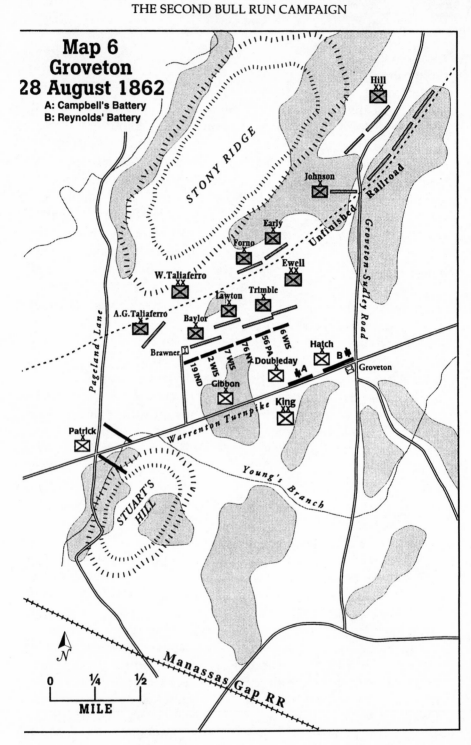

Map 6
Groveton
28 August 1862
A: Campbell's Battery
B: Reynolds' Battery

STONY RIDGE

Hill
XX

Johnson

Early

Forno

Ewell
XX

W.Taliaferro
XX

Lawton
X

Trimble
X

A.G.Taliaferro
XX

Baylor
X

Brawner

6 WIS

56 PA

7 WIS

76 NY

2 WIS

19 IND

Doubleday

Hatch
X

Groveton

Gibbon
XX

King
XX

Patrick
X

Warrenton Turnpike

Young's Branch

STUART'S HILL

Pageland Lane

Unfinished Railroad

Groveton-Sudley Road

N

0   ¼   ½
MILE

Manassas Gap RR

way behind schedule in coming up from Warrenton Junction. Pope did not wish to push Hooker's exhausted troops forward, so he sat and waited all morning for more troops to reach him.

Kearny's troops at last reached Bristoe late in the morning, whereupon they led a belated advance towards Manassas. The Union troops reached the Junction around noon and found only smoldering ruins and total desolation. Jackson was gone, having slipped off to the north through the unguarded back door that Pope had failed to close. So much for the Yankee trap.

Kearny's troops, though, did manage to bring in a number of stragglers from Jackson's command. These reported that Jackson's troops had just left Manassas at 1000 that morning and headed for Centreville. Hill's mistaken march the previous night was now to reap unexpected benefits. Pope impetuously decided to push his whole army in pursuit of Hill, and at 1400 sent out orders for all his commanders to converge at Centreville instead of Manassas.

The situation developed a new wrinkle a short while later when Pope received information that Longstreet was heading for Thoroughfare Gap. He now faced a dilemma, whether he should continue to pursue Jackson or should turn aside towards Longstreet's strung out column. He had sufficient force to deal with either Confederate force separately, but had to make his choice quickly. His first reaction was to attack Longstreet and prevent him from joining Jackson. To do this, he sent orders to McDowell to halt his march to Centreville and wait near Gainesville. Pope would then move to join him there with Heintzelman's and Reno's commands. Pope's thinking at the time, though, was a bit muddled. He said that he would join McDowell personally, "unless there is a large force of the enemy at Centreville, which I do not believe." McDowell was instructed to advance towards Green Spring, unless he felt that this was too dangerous, and he was to look out for Jackson's trains, "which certainly should be captured."

A short while later, Pope changed his mind again and decided that it was better to pursue Jackson to Centreville, as he earlier had intended. Between 1500 and 1600, he sent out yet another set of orders. He now directed Heintzelman and Reno to go directly from Manassas to Centreville. Sigel, who had managed to proceed barely four miles past Gainesville towards Manassas, was to swing over to the Sudley Road and there turn north until he reached the Warrenton Turnpike, where he was to turn east towards Centreville. McDowell was ordered to march "directly upon Centreville from where you are." The orders to head for Centreville rankled McDowell, since they contained no provision to watch out for Longstreet. Pope's continuous changing of orders and his lack of concern for Longstreet, both seemed to McDowell to indicate that the army commander was "befuddled" and had no master plan of action.

McDowell's corps was greatly spread out when he received Pope's latest orders. Ricketts' division was beyond Gainesville; his march will be discussed later. King's division, which had been following Reynolds', had been delayed by the morning's traffic jam and then by Pope's changes of orders. In midafternoon, King had stopped on Pageland Lane about a mile south of the Warrenton Turnpike, having covered about seven miles in fits and starts. His men had just cooked supper and were stretching out to rest when they received orders at 1700 to head back to the Turnpike and head for Centreville.

King had four brigades in his column, which stretched out for about a mile on the road. Hatch's brigade led the way, followed by Gibbon's brigade of westerners, then Doubleday's and lastly Patrick's brigade of New Yorkers. McDowell rode for awhile with Hatch's vanguard, anxious because of the morning's skirmish near the Brawner farm. After Hatch's men reached the Warrenton Turnpike and turned to the east, he sent out the *14th Brooklyn* as flankers to the left. The men of the *14th*, colorful in their distinctive red trousers, reported that there were no Confederates on the Brawner farm. This eased McDowell's mind enough that he left the column to ride to see Pope and try to find out the army's plans.

King's men did not know that their march to Groveton was taking them right across the front of Jackson's command, who were resting in the woods less than a mile to the north. Jackson, on the other hand, was well aware of King's movements. His scouts had kept him well informed of the confusing Union movements along the Turnpike, and at about 1800 he rode forward alone to survey King's column. Brigadier General

Abner Doubleday later claimed to have seen Jackson conduct this reconnaissance, but he could not get anyone to take a shot at the solitary horseman.

Jackson had been waiting for exactly such an opportunity to pounce on a portion of Pope's command. He was not so much interested in inflicting a defeat on one of the enemy's detachments as he was in revealing his location to the confused Union commander. As previously discussed, Jackson did not want Pope to move towards Washington and link up there with the remainder of McClellan's command. Now that Longstreet's wing was only a day's march away, Jackson felt that the Confederates now had one last chance to defeat Pope, if only the Yankees could be halted short of Centreville and Fairfax. The only trick was to get Pope's attention. Since Pope's confused marches the previous two days showed clearly that the Union commander was having a difficult time locating Jackson, Stonewall felt that he had no choice but to resolve the situation by taking direct action himself to reveal his presence to the enemy.

THE BATTLE OF GROVETON

Jackson returned to his lines shortly after 1600 and calmly told his officers, "Bring up your men, gentlemen." Taliaferro at once sent his men forward with a cheer. His four infantry brigades advanced to the northern edge of the Brawner farm, fronted by a swarm of skirmishers. At the same time, three batteries rolled up and began to take position on the lower slope of Stony Ridge. Garber's battery opened fire first, and had the range of Hatch's rear troops by its third shot. The Union infantrymen at once dove for cover along the roadside. Hatch ordered Gilbert Reynolds' New York battery to deploy just to the northwest of Groveton (which was just a crossroads with six plain houses) and return the Confederate fire.

The growing artillery duel and appearance of Confederate skirmishers meant serious business, but there was no Union commander on hand to take charge of the situation. Hatch's division commander, Brigadier General Rufus King, was not well enough to take the field that day. He had suffered a bad epileptic seizure five days earlier, but he refused to leave his

Feisty Brigadier General John Gibbon refused to decline Jackson's challenge to battle at Groveton on 28 August. His command fought so well there and in the Antietam Campaign that it was christened the "Iron Brigade." He rose to command the XVIII Corps at the end of the war.

troops and was accompanying them in an ambulance. (If King went to the hospital, he would have been replaced by his senior brigadier, Hatch, whom neither King nor McDowell nor Pope liked.) Just before the fighting started, King had left his ambulance in order to have dinner, during which he suffered another seizure that would render him useless for several hours. Since McDowell had just left half an hour earlier to look for Pope, there was no senior Federal officer on the field to take charge of the situation.

Reynolds' battery soon found itself overwhelmed by Taliaferro's guns, and Hatch had no interest in sending his infantry into the unequal action. Brigadier General John Gibbon, whose brigade was on the roadway behind Hatch's, was made of sterner metal. When the Confederates opened fire on his lead regiment, the *6th Wisconsin,* he formed it into battle line and sent his battery, Campbell's, into action on a rise just east of the Brawner farm. The rest of his brigade momentarily enjoyed cover from Brawner Woods. By now two more Confederate batteries opened up on the Federal column. Brigadier General Abner Doubleday, commander of the brigade behind Gibbon's, quickly headed his men to the nearest cover in the Brawner Woods, while Brigadier General Marsena Patrick's men, who were last in the divisional column, hurried into a woods south of the roadway.

Since there was no division or corps commander on hand to give orders, the four brigades stood inactive for several tense minutes. At last Gibbon took matters into his own hands and rode to consult with Doubleday at the edge of the Brawner Woods. Doubleday felt that the Confederate troops must be cavalry, since Jackson was supposed to be at Centreville. If that were the case, the Confederates could easily be driven off, since they probably did not have much support. Gibbon agreed, and offered to make an attack on his own authority.

Gibbon selected his only veteran regiment, the *2nd Wisconsin*, to deal with the Confederate cannons. The Badgers advanced in good order towards the Brawner farm buildings, only to see the enemy guns pack up and withdraw. Their mission, though, was far from over. Much to the Yankees' awe, they saw Taliaferro's entire division of over 5000 men marching out of the woods a quarter mile distant in full battle order, their red flags leading the way.

The men of the *2nd Wisconsin* did not flinch at this spectacle, even when their startled skirmishers came scurrying back to their lines. They simply held their ground as an entire Confederate brigade—the 800 men of the vaunted Stonewall Brigade, commanded by Colonel William Baylor—bore down on them. The Virginians fired first, a volley that sailed over the retreating Union skirmishers. Colonel Edgar O'Connor bravely had his regiment hold their fire until the Confederate line was just 150 yards away. When he gave the command, the *2nd's* 450 muskets let loose a horrendous volley at Baylor's men. The Confederates boldly continued their advance until they came within 80 yards of the Union line, where they stopped and fired a devastating volley of their own.

The two opposing forces stood eye to eye for the next twenty minutes in an old fashioned stand up fight that one participant described a as "one of the most intensely concentrated fires of musketry ever experienced by any troops." Gibbon by then moved to bring up his *19th Indiana* to support O'Connor's left,

The battle of Groveton, as seen from Centreville. Pope was having such a difficult time locating Jackson's troops that Stonewall had to emerge from his hiding spot and attack King's division near Groveton on the evening of 28 August.

which was in danger of being outflanked. Then pressure rose on the Federal right, where Starke's Louisiana brigade was entering the fight. Next Jackson personally ordered half of Lawton's Georgia brigade to come up and extend Taliaferro's line. They were in turn met by the *7th Wisconsin*, which Gibbon now committed on the right of his line.

The two battle lines continued to bang away at each other at a deadly distance of less than 100 yards. Though the Union troops were not all veterans, they fought as such, and neither side would pull back and admit defeat. Both sides now rushed more men into the fray as the fighting spread and intensified.

Trimble's brigade of Ewell's division came up next, just in time to meet Gibbon's last regiment, Colonel Lysander Cutler's *6th Wisconsin*. Cutler had been at the head of Gibbon's column, and now much up the eastern edge of Brawner Woods into the growing maelstrom. His regiment, though, was not a sufficient match for Trimble's brigade, particularly since there was a large gap to his left, between the *6th* and the *7th Wisconsin*. To Cutler's relief, two of Doubleday's regiments, the *76th New York* and *56th Pennsylvania*, appeared to plug the gap. Colonel Dawes later recalled the scene: "Through the intense smoke, through which we were advancing, I could see a blood red sun sinking behind the hills... The two crowds, they could hardly be called lines, were within, it seemed to me, fifty yards of each other, and they were pouring musketry into each other as rapidly as men could shoot."

The bloody battle had been going on for about 45 minutes on even terms. There was every reason for the Confederates to gain the upper hand, since Jackson had his entire command in the vicinity, and Hatch and Patrick declined to enter the fight on the Union side without orders from a superior. Even so, it seemed for the moment that the growing darkness might enable Gibbon and Doubleday to hold the field and so claim a victory, or at least a draw.

Jackson was bound and determined not to lose the day. The fight would have been over by that point if he had taken the time to form all his men before starting his attack. But here, as at Port Republic and Cedar Mountain, Jackson rushed into action in his haste to meet the enemy, and so suffered large unnecessary losses as his units entered the fight one by one. By 1915 Stonewall had the remainder of Ewell's command, plus Hill's large division, moving up to join the fight, but it was uncertain if they would be able to come up and deploy before dark.

At around 1930 Jackson sent out orders for a frontal assault, in hopes that his troops already on the field might be able to overwhelm the weary Federals in one final attack. Trimble's "Twin Twenty-ones" rushed to the attack first. They struck the right end of the Union line, where the Federals held their fire in the growing darkness until their foes were but 30 yards away, a distance at which their shots could not miss. The colonel of the 21st North Carolina was shot dead, and the 21st Georgia lost 146 of its 242 men. Lawton's brigade suffered equally heavy losses on Trimble's right. The Union line still held.

Attention now shifted to the left end of the Union line. Gibbon was well aware that his position was a vulnerable one, and for this reason he spent the entire fight on his left flank with his *19th Indiana*. Affairs began to go badly for the Yankees when Captain John Pelham, one of the South's most intrepid artillerists, came dashing up to within 100 yards of the *19th's* left flank. His

The battle of Groveton, from a sketch by Edwin Forbes from the Union lines.

cannon blasts shook the Hoosier line, which then felt the weight of a belated attack by three regiments from W.B. Taliaferro's last brigade, Colonel A.G. Taliaferro's. Gibbon reluctantly pulled the *19th* back, but was still able to put out enough fire power to stall this new Confederate attack.

The firing now began to die out at last, as if the two exhausted armies were ready to call the fight a draw by mutual consent. King, who had by now recovered some of his faculties, began trying to seek instructions from McDowell, but could not locate him. He was inclined to continue his march to Centreville, as previously ordered, but Gibbon persuaded him to stay where he was. King's resolve was stiffened when he learned that Ricketts was approaching Gainesville, three miles to the southwest, and that Reynolds had marched to the sound of the guns and would be up at first light in the morning. However, interrogation of some Confederate prisoners taken during the engagement persuaded him to withdraw rather than face Stonewall's force of "60,000 or 70,000 men." But where should he withdraw to? After some discussion, King and his brigadiers decided that it was best to head for Manassas, where they could surely find some support. The entire division then left Groveton at about 0100 after a very, very long day.

The battle of Groveton decided little in the long run. Jackson certainly could have revealed his location to Pope's men at much less cost. As it was, he did not manage the action well, particularly when he ordered artillery to open fire before his infantry was fully deployed. Nor did the Confederate division commanders have a good day. Brigadier General W.B. Taliaferro held one of his brigades, Johnson's, out of the fight because it had been engaged that morning, and he committed his other three brigades to action one by one. In return for his troubles, he received three wounds, one in the foot, one in the neck and one in the arm. Ewell, who was usually an aggressive and reliable commander, was also slow at committing his troops, so much so that half of his division came up too late to enter the fight. He, too, fell wounded in the action. He was struck in the left knee while leading one of Lawton's regiments to the attack, and the leg had to be amputated. The injury would put him out of action until after Chancellorsville, eight months later.

Confederate casualties in the battle numbered some 1250. Their losses could be ill afforded, since they came from veteran troops. The Stonewall brigade lost 40 per cent of its strength, and Trimble's "Twin Twenty-ones" lost a whopping 70 per cent. Union losses were just over 1000. The *2nd Wisconsin* lost heaviest, as 276 of its 430 men fell casualty, many of them with more than one wound. All told, Gibbon's black hatted brigade lost one-third of its strength in its first major action, and thus was well on its way to becoming the *"Iron Brigade"* of the Union army.

Thoroughfare Gap

Despite Jackson's exposed position in the proximity of most of Pope's army on 28 August, Lee and Longstreet appeared to be in no particular rush to reach him. In fact, their advance from the Rappahannock had been only at about half the speed that Jackson had marched. Longstreet covered about 14 miles on the 26th, proceeding from the Rappahannock to Orleans, which was a fair day's march. But he covered only six miles on the 27th before encamping at White Plains, eight miles west of Thoroughfare Gap. His column then did not break camp until 1100 on 28 August, and by midafternoon still had not reached the important gap. A message from Jackson, who by then had at last gathered all his troops near Sudley Church, assured Lee that all was going well on his front, so Longstreet felt no need to push on any farther that day. He let his troops go into bivouac at 1500 at the western approach to Thoroughfare Gap, and sent just one brigade, Anderson's, to secure the critical passage for the morrow.

Lee's scouts had already assured him that the Federals had not taken care to block the gap. This was a great reassurance to both Lee and Jackson, since the passage through the gap provided the most direct route for Longstreet to join Jackson's wing, then some ten miles to the east at Sudley Church. Pope had simply been too preoccupied with trying to catch Jackson at Manassas and Centreville, and for the moment was blocking out any thought of where Longstreet might be. Since it was highly unlikely that Longstreet was going to remain inactive once Pope left the Rappahannock, Pope should have prepared for either of the two most likely possibilities: that Longstreet might cross the Rappahannock and attack Pope's troops as they pulled back, or that Longstreet might follow Jackson's column eastward through the Bull Run Mountains. Pope erred greatly by not taking precautions against either event.

McDowell had been much more perspicacious than Pope in this regard. Since he had been posted on the army's northern flank, McDowell for the sake of self preservation had to keep an eye out to the north. As already noted, his cavalry scouts had kept him well informed on Longstreet's slow progress towards Thoroughfare Gap. Late on the 27th, McDowell had decided after much deliberation to move most of his command to face Longstreet near Thoroughfare Gap, but he had canceled these plans when he received Pope's orders to head for Manassas, as previously discussed. Even so, McDowell had decided to leave Ricketts' division behind near Gainesville when he left for Manassas at 0245 on 28 August.

Ricketts, in compliance with McDowell's orders, was ready to "march to resist" Longstreet at Thoroughfare Gap if the need arose. His call came at 1015 on the 28th, when he received word from Sir Percy Wyndham, who was then holding the gap with the *1st New Jersey Cavalry*, that Longstreet's vanguard had begun approaching his position at 0930. Wyndham set his men to work felling trees in order to block the road into the gap, and was anxiously awaiting help.

Ricketts set his 5000 man division into motion at once. He reached Haymarket, three miles east of the gap, at 1400, only to run into Wyndham's troopers, who had just been pushed out of the gap by the Confederates. Undeterred, Ricketts continued to push his infantry forward in an effort to halt Longstreet. His advance, led by Colonel Richard Coulter's *11th Pennsylvania*, moved forward confidently and ran directly into Anderson's lead regiment, the 9th Georgia, about one-quarter mile east of Thoroughfare. The Confederates were not exactly expecting a fight, and were in the process of setting up camp after their successful confrontation with Wyndham. As a result, the Yankee attack had an initial advantage and drove the Georgians back into the heart of the pass.

D.R. Jones, however, had seen the progress of the Union attack, and by the time the 9th Georgia reached Thoroughfare, he had the rest of Anderson's brigade drawn up in battle line there, with Benning's brigade in support. Even so, the Yankees almost gained control of the situation. A detachment of the *13th Massachusetts* hurried up the steep mountainside to try to seize the commanding summit of Pond Mountain, located on the south side of the gap. They were halted near the crest by two of Benning's regiments, which had arrived there just moments before.

The situation quickly developed into a stalemate when Ricketts drew up his men into a strong defensive position in the rugged terrain at the eastern end of the pass. Lee appreciated the seriousness of the situation and ordered Colonel Evander Law of Hood's division to try to take his brigade over the steep heights of the mountain north of the gap (which had the curious name of "Mother Leathercoat"), in order to turn Ricketts' right flank. In case Law could not accomplish his mission, Lee also sent Wilcox's division on a march to the next pass to the north, Hopewell Gap, which was about six miles distant. Wilcox could then return southward to turn Ricketts' right flank if this pass were not also held by the Yankees.

Law's men had an arduous climb and had to proceed single

file much of the way. By great effort they succeeded at crossing the mountain north of the pass, and then formed quietly into battle line at its eastern base. Ricketts moved part of his command to face this new threat, only to learn that Benning's two regiments had managed to descend from Pond Mountain and turn his left flank. He was now outflanked at both ends of his position, and found that he had no choice but to retreat and leave control of Thoroughfare Gap to Jones' Confederates.

This action at Thoroughfare Gap on the late afternoon of 28 August was not as bloody or intense as some sources claim. Ricketts actually committed only four of his regiments to the fight, and casualties on each side were probably not more than 100 each. Nor had Buford's cavalry been engaged in any last ditch effort to hold the gap and thereby save Pope's army from destruction. The only Union cavalry engaged in the gap was Wyndham's *1st New Jersey* of Bayard's brigade, which was only briefly engaged before Ricketts came up.

There is no question that Ricketts could have made a better defense of Thoroughfare Gap if he had arrived sooner and committed more of his troops to the fight. Even so, he could not have held the pass indefinitely against Longstreet's entire command of over 20,000 men. There were other passes not too far away that were available for the Confederates to use and thereby flank Ricketts' position. Pope's failure to attempt to hold the passes in the Bull Run Mountains in force meant that he would forfeit his best chance to slow down Longstreet and so win enough time to defeat Jackson or at least drive Stonewall back. As affairs developed, McDowell had the right idea on his own, but he lacked the manpower sufficient to carry it out. Ricketts arrived at Thoroughfare Gap too late with too little. As it turned out, Ricketts did not even succeed at delaying Longstreet's march one hour. Longstreet's troops had already started going into camp west of Thoroughfare Gap before the fight with Ricketts started. These troops, along with those who had been engaged in the fight, simply resumed their march eastward in the morning as originally scheduled.

The Two Bull Runs

Bull Run's proximity to Washington destined its banks to be the scene of two great battles of the war, both Union defeats and each the bloodiest engagement of the war until that point. First Bull Run was fought on 21 July 1861, the first major battle of the war. Here Brigadier General Irvin McDowell's *Army of Northeastern Virginia* was defeated by the combined and slightly larger Confederate armies of the Shenandoah and the Potomac, led by Generals Joseph E. Johnston and P.G.T. Beauregard, respectively. The battle of Second Bull Run, fought on 29-30 August 1862 between Major General John Pope's *Army of Virginia* and General Robert E. Lee's Army of Northern Virginia, involved almost twice as many men and five times as many casualties as First Bull Run.

The two battles were fought on completely different axes, but still covered much the same ground. In First Bull Run, McDowell's army approached the field from the northeast with the goal of defeating the Confederate troops who were posted along the east-west course of Bull Run. McDowell sent most of his command on a wide flank march that crossed Bull Run at Sudley Ford, and the battle's fighting then flowed southeastward from Matthew's Hill to its climax on Henry House Hill.

At Second Bull Run, Pope's Union forces approached the field from the south and west and spent two days attacking Jackson's position, which was posted behind the unfinished railroad line that ran southwestward from Sudley Church past the Brawner farm. Late on the second day of the battle the fighting spread to the south as Longstreet's troops attacked from the west and fought the Union troops posted on Chinn Ridge and then on a north-south line on the edge of Henry House Hill. After the battle the defeated Federal forces withdrew across Bull Run towards Centreville, just as they had done after the battle of First Bull Run, but in much less confusion than they did in 1861.

Much of the two battles, then, was fought over the same ground, though Second Bull Run covered more area simply because of the greater number of troops involved. Both battles saw their climaxes played out on Henry House Hill, though the opposing sides had different roles and alignments there in the two battles. At First Bull Run, the Confederates successfully held the hill against several Union attacks from the northwest, while at Second Bull Run the Yankees attempted unsuccessfully to hold it against Longstreet's attacks from the west. Matthew's Hill, Buck Hill and Chinn Ridge also saw important fighting in both battles. In addition, Sudley Ford played a key role in each battle, as did the Stone Bridge and the Warrenton Turnpike.

First Bull Run 21 July 1861

Army	Strength	Losses
Union	28,000	2900
Confederate	32,000	2000

Second Bull Run 29-30 August 1862

Army	Strength	Losses
Union	73,000	15,000
Confederate	55,000	9500

The Big Battle Picture

Large cylindrical paintings called cycloramas were popular attractions in the late 1800s, and none attracted more attention than the specially prepared canvases of significant Civil War battles. The most famous of these is the Gettysburg cyclorama created by the Frenchman Paul Philoppoteaux in 1884. The artist did detailed studies of the battlefield terrain and interviewed numerous generals and other battle participants in order to ensure accuracy. He needed 16 assistants to help him complete the canvas which was 370 feet in circumference and 30 feet in height, covering a total of 11,100 square feet and weighing six tons. Similar cycloramas of Shiloh, Lookout Mountain, Atlanta, and other battles toured the country and attracted great crowds. Often the spectators were given historical lectures while they stood in the middle of what was called "an astoundingly convincing impression of unlimited space and of action, suspended but animate."

Second Bull Run was as apt a subject for a cyclorama as any other Civil War battle, and indeed one was prepared in 1886 by the French artist Theophile Poilpot. Most of Poilpot's groundwork apparently was done by a fellow Frenchman, Louis Kowalsky, who rented a room near Groveton for six months in 1885 in order to study and sketch the field. He chose as his focal point a spot on Douglas Heights, just northwest of Groveton, where he made sketches which he transferred to larger painted canvases at night or on bad weather days. Kowalksy's work probably served as a basis for Poilpot's final project, though some sources claim that Kowalsky's paintings were shown separately as a traveling exhibition.

Poilpot's completed work, which according to one source used 7000 pounds of paint on a 20,000 square foot canvass, depicted the battle at the height of Porter's attack on the afternoon of 30 July. It was exhibited in Washington for fifteen years until 1901, when it was purchased by Everett W. Connell, the "Panorama King," who owned and exhibited no less than 31 different cycloramas throughout the world. The Bull Run cyclorama seems to have been displayed in New York for awhile, after which it disappeared. One art historian believes that it fell into the custody of Emmett's creditors at one point and that they cut it up in order to sell it piecemeal in an effort to recoup their money. All that remains today of Poilpot's cyclorama of Second Manassas are a few photographs of selected scenes, and some copies of its descriptive souvenir pamphlet, which contains a rough sketch of the entire work.

The cyclorama fad faded away after the turn of the century, when public taste changed to favor other mediums such as "moving pictures." Most of the great cycloramas disappeared, either cut to pieces or molding away in warehouses. Today only two survive intact. One version of Philoppoteaux's Gettysburg cyclorama has been preserved at the Gettysburg National Battlefield Park since 1942. The Atlanta cyclorama was restored in 1935. It features manikins and other props placed in its foreground to give a realistic three-dimensional effect to its scenes.

Number of Units From Each State at Second Bull Run

State	Union Regiments	Batteries	Independent Companies
U.S. Regular Army	16	12	
Connecticut	2		
Delaware	1		
District of Columbia	1		
Indiana	5	1	6
Maine	5	5	
Maryland	4		
Massachusetts	12	2	
Michigan	8		1
New Hampshire	2	1	
New Jersey	9		
New York	54	11	
Ohio	15	3	2
Pennsylvania	44	7	4
Rhode Island	1	3	
Vermont	1		
West Virginia	6	1	3
Wisconsin	4		
TOTAL	190	46	16

Confederate

State	Regiments	Batteries
Alabama	10	
Florida	2	
Georgia	31	
Louisiana	11	6
Maryland		3
Mississippi	6	
North Carolina	14	2
South Carolina	21	6
Tennessee	3	
Texas	3	
Virginia	54	27
TOTAL	155	44

CHAPTER VIII

The First Day of Second Bull Run

Jackson's bold announcement of his position to the Federals through his attack on King's division at Groveton quickly achieved its desired effect. During the evening of 28 August, Pope was maintaining his headquarters near Blackburn's Ford and was still looking for Jackson to be near Centreville. He heard the noise of King's fighting some eight miles distant, but was unaware of its significance until he received a message from King at 2130. This note bore the ominous news that King had met and engaged a large portion of Jackson's command in a sharp fight near Groveton. Pope at once jumped to the conclusion that King "had met the enemy retreating from Centreville," and rejoiced that the elusive Jackson had at last been found. Furthermore, he was led to understand that King's men "had remained masters of the field," so "interposing between Jackson's forces and the main body of the enemy [Longstreet]." Pope exclaimed at once to his staff officers "that the game was in our hands, and that I did not see how it was possible for Jackson to escape without very heavy losses, if at all."

Pope's plan, then, was to catch Jackson's command at Groveton in-between McDowell's corps to the west and Heintzelman's and Reno's advancing from the east. Once again, he had misread the situation. The center of Jackson's force was not at Groveton, but was instead farther to the northeast, near Sudley Church. If Pope put any pressure on Jackson's position, Stone-

Sudley Church stood just to the northeast of Jackson's left during the battle of 2nd Bull Run. It served as a hospital during the fighting, as it had a year earlier at the time of First Bull Run.

wall would have the choice of fighting or simply withdrawing to the north via the Sudley Road; Pope once again had left an open back door that would foil his trap.

Pope's plan also showed a severe misunderstanding of the position of his own troops. His trap was predicated on the belief that McDowell's entire command was near Groveton and in a position to stop Jackson from marching westward to Gainesville. In fact, half of McDowell's corps had never been near Groveton all day. Ricketts' division, after facing Longstreet briefly at Thoroughfare Gap, was then on its way to Bristoe. King apparently never received his orders to maintain his position at Groveton, and at 0100 on the 29th decided to withdraw to Manassas Station, as already discussed. Pope also believed that Sigel was with McDowell, somewhere to the west of Groveton, when in reality Sigel was southeast of Groveton. These dispositions meant that there were in actuality no Federal infantry in place to block Jackson from heading westward to

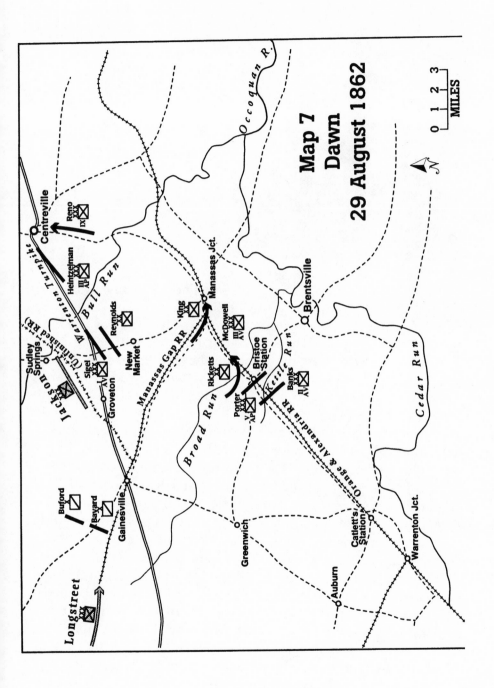

Map 7
Dawn
29 August 1862

Major General Irvin McDowell, who had led the Union Army to defeat at 1st Bull Run in July 1861, commanded Pope's III Corps at 2nd Bull Run. He was not very popular with his troops, and was later investigated (but exonerated) for his role in the 1862 battle.

Gainesville or Thoroughfare Gap — and none to prevent Longstreet from marching directly to join Jackson.

Pope realized that something was terribly amiss at around dawn on 29 August, when he found out that both King and Ricketts were withdrawing to the southeast of Groveton. He at once became furious with McDowell, whom he had not heard from for some time; he did not know that McDowell had gotten lost after he left Groveton at 1800 the previous evening, and consequently had been out of touch with everyone during the ensuing twelve critical hours. Soon after dawn, Brigadier General John Gibbon of King's division rode into Pope's headquarters to give a personal report of his fight at Groveton. Gibbon apparently had realized that King was too sick to grasp the situation, so he decided to report directly to Pope after he could not locate McDowell. Before Gibbon was able to say more than a few words, Pope interjected, "Where is McDowell?" When Gibbon replied that he did not know, and that McDowell had not been present during the Groveton fight, Pope exclaimed, "Goddamn McDowell, he is never where he ought to be!" Gibbon later recalled how much "the remark struck me with surprise, for it was generally supposed in the army that Pope liked, trusted and leaned upon McDowell very much."

Pope recovered his composure after awhile, and decided to

continue his push against Jackson from the east and the south. Since McDowell's troops were no longer near Groveton in order to block Jackson there, he would have to send other troops to do the job. Pope dictated an order for Porter, then at Manassas Junction, to take his corps and King's division directly to Gainesville. Pope knew that speed was of the essence, and warned Porter to "be expeditious or we shall lose much." Gibbon understood the urgency of the situation and offered to deliver the order personally.

Gibbon rode at once to Porter's camp at Manassas Junction, and was surprised to find McDowell there. McDowell did not like Pope's order to Porter at all, since it assigned half of his own corps to Porter, and immediately penned an objection to Pope. Little did McDowell stop to think that it was his own inaccessibility for the previous twelve hours that had gummed up Pope's plans so much. While he waited for a reply from Pope, McDowell persuaded Porter to delay his march to Bristoe. Porter agreed because his troops needed to cook breakfast, and King welcomed the time for his men to get some additional rest from the previous evening's battle and the ensuing night march. King then at last decided that it might be best for him to step down and get some medical attention, so yielding command of his division to Hatch.

Porter eventually started his column moving at 1000, accompanied by McDowell. They had not proceeded far when they received from Pope a new order to them both that had been prompted by McDowell's recent note. This "joint order" began by restating that Pope was advancing with half the army from Centreville towards Gainesville. Porter and McDowell were directed to continue their march towards Gainesville as previously ordered, but they now were instructed to be ready to halt as soon as they made contact with Pope's column. Pope did not know where Ricketts was, and desired McDowell to "instruct him to rejoin the other divisions of his corps as soon as practicable."

Pope later explained that he wanted Porter and McDowell to be able to move quickly in order to be able to turn the enemy's flank near Gainesville. This intent, however, was nowhere stated in the "joint order," which instead gave a quite contrary caveat: "It may be necessary to fall back behind Bull Run at Centerville tonight. I presume it will be so, on account of our supplies." Pope's orders were further muddled by their closing paragraph, which stated, "If any considerable advantages are to be gained by departing from this order, it will not be strictly carried out. One thing must be had in view, that the troops must occupy a position from which they can reach Bull Run tonight or by morning." This strange wording only seemed to confuse Porter and McDowell, as will be seen shortly.

Pope's right wing was not moving as scheduled on this fateful day, either. Kearny, it will be recalled, was supposed to start moving west from Centreville at 0100 and then be ready to attack at early dawn. According to one source, Kearny was not at all pleased with Pope's constant changes of plans, and carped at Pope's courier, "Tell General Pope to go to Hell. We won't march before morning." Whatever were his reasons—perhaps he was waiting for Hooker to come up first—Kearny did not begin moving until dawn. This delay would put his arrival at Groveton at least two or three hours behind schedule. Nor did Hooker and Reno move quickly to the front. Their orders were to proceed to Groveton via Centreville, which, at least in Reno's case, necessitated a detour when more direct routes were available.

The end result of these circumstances was that only one side of Pope's second "Jackson trap" was in position to be sprung at the appointed hour. This was Sigel's corps, which Pope initially thought was west of Groveton with McDowell. Instead, as had been noted, Sigel's men had spent a nervous night at and near Henry House Hill. Sigel had witnessed King's fight the previous evening, but declined to enter it because he had no direct orders to do so. Since King's withdrawal at 0100 left Sigel as the front line force facing Jackson, he sent out a number of skirmishers to secure his front and identify the enemy position. All he could learn for the moment was that the Confederates were present in "considerable force" on the wooded ridge north of the Warrenton Turnpike.

Since Sigel did not know the length or exact location of Jackson's line, he decided to advance at dawn on a wide two mile front in order to develop the enemy's position. His right would be held by Brigadier General Carl Schurz's division, which was to advance astride the Manassas-Sudley Road. Schurz had instructions to "attack the forces of the enemy supposed to be concealed in the woods immediately on my front," and moved forward with Schimmelfennig's brigade on the right of the road and Krzyzanowki's on the left. Brigadier General Robert Milroy was to move his independent brigade on Krzyzanowski's left, and Brigadier General Robert Schenck was to advance on the corps' left, along the Warrenton Turnpike. Just before the attack began, Sigel learned that Reynolds was moving his independent division forward to help, as he had promised the now departed King the night before. Sigel suggested that Reynolds form on Schenck's left, to the south of the Turnpike. Reynolds' arrival would give Sigel about 15,000 men, a force significantly smaller than Jackson's command of about 24,000.

Jackson was aware of Sigel's location because Sigel's cannons had drawn up and fired occasional shots in Stonewall's direction during the engagement at Groveton the previous evening. Jackson's first concern at dawn on 29 August, though, was that King might have been reinforced after he disengaged the night before. When he found out that King had withdrawn and that no Yankees were in the immediate area, Jackson was able to shift his troops to face the threat that Sigel posed to the Sudley Road, the principal Confederate withdrawal route to the north.

Jackson decided to form most of his troops along the course of an unfinished railroad line that ran on a northeast to southwest course from just south of Sudley Church to the northern edge of the Groveton battlefield about one-quarter mile north of the Brawner farm buildings. The railroad line had been started by the Manassas Gap Railroad Company in the mid 1850s, but had to be abandoned for lack of funds before the war broke out. Since much of its grading and fills had already been completed, the abandoned railroad line furnished ready made defensive positions facing the direction of the anticipated Union attack.

Jackson stationed his biggest and freshest division, Hill's, on his left in order to guard the critical ford at Sudley Springs. Hill posted his six brigades on a three-quarter mile front, three in the front and three in the second line. Brigadier General A.R. Lawton, who had succeeded to the command of Taliaferro's division, held the center of Jackson's line, and Brigadier General W.E. Starke, who had replaced Ewell, held the right of the position, where the unfinished railroad line crossed Stony Ridge.

Jackson's position was reasonably strong, but by no means ideal. Stonewall was aware that his line was vulnerable at both its flanks. On the left end of his position, the railroad line was generally lower and less protected by woods cover than the rest of its course. The best that Hill could do there was to post his left brigade, Gregg's, on a small knoll just west of the Groveton-Sudley Road, about 300 yards south of Sudley Church. Gregg was supported on his left rear by Branch, who was positioned nearer the ford, and also by Fitz Lee's cavalry, which deployed skirmishers on the northern side of Bull Run a short while later in the morning. On the right end of his position, Jackson's line was readily approachable by Pageland Lane, which offered an easy route to turn Starke's right. In order to forestall such a move, Jackson boldly placed two of Starke's brigades (Early's and Forno's) on the Warrenton Turnpike a mile to the west of Pageland Lane. Their purpose was to forestall any Union advance in the area, and also watch for Longstreet's expected approach from the west.

Jackson's position was also weak because the heavily wooded terrain along the left and center of his line precluded the deployment of artillery to support his infantry. Only on the right, on Stony Ridge north of the Brawner farm, was there sufficient open space with a clear field of fire for artillery. Here Jackson formed Shumaker's battalion of eight batteries to help cover the large gap in Starke's line. Jackson's other 50 guns would have to be held in reserve for the moment.

Lastly, it should be noted that the unfinished railroad did not furnish a consistently good course on which Jackson could align his front. Some of the cuts through which the railroad line ran were too deep for men to see out of, and at other points the line passed through open fields or was level with or even lower than its immediate surroundings. For this reason, Gregg's and Thomas' brigades on Hill's far left had to be posted some 60 to 100 yards north of the railroad line. Likewise, Starke had to post most of his men on higher ground some 200 yards north of the railroad line, with only a weak skirmish line along the railroad's course itself. The only section of Jackson's line that was actually posted along the railroad was his center, where Trimble's and Douglass' brigades of Lawton's division and Field's brigade of Hill's formed astride the Sudley-Groveton Road.

Jackson's line was reasonably well formed, then, when Sigel began his attack at around 0800. Sigel, it will be remembered, had been ordered to attack at dawn, and it took him a couple of hours to send out skirmishers and develop his front. Another hour was consumed in advancing the two mile wide battle line previously described.

Schurz's division on Sigel's right struck Jackson's line first. Jackson was by no means eager to begin the battle until Longstreet came up, but Gregg felt that he had to meet Krzyzanowksi's attack in order to hold on to his position, He sent his 1st South Carolina to reinforce his skirmish line, whereupon Krzyzanowski pushed his *54th* and *58th New York* regiments to the attack. When the New Yorkers gained the upper hand, Gregg sent in his 12th South Carolina, which was soon matched by the Union *75th Pennsylvania*, to which Gregg replied with his 13th South Carolina. The escalating fight continued for an hour on fairly equal terms.

Meanwhile, the Union troops to Schurz's left were moving to the attack. Before they could reach the Confederate lines, they found themselves under the punishing fire of Shumaker's artillery. To counter these cannons, Schenck and Milroy began forming a 20 gun battery northeast of Groveton. In addition, Reynolds boldly pushed Cooper's battery past the Brawner farm, where it unlimbered on Shumaker's flank and began raking the Confederate line. Shumaker had to move Poague's Virginia battery to face Cooper, and the two units began banging away at each other at a distance of only 600 yards. At the same time, Meade's brigade of *Pennsylvania Reserves* began engaging Early's infantry. In the midst of all this fighting, some of the Union troops endeavored to begin removing King's wounded, who had lain on the Groveton battlefield untended since the previous evening's fight ended.

Schenck's division had not yet become engaged, other than its skirmishers. Milroy, on Schenck's right, pulled up closer to the

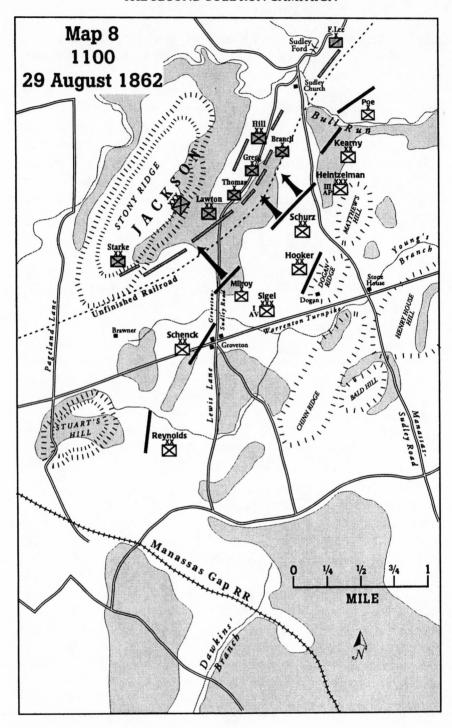

Map 8
1100
29 August 1862

Confederate center with his solitary brigade, and then decided to send two of his four regiments, *82nd Ohio* and *5th West Virginia*, to help Schurz. The commanders of these two regiments, however, either misunderstood their orders or lost their way, and instead began heading straight towards the center of Jackson's line. Even though they unexpectedly ran into heavy Confederate fire, the two isolated Union units continued their attack. Part of the *82nd Ohio* even managed to penetrate Jackson's line at a spot called "The Dump," which was a pile of stones and other debris left by the workers who had constructed the railroad line. This rough area marked the boundary between Lawton's and Starke's divisions, and was only lightly defended, reportedly by assorted skulkers and stragglers posted there by Jackson himself. The Federal success turned out to be only fleeting. Trimble's brigade soon made a counterattack and sent the Yankees reeling.

Milroy, meanwhile, was entertaining a foolish idea to assault Shumaker's guns with his two remaining regiments. However, when his first attackers were repulsed, he found that he had no choice but to reinforce them. His *2nd West Virginia* arrived first and met such a heavy Confederate fire that it lost 120 of its men. The *3rd West Virginia* managed to get within 50 yards of the railroad line before it ran into a withering fire from Starke's unseen troops. The regiment managed to return just one volley before it broke and headed for the Groveton Woods to its rear.

Milroy's entire brigade was now in disorder, and Milroy endeavored to rally it as best he could. The Confederates followed with a counterattack that was limited but still posed a threat to Shenck's left. Fortunately for the Yankees, Brigadier General Julius Stahel saw the enemy counterattack develop and moved to check it. The Confederates in turn saw Stahel coming, and pulled back. The fighting in the Union center was over for the moment.

While Milroy was being repulsed, the fighting intensified on Sigel's right. Here Krzyzanowski, as has been already discussed, opened the Union attacks at about 1000. Schurz's other brigade, Schimmelfennig's, did not enter the conflict until 1100, when Krzyzanowski's units were beginning to be played out. Schimmelfennig's three regiments were supported by the *1st*

New York of Heintzelman's corps, which was just beginning to reach the field following its march from Centreville. Sigel had suggested to Heintzelman that he deploy Kearny's division on Schurz's right, and Hooker's division on Schurz's left, and Heintzelman complied.

Schimmelfennig's 2000 fresh men went into action facing the three South Carolina regiments of Gregg's brigade that had been fighting Krzyzanowksi for the previous hour. By all rights, they should have overwhelmed the weary and outnumbered Confederates, but Colonel Dixon Barnes of the 12th South Carolina had other ideas. He boldly ordered his 300 men to charge and break up the enemy attack. The suddenness of his charge flanked and broke the *1st New York*. As the New Yorkers retreated, Barnes turned his men against the exposed right flank of Krzyzanowski's *54th New York* and Schimmelfennig's *8th West Virginia*. These two units collapsed also, leaving a huge hole in Schurz's center. Schurz then rushed his only reserve, the *29th New York*, into the gap, only to see it driven back, too.

Barnes' counterattack finally sputtered out when his men came under the fire of Roemer's New York battery. These Yankee guns persuaded Barnes to fall back to the woods near the railroad line, where he was reinforced by the 1st South Carolina Rifles. It was at this point that Gregg decided it was time to retire. His troops were tired from two hours of fighting, and had received no help from their neighboring brigades, perhaps because of Jackson's orders to avoid a general engagement until Longstreet arrived. For these reasons, Gregg pulled his command back to the knoll from which he had first advanced to start the fight.

Schurz, however, was not about to let Gregg withdraw in peace. He had received word that Kearny was about to launch his entire division against Jackson's left flank, so he moved his regiments back into action to support him. Schimmelfennig's *61st Ohio* and *74th Pennsylvania* led the attack, and even managed to cross the railroad line. They were promptly met by heavy fire from Crenshaw's Virginia battery and two of Branch's regiments, and so had to withdraw to the railroad line, which the rest of Schurz's men had now reached. Schurz now understood that he could not break the enemy line alone, so he held a defensive posture and waited for Kearny to come up.

Kearny, though, was in no hurry to rush to the attack, particularly after his *1st New York* had been so quickly repulsed. Instead, he pushed Colonel Orland Poe's brigade forward to try to turn Jackson's line. Poe's men advanced with their left on the Sudley-Groveton Road, and then turned northwest to cross Bull Run a half mile downstream from Sudley Ford. They then formed a skirmish line and began heading towards the Sudley mansion. This advance startled the wagoneers in the Confederate rear, who started rushing their exposed wagons away on the road to Aldie. Jackson hastily dispatched the 1st Virginia Cavalry (dismounted) and Pelham's battery to oppose Poe, and their combined fire succeeded at bringing the hesitant Union line to a halt. Kearny then became concerned for Poe's exposed position, and ordered him to fall back to the south side of Bull Run.

Kearny had held Robinson's brigade back as support for Poe, so leaving only one brigade, Birney's, available to support Schurz. Birney originally had seven regiments under his command, but their number had been quickly whittled down when two were detached to support the division's artillery line on Matthew's Hill, one was ordered to stay back as a reserve, and another, the *1st New York*, wandered off prematurely to aid Schimmelfennig, as already discussed. This left Birney with only three regiments under his immediate command. When he advanced northward with them towards Sudley Church, Birney ran into heavy Confederate artillery fire and had to withdraw into the woods to his left for cover. Then, oddly, he moved still farther to his left and ended up engaging in a long distance fire fight with Thomas' brigade, located to Schurz's left. Birney's strange odyssey ended when he decided to disengage and pull back to Matthew's Hill.

Kearny was one of the North's most aggressive division commanders, so his strange behavior is difficult to explain. He may have been motivated by an intense dislike for Sigel. The two had a run in earlier that summer when Kearny wrote some deprecating remarks about the German soldiers from New Jersey. Sigel, as champion of the German-Americans, had taken offense, and a personal feud quickly arose between the two generals. That is probably why Kearny reportedly spoke a bit of foul language when he received orders from Heintzelman to go to Sigel's support. He complied with a half hearted attempt to turn Jackson's left flank, as already discussed, and then left his brigades on their own. Heintzelman, of course, should have kept closer control of Kearny's actions, but he also was not having a good day. He did not care much for Sigel, either, probably because the German outranked him as a major general by six weeks. Heintzelman for this reason chose to defer to Sigel concerning the deployment of his own troops, and apparently did not really care that Sigel already had his hands full.

The collapse of Milroy's brigade and Kearny's passive support on Schurz's right forced Sigel to commit his reinforcements piecemeal as they came up. Hooker's division, as already noted, was sent in on Schurz's left to fill the gap between Schurz and Milroy, and was not yet engaged. When Reno's lead division of the *IX Corps* came up at about 1130, Sigel broke it up and scattered its regiments to support various points along his line as needed, particularly on Schurz's beleaguered front. Reno's second division was held back as a reserve on Dogan Ridge, southwest of Matthew's Hill.

The situation, then, was static on Jackson's front when Pope arrived at about 1300 and set up his headquarters near the Dogan House. He certainly was not displeased with the day's progress, since his goal had been to locate Jackson and distract him near Groveton until Porter and McDowell could reach Bristoe and then begin rolling up Stonewall's right flank. Jackson was not unhappy with the situation, either, since he simply wanted to hold Pope's attention until Longstreet came up.

As events would show, it was Jackson who clearly held the upper hand at the moment. Pope's perception of the situation was clouded by the fact that he had failed to specifically order Porter and McDowell to march against Jackson's flank. Nor, indeed, was Pope even aware that Porter had halted his advance far short of Gainesville, and that McDowell had left Porter's side in order to march to Groveton. Just as significantly, Pope had no idea where Longstreet was, nor did he seem to care.

Longstreet's troops going into bivouac near Thoroughfare Gap on 28 August. Contrary to common belief, Longstreet did not have to fight his way through Union cavalry in order to pass through the gap.

Longstreet's Arrival

As previously discussed, Lee, who was with Longstreet's wing, had used couriers in order to keep in regular touch with Jackson. Longstreet's march to Thoroughfare Gap had so far not been a speedy one, since Jackson had managed to avoid serious trouble and the situation on Stonewall's front seemed to be under control. However, Jones' fight at Thoroughfare Gap on the afternoon of 29 August, and the news of Jackson's sharp fight at Groveton that same evening, convinced Lee that he ought to hasten Longstreet's march on the 30th. As a result, Longstreet had his lead troops (Hood's division) on the road by 0600 on 30 August.

Hood's veterans pushed forward steadily, but with no sense of urgency. As Longstreet later put it, "Our communications with Jackson were quite regular, and as he had not expressed a wish that we should hurry, our troops were allowed to take their natural swing under the inspiration of impending battle."

Longstreet's troops march through Thoroughfare Gap en route to rejoining Jackson's wing. Confederate control of this critical pass was essential for their success in the campaign as it developed.

Longstreet's lengthy column was already raising a great deal of dust on what promised to be another beastly hot day, when Hood reached Gainesville and was directed to turn left on the Warrenton Turnpike towards Jackson's position, which was reported to be near Sudley Ford. Lee had by now heard the din of the fighting on Jackson's front, and urged the troops behind Hood to hasten their pace. Stuart, who had been screening the right of Longstreet's column, was directed to head towards Manassas and shield whatever enemy forces might be there.

When Hood's men entered the edge of the battle area, Lee decided to ride to the head of their column in order to inspect the situation personally. In the process, he got a much closer view of the battle than he ever anticipated. A Yankee sharpshooter saw him coming, and took a shot at him that grazed his cheek and just missed killing him. It was to be the closest brush with death in battle that Lee would have during the entire war. He was under fire several times and had to be hustled to the rear by his staff on more than one occasion, but was never hit while in action except on this occasion. (He would also suffer a debilitating fall from his horse on the morning of 31 August, the day after the battle of Second Bull Run ended, when he broke one wrist and sprained the other, and so had to ride in an ambulance during most of the Antietam campaign.) It is indeed difficult to imagine how the war would have turned out if this Union sharpshooter had hit his target, and Robert E. Lee had fallen, killed in the opening hours of Second Bull Run.

Jackson had received word of Hood's approach at 0800, and requested Hood to post his command with his left on the Warrenton Turnpike near Groveton. This was a significant tactical decision. Jackson clearly felt that he had a strong enough position to hold back Pope's threatened attacks, at least long enough for Longstreet to come up and form on Stonewall's left. He felt no need to have Longstreet reinforce his line directly. Instead, Longstreet could support his line by strengthening his vulnerable right flank at Stony Ridge. Then, hopefully, Longstreet would be able to swing his whole command so as to strike Pope's troops on their left flank and rear. These plans were in fact discussed and agreed upon in a brief conference that Lee, Longstreet and Jackson held late in the morning. Unfortunately, the details of their meeting were not recorded. Nor, apparently, was any timetable set for Longstreet's planned attack.

As Hood advanced to deploy, he sent forward some skirmishers, who promptly ran into an unidentified line of skirmishers already stationed near the roadway. The situation was tense for a moment until Hood's men learned that the other line was friendly, being part of Early's command. It will be recalled that Jackson earlier in the day had detached half of Starke's division (Early's and Forno's brigades) to his far right in order to guard his flank and watch for Longstreet's arrival. So far Early had not been attacked, though he was painfully aware of the large build up of enemy troops all across his front. For this reason, he and Forno had no complaints about returning to the rest of Starke's division, a mile or so to their left, when Hood came up.

Hood formed his famed Texas Brigade near Pageland Lane, with its left on the Warrenton Turnpike as Jackson had requested. He then posted his other brigade, Law's, on his left, north of the Turnpike, with instructions to Law to send flankers out to connect with Jackson's right. The next unit to reach the field was Evans' independent brigade, which was placed on Hood's right, with the understanding that the rest of Longstreet's command would form on Evans' right as it came up.

This deployment meant that Longstreet's line would be almost at a ninety degree angle to Jackson's right, which was posted along the unfinished railroad line as far as Shumaker's position on Stony Ridge north of the Brawner farm.

The arrival of so many troops under Longstreet could not avoid catching the attention of the Union troops moving up on his front. Hood's skirmishers moved forward along the Turnpike and began engaging the Union skirmishers of Reynolds' division, which had been moving forward to attack the gap in Starke's line at the Brawner farm. (Had Longstreet not arrived when he did, Jackson's right might have been in serious trouble, though it could be argued in reply that Jackson would not have held his right in such an awkward position if he had not been expecting Longstreet's arrival at that point.) Reynolds quickly found that he had no choice but to abandon his forward movement and form to meet this unanticipated threat to his left. A determined advance by Hood and Evans to the Cundiffe farm then forced Reynolds to fall back a quarter mile to Lewis Lane. Reynolds must have been relieved that Hood did not advance any farther, since he had no support at all on his left (southern) flank. A pregnant lull followed on this stretch of the front, punctuated by the continued popping of the blue and gray skirmishers.

While Hood was deploying on the Warrenton Turnpike, Stuart's cavalry made contact with Porter's Union corps about two miles to the south. As previously discussed, Porter and McDowell had begun marching up the Manassas Road to Gainesville at about 1000 as part of Pope's plan to turn Jackson's left. Around 1100, some of Griffin's troops, who led Porter's advance, ran smack into the forerunners of Stuart's command near the bridge over Dawkins' Branch. Stuart appreciated the seriousness of the situation at once. The huge enemy force he had run into would cause a serious problem if it struck Longstreet's troops before they were formed. Since he had only six regiments with him, Stuart knew that he would not be able to hold off the Union column for long. He sent to Longstreet for help, but he knew that it would take an hour or more for any infantry reinforcements to reach him. Faced with this crisis, Stuart decided to try a bit of trickery. He ordered the cavalrymen

Pope's attack on the Confederate left, which was posted in the woods in the background. The Stone House and Warrenton Turnpike are in the foreground.

of the 5th Virginia to cut all the brush they could and drag it along the roadway to his immediate rear, so raising enough dust to make it appear that a very large Confederate force was coming to his aid. The ruse worked perfectly. Porter halted his advance when it met Stuart's skirmishers near Dawkins' Branch, and declined to advance farther for the moment because of all the dust he saw on the roadway behind the enemy position.

Stuart's trick was to have much greater results than just the temporary halting of one-third of Pope's army. By chance, Porter and McDowell had just received Pope's complicated "joint order," which their army commander had sent out at 1000. As previously discussed in this chapter, the "joint order" directed the two officers to proceed to Gainesville, though they were to be prepared to fall back to Bull Run or to take other lines of action if necessary. The order was confusing and certainly gave no instructions on what to do if the enemy were encountered. McDowell, who had an agenda of his own this day, suggested to Porter, "You are too far out already; this is no place to start a battle." What McDowell wanted to do was to take his own two divisions and march up the Manassas-Sudley Road in order to link up with Pope's advance near Groveton. Once there, he could move to Sigel's left and then try to link up with Porter's right.

Since McDowell outranked Porter, he marched off and turned his troops back on the Gainesville Road in the direction of the Manassas-Sudley Road. Porter, now denied any support for his two divisions, still had to determine the size of the Confederate force on his front before he could even consider resuming his advance. He drew up two batteries behind Dawkins' Branch in order to support his skirmishers, and sent Griffin's brigade to the right in order to try to get around Stuart's left. Griffin, however, soon was turned back by unfavorable terrain. Porter then recalled him to the Dawkins' Branch line, and sent a message to McDowell to ask for one of his divisions as reinforcement. McDowell, of course, declined to break up his command, and told Porter, "I think he had better remain where he is; but if it is necessary to fall back, he can do so on my left."

Porter complied with the advice of his senior officer, and held his troops where they were, with Griffin's brigade drawn up in battle line along the eastern side of Dawkins' Branch and the rest of the corps lined up on the road to Manassas. This halt gave Lee the time he needed to rush Corse's Virginia brigade to support Stuart. Corse took over and expanded Stuart's front when he arrived, so giving Porter all the more reason to continue maintaining his position. To be certain, Porter could have pushed both Corse and Stuart aside had he wished, in compliance with Pope's orders to march to Gainesville. Such a move, however, would have brought on an early, and possibly disastrous, confrontation with Longstreet's wing. Porter's decision to stand firm and not press forward would be debated for years, and certainly would have a significant effect on the course of the battle, as well as on the rest of Porter's life.

With the danger on the army's tight checked for the moment, Longstreet devoted all his attention to bringing up the rest of his command. D.R. Jones' division was sent to reinforce Corse's left near the line of the Manassas Gap Railroad, and Kemper's small division (less Corse's brigade) was stationed between Jones' left and Hood's right. Wilcox's division, which arrived late because it had been sent northward to Hopewell Gap the previous evening, was held in reserve behind Law's brigade on the left of the line. Longstreet also placed 19 guns of his artillery on his left, since the open slope of Stony Ridge offered the best field of fire on his front. Most of the rest of his line, which ran for about one and one-half miles from the Brawner farm south to the Manassas-Gainesville Road, was too wooded and rough for artillery.

Longstreet's dispositions were basically completed around 1200. Lee wished to move to the attack at once, but Longstreet was reluctant to do so without reconnoitering his front first. Lee granted him permission to delay, and Longstreet went out on a lengthy scouting trip. He did not like what he found. Schenck had moved to support Reynolds' right, and any attack in that direction faced the prospect of being flanked by Porter. Longstreet was discussing his reservations with Lee when Stuart brought word of more Union movements on the Manassas-Gainesville Road. This persuaded Lee to hold Longstreet's troops back until the situation on the Union left was investigated more.

Incredibly, Pope was even less informed than the Confederates about what was happening on the Union left flank. He had reached the field at about 1300, as already mentioned, and set up his headquarters behind Sigel's center. His assumption was that McDowell and Porter were on their way to Gainesville, and he certainly had no idea that Longstreet was on the field. Most of the fault for this immediate situation was McDowell's. McDowell did not at first inform Pope of his changed line of march, nor did he inform his commander where Porter was. To make matters worse, Porter sent several messages to McDowell explaining the situation on his front and requesting McDowell to forward this information to Pope, but McDowell did not do so.,

Most incredible of all is the fact that McDowell knew that Longstreet was on Porter's front, and did not inform Pope at once. Buford's cavalry had been closely monitoring Longstreet's line of march all morning, and at midmorning saw seventeen regiments, one battery, and 500 cavalry pass through Gainesville. He reported this intelligence to Ricketts at 0930, with a request to "Please forward this." Ricketts sent the note to McDowell, but McDowell for various reasons did not deliver it to Pope until 1900 that evening.

This confusion on the Union left flank is as difficult to explain as it is to understand. Much of the problem seems to stem from the fact that there was a confused Union chain of command. Porter was not officially part of Pope's army, but was serving under his command and should have reported to him directly. Instead, Porter chose to forward his messages through McDowell, who was senior to him, either to keep him abreast of the situation, or because he believed that he belonged to an ad hoc wing commanded by McDowell. Whatever was the case, McDowell clearly erred by not forwarding Porter's messages and by not keeping in constant communication with Pope as to his own movements. This is not surprising, though, in view of his disappearance for twelve hours following the start of the fight at Groveton. Some of the blame for the situation also must rest on Porter. He definitely could have been more aggressive to develop the enemy forces on his front, and he could have sent separate dispatches directly to Pope instead of sending them via McDowell. Lastly, Pope must be found at fault for not sending out couriers to confirm the location and activity of each of his corps commanders,

Thus Pope falsely assumed that his battle plan was at last proceeding as he had anticipated. His purpose remained as before, to preoccupy Jackson's front while Porter and McDowell reached Gainesville and then turned the Confederate right. Yes, Sigel's attacks had not gone well that morning, but they did not need to succeed in order for Pope's master plan to be a success, All Pope needed to do was to continue to engage Jackson so that Stonewall could not slip away again.

Since Hooker's division had not yet been engaged, Pope at 1400 sent it forward to relieve Schurz's exhausted troops, who were by then quite hungry and almost out of ammunition. Hooker, who had been deployed on Schurz's left earlier in the day, sent Carr's *Second New Jersey Brigade* to the attack first.

Carr's men were ordered, as a private in the *5th New Jersey* recalled, "to fire away wither we saw the enemy or not, so as to make as much noise as possible." Schurz's tired troops gladly withdrew under cover of this racket, and began reforming on Dogan Ridge.

At about 1430, Pope decided that stronger measures were needed, so he directed Hooker to move his entire division forward. Hooker, though, had little interest in conducting an unsupported assault, so he rode to Pope's headquarters and persuaded him to order Kearny to furnish some support by moving against the Confederate left flank in order to "agitate them a little." Kearny complied by sending Robinson's brigade against Gregg's left at about 1500.

Brigadier General Cuvier Grover was far from excited when he received Kearny's orders to conduct what he was certain would be a suicidal attack against Jackson's line. Acting on advice from Milroy, who had been repulsed on this same section of line a few hours earlier, Grover felt that the only way to dislodge the enemy was to punch a hole through their line using a rapid, direct assault. To achieve this, he formed his 1500 men into two lines and directed them to advance slowly until they encountered Confederate fire. They were then to rush forward, let loose a volley, and then charge with their bayonets fixed, without pausing to reload.

Grover's intended line of advance led him into an open area along the Groveton-Sudley Road that was swept by Jackson's artillery fire, so he moved into a woods to the right and altered his orders. His men were now to advance under cover of the woods and then conduct a charge with bayonets only. When the order to attack was given, the *11th Massachusetts* endured the first Confederate volley and then succeeded at piercing the center of Thomas' line. Then the unexpected happened. It seems that the right wing of Grover's attack struck a 100 yard gap in Hill's line, a low area between Thomas' and Gregg's brigades that the Confederates had neglected to cover because it was too marshy. Here the *1st Massachusetts* crossed the railroad line and fell savagely on the rear of the 49th Georgia, sending it and the rest of Thomas' front line scurrying to the rear. After pausing to regroup, Grover's men charged Thomas' second line, which was

THE SECOND BULL RUN CAMPAIGN

stationed some 80 yards beyond the railroad line. The fighting here was more intense than their original attack, and once again the Confederates were driven back.

Quite unexpectedly, Grover's attack had broken Hill's line. All he needed were some reinforcements to enable him to turn against Gregg's tired troops and exploit this success. But no reinforcements were to come. In addition, Robinson's brigade, which Kearny had sent to support Grover's attack by making a diversion on Hill's left, had been so passive that Gregg actually was able to move his 12th South Carolina from Robinson's front to deal with Grover's breakthrough on his right.

By now, Grover's attack was beginning to run out of steam, even though he committed his second line of troops. Thomas' men began to rally, bolstered by Gregg's 12th South Carolina, and halted Grover's forward advance. Then Pender's fresh brigade from Hill's second line came up and entered the fray. The Yankees were caught in a pocket that made them suffer from a heavy crossfire. Then Pender turned Grover's left flank, forcing the *11th Massachusetts* and the rest of the Union brigade to break and run. Grover's attack, which had begun with such success, was totally defeated in less than 30 minutes, at the loss of 33 per cent casualties.

Grover's defeat enabled the Confederates to turn their attention to Robinson's brigade, and it, too, was forced back. Pender then boldly rushed to pursue the fleeing Yankees. He chased them through the woods near the railroad line and then into the open field beyond. Here his counterattack was exposed to Union artillery fire, as well as a flanking fire from Schurz's troops, so he withdrew.

At the same time that Grover was attacking, Pope decided that he should also put pressure on Jackson's right. Orders were accordingly sent for Reynolds, who was on the far left of Pope's line, to advance on the south side of the Warrenton Turnpike and "threaten the enemy's flank and rear." Reynolds had become increasingly concerned over the growing number of enemy troops on his front, and had told Pope of this problem. Of course, Reynolds had no idea that he was facing most of Longstreet's command, nor did Pope. Reynolds dutifully began his advance at about 1500, only to meet heavy artillery fire that was well supported by infantry. He wisely suspended his attack and sent a staff officer to tell Pope of the large number of enemy battle flags that had been spotted in the woods on his front. Pope only responded curtly, "You are excited, young man; the people you see are General Porter's command taking position on the right of the enemy."

Pope would have done well to cease his attacks for the day until he had all his troops up or accounted for, but he would persist in making additional disjointed attacks until well after dark. Just before 1600, he decided that something needed to be done about the enemy troops (probably part of Pender's command) who were occupying the woods east of the Manassas-Sudley Road and annoying the Union artillery drawn up on that front. Colonel James Nagle's 1500 man brigade of Reno's division was selected for the task. Nagle's men had been standing by idly since they reached the field at around noon, and were actually eager to enter the action, despite all the carnage that they had already witnessed.

Nagle's three regiments had a front of about 700 yards, and in their advance passed over and relieved Carr's brigade of Hooker's division, which had been skirmishing against Jackson's center for two hours. They easily over ran the Confederate skirmishers on their front, and then charged the railroad line with a shout. Lawton's Georgians thought that they had an excellent defensive line in a fair sized railroad cut, but their position proved to be a liability when Nagle's men climbed to the edge of the cut and began firing volleys into it. Lawton's front line had to retreat, and carried with it part of Field's brigade of Hill's division, which had been posted to their left. As Nagle expanded his bridgehead into the Confederate lines, Trimble's brigade also had to fall back on Lawton's left. Trimble himself had been wounded shortly before this attack by an explosive bullet that hit him in the leg. Command of his hard fighting brigade devolved on the next highest field officer still standing, Captain W.F. Brown of the 12th Georgia.

Nagle's attack soon ran the course of Grover's. His advance soon slowed as the Confederates regrouped in the woods behind the railroad line, and pressure began to mount on his unsupported flanks. Then Jackson brought up fresh troops from his second line in a massive counterattack. Forno's Louisiana brigade of Lawton's division struck Nagle's right, and Johnson's brigade of Starke's division crashed in on the flank of Nagle's left regiment, the *6th New Hampshire*. Colonel Simon Griffin of the *6th*, whose command had actually managed to advance about 100 yards beyond the railroad line, for awhile believed that the troops moving past his left flank were friendly. However, when he grabbed his regimental flag and waved it in that direction, he was greeted by a hail of bullets that convinced him otherwise. His three regiments were rolled up from the left, and soon had no choice but to retreat. Nagle's brigade was already retiring when he belatedly received support in the form of Taylor's *Excelsior Brigade* of Hooker's division, which arrived just minutes too late to be of any help. Soon the New Yorkers, too, were overwhelmed from the left and forced to retreat in disorder.

The defeat of Nagle's and Taylor's attack encouraged Colonel LeRoy Stafford of Starke's division to enter the fight. Stafford advanced on Johnson's right, crossed the railroad line, and ran into the *3rd West Virginia* of Milroy's brigade, which Milroy had belatedly sent to help Nagle. The Mountaineers were no match for Stafford's entire brigade, and quickly withdrew to the Groveton Woods.

The entire Union center was by now in disarray as Law's brigade of Hood's division pushed up towards Groveton in order to join in the expanding counterattack. The successful Confederates pushed Milroy back from the Groveton Woods, and then entered the open fields beyond. They managed to overrun a Union battery posted just 100 yards east of the woods, capturing two of its guns, but their counterattack soon ran out of steam in the face of the rallying Union forces and heavy fire from the Yankee guns posted on Dogan Ridge. It did not take much time for all the attacking Confederates to begin pulling back to their original lines. Since they lacked horses to withdraw the captured cannons, they found some ropes and made some fifty Yankee prisoners pull them off the field.

The successful Confederate counterattack just described forced Pope to withdraw his center from the Groveton-Sudley Road and concentrate it on a shorter line near the Manassas-

Sudley Road, where the weary brigades could get better support from the cannons drawn up on Dogan Ridge. Since Law's advance had forced Schenck to withdraw from Groveton, there was now a gap of at least a mile between the troops on Dogan Ridge and Reynolds' division, which was still posted south of Young's Branch on the east side of Lewis Lane. The fact that Pope continued to leave Reynolds in such an exposed position shows how much he still believed that Porter would be attacking Jackson from the direction of Gainesville at any moment. Pope wanted Reynolds to serve as a pivot for Porter's advance, so he planned to hold him near Lewis Lane as long as possible.

By now Pope clearly should have realized that something was amiss with Porter. McDowell's troops, which were supposed to be with Porter, began to wearily arrive at Henry House Hill at about 1500, so signaling that Pope's "joint order" had miscarried. Even so, Pope did not attempt to find out what happened to Porter until 1630, when he sent the following blunt directive to him: "Your line of march brings you in on the enemy's right flank. I desire you to push forward into action at once on the enemy's right flank, and, if possible, on his rear, keeping your right in communication with General Reynolds. The enemy is massed in the woods in front of us, but can be shelled out as soon as you engage their flank. Keep heavy reserves, and use your batteries, keeping well closed to your right all the time. In case you are obliged to fall back, do so to your right and rear, so as to keep you in close communication with the right wing."

Quite amazingly, Pope still figured that he needed to continue to keep Jackson occupied, so soon after 1630 he directed Kearny to lead yet another attack against the Confederate left near Sudley Church. Kearny decided to spearhead his attack with Robinson's brigade. He would not, though, doom his attack by advancing on too narrow a front, as others had been conducted earlier in the day. In order to conduct a broader attack, he directed Birney's brigade to move forward on Robinson's left in what would be the largest single Union assault of the day.

Though Jackson's men had repulsed every Union attack already made on their lines, most were by now quite exhausted. Some units had been engaged virtually all day, and many commands had suffered heavy losses, particularly in officers.

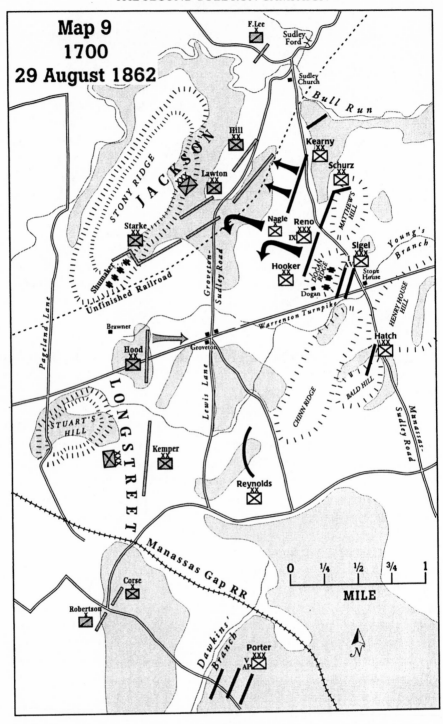

Map 9
1700
29 August 1862

Jackson in fact had only three brigades that had not yet been heavily engaged, Archer's and Branch's of Hill's division and Early's of Starke's. These he held in reserve to meet any Union breakthroughs or conduct any local counterattacks as needed.

Kearny's attack commenced at around 1700. On the left of the line, part of Birney's brigade struck Archer's regiments just as they were coming up to relieve Pender's North Carolina brigade. The Confederate line was shaken, but managed to hold, and a heavy fire fight developed in the woods along the railroad line. Meanwhile, Kearny's right, under Robinson, managed to drive back Gregg's far left regiment, the 1st South Carolina Rifles. Their retreat unsettled the rest of Gregg's left flank, just when his right was being struck by three more of Kearny's regiments. Before long, Gregg's entire command was forced to fall back, flanks first.

Gregg frantically tried to rally his men, as he waved his sword and cried out, "Let us die here, my men." At last he managed to form most of them a couple hundred yards behind the railroad line. He could not have done so had it not been for the arrival of the 37th North Carolina of Branch's brigade. With their aid, Gregg was barely able to check Kearny's advance for the moment.

Affairs were now at a crisis. Kearny searched desperately for reinforcements and finally located Leasure's brigade of Stevens' division on his left. Leasure had not yet been engaged, and was more than willing to pitch in to help. His two fresh regiments crashed into the part of Archer's brigade that was still clinging to the railroad line, and drove most of it back. Leasure, though, refused to face the Confederate fire beyond the railroad line, and held his troops in place along the part of the enemy line that they had captured.

The pendulum now swung in the Confederates' favor as Jackson committed his last reserves. First, Branch's four regiments were sent in to stiffen Hill's line and attempt to blunt the Yankees' momentum. Two of Branch's regiments struck Kearny's right flank and in this way managed to halt his advance. Branch's other two regiments went into action on Archer's front. Their arrival prevented Hill's right from collapsing long enough for Early to come up. Lawton had been holding

Early back until he was really needed, and now at 1730 the proper moment had come. Early also picked up two additional regiments from neighboring commands, and led 2500 new troops into the action.

Early's counterattack could not have come at a more opportune time. Hill's men were even more exhausted than Kearny's attackers, who were themselves starting to run out of steam. The weary Yankee regiments collapsed as Early's fresh troops charged, their Rebel yell echoing in the woods. By 1800 the fighting was over, just an hour after it had been renewed. Early had a difficult time halting his exhilarated troops at the railroad line and had to give them strict orders not to proceed farther; Jackson had learned a lesson from his previous counterattacks, that Pope's rear lines were too strongly studded with artillery to be challenged.

There indeed had been a terrible butcher's bill on Jackson's line. Every Federal attack had been repulsed after an initial success, but at the cost of horrible losses on both sides. Kearny's division had lost 25 per cent of its men, and some Confederate units had lost even more, as much as 50 per cent in Gregg's brigade. When he reformed his men, General Branch was astonished to learn that there were only 24 rounds of ammunition left in the entire brigade. It would seem that Pope might actually have been able to carry the day, despite the bloody repulse of all his disjointed attacks, if he only had some more troops to throw into the fight.

In spite of the repeated setbacks on Jackson's front, Pope persisted in believing that he was winning the day. Kearny exaggerated his success against the Confederate left, falsely stating that he still held key ground there, and Pope still believed that Porter would begin to roll up Jackson's right at any moment. Around 1830, Pope heard a report that the Confederates were withdrawing, so he rode to a hill near the Warrenton Turnpike with one of his staff in order to see for himself. He looked to the west and spotted some enemy wagons heading away from the battlefield. His Chief of Staff, Colonel George Ruggles, properly interpreted that these wagons were just ambulances taking wounded to the rear. Pope, though, overruled him, and deemed that the Confederates were "retreating toward the Pike from the direction of Sudley Springs."

Pope got excited and promptly decided to organize a pursuit. Since Reno's and Sigel's corps were totally fought out, he ordered McDowell to send one of his divisions after the Confederates. McDowell, who had just reached the battle area late in the afternoon following his circuitous march from Porter's front, sent Hatch's division forward with the order, "The enemy is in full retreat down the Warrenton Turnpike...Overtake and attack him!"

Hatch was selected for the task, and rushed his division westward on the Turnpike, with Doubleday's brigade in the lead. When Doubleday's vanguard reached the rest of the small ridge just east of Groveton, Hatch halted in order to survey the situation. He expected to see the Confederates in retreat, with perhaps only a small rear guard left behind, so he ordered up Gerrish's four gun battery to shell them if necessary. A few moments later Hatch spotted the enemy, and was astonished to see that they were not in retreat, but were moving to attack him in force!

The command that was attacking Hatch's was Hood's fresh division of Longstreet's wing. As previously discussed, Longstreet had reached the field at around noon and had deployed at almost a 90 degree angle to Jackson's right. Lee had wanted Longstreet to strike Pope's left flank at once, but Longstreet was concerned about Porter's presence south of the Manassas Gap Railroad, and persuaded Lee to refrain from ordering him to attack until Porter's intentions were disclosed. Lee even went to Longstreet's front at 1500, and from his observations agreed that Porter needed to be reckoned with. He then sent Wilcox's small division to support Stuart and Corse on Porter's immediate front, and held D.R. Jones' line back to aid Stuart if needed. These dispositions left Lee with only seven brigades posted near the Warrenton Turnpike, Evans' independent brigade plus Hood's, Kemper's and Wilcox's mini-divisions of two brigades each. These forces were too few, he felt, to assault Pope at the moment, so Lee agreed with Longstreet to postpone his counterattack until morning.

This situation changed greatly after 1600. By then Wilcox and

Stuart were reporting little activity on Porter's front, and Longstreet had noted the dust being raised by troops marching away from Porter's front towards Pope's. Longstreet rightly interpreted that Porter no longer posed much of a threat because part of his command had gone to Pope's aid. In this he was largely correct, since the dust Longstreet saw had been raised by McDowell's troops and wagons as they headed to the north.

This intelligence sparked Lee to revive his plans to attack Pope at once along the Warrenton Turnpike. Longstreet, however, again disagreed, this time because of the lateness of the hour (after 1700). He argued that by the time he got everyone into position, it would be too late to attack, and would certainly be too late to reap any benefits from a victory. Lee reluctantly agreed, on condition that Longstreet would conduct a "forced reconnaissance" toward the Union lines in order to secure a favorable position from which to "have all things ready for battle at daylight the next morning."

Longstreet now made plans to move Hood's two brigades eastward to Groveton, supported by Wilcox's division and Evans' brigade. Hood's men, with Law's brigade leading the way, moved forward at 1830 and just missed by a few minutes at seizing the ridge east of Groveton before Hatch's Union troops arrived there.

Law's skirmishers ran straight into Doubleday's, which consisted of a detail from the *2nd U.S. Sharpshooters*. This command had never been in combat before, and was soon chased to the rear. Hatch quickly began deploying the rest of Doubleday's regiments on Law's front, only to be struck south of the Turnpike by Hood's Texas brigade, which outflanked his left by several hundred yards. Had it been daylight, the Confederates would have outflanked and overrun Doubleday's entire line, which was having difficulty deploying. But the darkness prevented them from pressing their advantage. Likewise, Hatch could not see all the Confederate troops deployed against him. If he had, he would have ordered an immediate retreat. For the moment, however, he did sense that something was not right, since the enemy was attacking him instead of retreating as expected. He sent an aide back to McDowell to explain his uncomfortable situation, only to again be told that "the enemy is in full retreat, and to pursue him!"

Despite these renewed orders, Hatch had his hands full simply trying to hold his ground. He tried to bring up his old brigade, now under Colonel Timothy Sullivan, but Sullivan in the darkness mistakenly formed behind Doubleday and then tried to move forward through Doubleday's line. This error threw both brigades into total confusion. Affairs now came to a climax on Hatch's left, where the troops on both sides met difficulty telling friend from foe in the dark. At length, Hood managed to advance three of his regiments to a position from where they could get a good flanking fire on the Union line. Their volleys devastated Hatch's line, and the Yankee position began to unravel from the left.

By 2000 Hatch's entire command had retired in confusion to Dogan Ridge. His withdrawal enabled Hood to advance past Young's Branch to the western slopes of Chinn Ridge. Hood was followed at 2100 by Wilcox's division and Evans' brigade, which groped their way forward in the dark. Little did the Confederates know that they now had some 10,000 men within an easy cannon shot of Pope's headquarters. Confusion flourished because of the darkness. Brigadier General Marsena Patrick and his staff accidentally rode right into part of Evans' line; the resulting Confederate volley wounded one of Patrick's aides, Lieutenant John V. Bouvier, an ancestor of Jacqueline Bouvier Kennedy Onassis. At another point, Lieutenant Colonel Judson Kilpatrick for some reason ordered a squadron of his *2nd New York Cavalry* to charge down the Warrenton Turnpike towards the Confederate lines. The New Yorkers boldly rode forward, only to be blasted by Evans' infantry and then by Law's. These Yankee troopers were lucky that it was almost pitch dark, or else they would all have been killed or captured. As it was, only eleven of Kilpatrick's squadron managed to make it back to their own lines.

These successes persuaded Lee and Longstreet to attempt a Civil War rarity, a large scale night attack. They ordered Wilcox to move his command down the Turnpike past Hood's division, and lead the assault. Wilcox, though, met with Law before advancing in order to learn the situation on his front, and was

191

not pleased to be told that Hood had managed to defeat only a forward detachment of the Yankees (Hatch's force); strong Union forces lay behind, their exact positions unknowable in the darkness. This information induced Wilcox to think better of the idea of attacking, and he rode back to Lee and Longstreet to try to get his orders changed. Longstreet sided with Wilcox, largely because of a new report from Hood that he was unable to see well enough to secure a favorable jump off position for the morrow's attack. Lee at last concurred, and at about midnight ordered all of Longstreet's troops on this front to retire to their original positions, just west of Groveton.

Pope was not much concerned with the continued sporadic fighting along the Warrenton Turnpike, even though he at last came to realize that Longstreet was finally on the field. Sometime after 1700, McDowell reported to Pope in person for the first time in four days, and he was full of news. Among other things, McDowell now belatedly delivered Buford's 0930 note concerning Longstreet's passage through Gainesville even earlier in the day. This news probably led Pope to believe that it was Longstreet's troops who were making all the ruckus along the Turnpike. Since he had received no evidence that Longstreet was forming farther to the south, Pope erroneously concluded that Longstreet was directly reinforcing Jackson's line. This belief would control his plans for the next day, as will soon be seen.

McDowell also brought with him several messages that Porter had asked to be forwarded to Pope at various times during the day. These informed Pope that Porter was not advancing to Gainesville as he had been ordered, but that he was instead holding a position near Dawkins' Branch in the face of an enemy force of unknown size. In addition, Porter was concerned about whether or not Pope was withdrawing to Bull Run, as the morning's "joint order" had suggested he might do. Porter also complained that his men were running low on water and food.

At this news, Pope exploded. He called Porter a saboteur and a traitor, and threatened to have him arrested. McDowell at length calmed him down somewhat by arguing that Porter was just being incompetent. The two generals then agreed that Porter could no longer be trusted while so far afield, and that he

Collecting the wounded on the Union right on the evening of 29 August. Many of the Union wounded—particularly those who fell at Groveton on the 28th—lay in the field for an extended period, and were even struck again during later periods of fighting.

needed to be recalled to the army's main position. As a result, Pope at 2050 sent Porter the following unequivocal instructions: "Immediately upon receipt of this order, the precise hour of receiving which you will acknowledge, you will march your command to the field of battle of today and report to me in person for orders. You are to understand that you are to comply strictly with this order, and to be present on the field within three hours after its reception or after daybreak tomorrow morning."

These orders and others issued that night show that Pope was clearly planning to stay and fight in the morning. This certainly was not a good decision in view of the fact that he now knew that Longstreet had at last linked up with Jackson. Pope would have done much better to withdraw to Centreville and there link up with McClellan's advancing *II* and *VI Corps* of the *Army of the*

Potomac. If he had done so, Lee would probably have withdrawn to the lower Shenandoah Valley in order to keep the campaign going, and the center of the action would have shifted to the west of Manassas. But Pope refused to admit defeat, and he and some of his officers even dared to claim that the fighting on 29 August had been a Union victory! Pope's misreading of Kearny's claims to success near the Sudley Church as well as his misunderstanding of the nature of the fighting along the Warrenton Turnpike after dark, led him to believe that Jackson was broken and ready to retreat, if the Confederates were not actually doing so already. He simply felt that McDowell's and Porter's fresh troops, supported by McClellan's anticipated arrival from Alexandria, would be sufficient to deal with Longstreet and whatever part of Jackson's command still remained on the field. The next day's fighting would prove Pope's analysis to be wrong, deadly wrong.

The Porter Court-Martial

Major General Fitz John Porter came from a family with a strong military tradition: his cousins David Dixon Porter (1908-1891), William D. Porter (1809-1864) and David Farragut (1801-1870) were three of the most promising naval officers in the Civil War. Fitz John was born on 31 August 1822 in Portsmouth, New Hampshire, and graduated 8th in the West Point Class of 1845. After commendable service in the Mexican War, he remained in the army and was named colonel of the *15th U.S. Infantry* at the opening of the Civil War. Promoted soon to brigadier general, he was given a division in McClellan's new *Army of the Potomac*. Porter directed the successful (though long) siege of Yorktown, and as a reward was given command of the *V Corps*, which would grow to become the largest in McClellan's army. He handled his troops very well at Mechanicsville, Gaines' Mill and Malvern Hill during the retreat from Richmond, and was promoted to major general on 4 July 1862.

Porter was a fellow Democrat with McClellan, and soon became one of his commander's staunchest supporters. We do not know whether it was the luck of the draw or a deliberate choice by McClellan that sent Porter's corps as the first reinforcements to leave the Peninsula for the support of Pope's army. Porter left Fort Monroe on 19 August and landed the next day at Aquia Creek. From there, he marched to Fredericksburg and then headed west to guard Pope's left wing at Kelly's Ford on the Rappahannock, where his troops began arriving on the 23rd. During this march and afterwards, Porter kept in constant touch with McClellan, who arrived at Aquia Creek on 24 August. Their messages were constantly deprecating of Pope and his intentions, particularly after Pope began shifting his command to the north along the upper Rappahannock and neglected to keep Porter fully informed on his expectations.

Porter dutifully followed Pope's army in its withdrawal to Manassas on the 26th and 27th. His position on the army's far left on the Rappahannock line brought him up as the last of Pope's combat troops to reach the battle area. Porter camped at Warrenton Junction on 27 August, and reached Bristoe Station the next night. On the morning of 29 August, he began moving to Manassas until he was ordered at 1000 to march towards Gainesville and link up with the rest of the army as it headed west down the Warrenton Turnpike.

Pope later claimed that he intended for Porter to head for Gainesville via the Manassas-Gainesville Road, and then turn east to strike the right flank of Jackson's troops line, which was drawn up northeast of Groveton. Nothing in Pope's orders, though, indicated this purpose, nor did they instruct Porter on what to do if he ran into any Confederate troops. That is exactly what happened at 1100 when Porter's lead brigade struck Confederate pickets on the west side of Dawkins' Branch. It was at this point that Porter received Pope's rambling "Joint

Order," discussed in the text. This directed him to continue towards Gainesville, though he was to be prepared to halt or even fall back behind Bull Run under certain conditions. The last line of the Joint Order noted that, "If any considerable advantages are to be gained by departing from this order it will not be carried out."

Porter discussed the order with McDowell, whereupon McDowell pulled out his command to march over to join the main body of Pope's command. Porter, having lost his supporting troops, at first tried to push past Dawkins' Branch, but he met several obstacles and decided to hold where he was. He sent several notes to Pope to explain the situation, but for some reason he routed them through McDowell, and McDowell neglected to deliver them until he personally conferred with Pope that evening.

As a result, Pope spent all afternoon assaulting Jackson's front while anxiously awaiting news of Porter's anticipated attack on Stonewall's right. By 1630 Pope finally understood that Porter was not advancing as desired, so he sent firm orders for Porter to strike the enemy's flank and rear. Porter, though, did not receive these orders until 1800, by which time it was too late to accomplish anything decisive. Pope in the meanwhile vented his frustration by cursing out Porter and all McClellan supporters as traitors. It was all that McDowell could do to dissuade Pope from having Porter arrested.

Pope's anger subsided during the evening, and at 2050 he sent Porter strong and direct orders to bring his corps to the main body of the army

no later than first thing in the morning. Porter had no choice but to obey, despite his concern about the large number of Confederate troops that had gathered to threaten Pope's left, which would be mostly denuded once he marched north. Porter tried to explain this danger to Pope in person at about 0800 on the 30th, but Pope would not heed him or Brigadier General John F. Reynolds, who was also posted on the left and saw the same problem.

Porter ran afoul of Pope again that afternoon, when his corps was sent forward at 1500 as Pope's last grand assault on Jackson's line. Porter realized half way through the attack that success was unattainable, so he held back his second wave (about half his command) rather than send them forward to what he thought would be certain defeat. He halted his attack on his own orders, without consulting Pope, who was too busy to object at the moment because he was just coming to realize the severity of his mistake at ignoring the large body of unknown troops on Jackson's right.

After the battle was over, Pope refused to accept the fault for his disastrous defeat, and as early as 3 September began accusing Generals McClellan, Franklin, Porter, Ricketts and Griffin of deliberately trying to sabotage his campaign. He had Porter suspended from command on 5 September, and a military court of inquiry met a few days later to consider Pope's charges. Its members were Major General George Cadwallader, Brigadier Generals Silas Casey and J.F.K. Mansfield, and Colonel Joseph Holt as judge advocate. However, this inquiry was dissolved without taking any action, partly because of the pressures attending Lee's invasion of Maryland, in which all the principals except Pope were involved. McClellan even succeeded at having Porter returned to command of the *V Corps* during the campaign. Porter, though, was held at reserve at Antietam and was not actively engaged in the battle.

McClellan's removal from army command on 9 November 1862 changed the situation drastically. The same ax that struck McClellan also struck at Porter, his staunchest supporter, and on 10 November Porter found himself abruptly relieved of command pending investigation of Pope's charges against him for misconduct at Second Bull Run. A military commission set up by the Republican members of Congress was organized on the 12th, and on 17 November Porter was placed under house arrest, with instructions not to leave the capital.

The commission to hear Porter's case was announced on 25 November. It consisted of an assortment of second rate officers who happened to be available for such duty. The only really bright member was Brigadier General James A. Garfield, the future President, who was at the time in-between jobs after holding several minor field commands in the West. He was a strong Republican, and was eager to please the administration. So were Colonel Joseph Holt, a former Secretary of War who would serve as the government's chief prosecutor, and Major General David Hunter, a close friend of Lincoln and Pope who recently had been relieved of command of the *Department of the South.*

Major General Silas Casey was another commission member who was no friend of Porter. He had once been slated to take command of Porter's best division, the *Pennsylvania Reserves*, but Porter successfully fought the appointment on the grounds that Casey's age (55) and bad health made him unfit for command. Casey should probably have disqualified himself from sitting on Porter's tribunal for this reason. Brigadier Generals Rufus King and James Ricketts should probably have done likewise. Both had commanded divisions at Second Bull Run and were under investigation by a second commission that was meeting just down the hall from Porter's to investigate the charges that Pope had filed against McDowell and other assorted officers!

Two of the four remaining commission members were relatively innocuous. Brigadier General Benjamin Prentiss, who had been captured while defending the Hornets' Nest at Shiloh in April, had just been released from Libby Prison and was not yet in the best of health. Bookish Major General E. A. Hitchcock was 65 years old and more concerned with the court's procedures than with its content.

Only two of the court's members could be construed to be possibly biased in favor of Porter. Brigadier General Napoleon Buford was the half-brother of Pope's onetime cavalry chief, Brigadier General John Buford, whose actions had been one of the few Union bright spots in the campaign. Brigadier General W.W. Morris, a regular army officer in command of the military defenses of Baltimore, was the commission's only member to voice a protest over the court's integrity. This bold move only got him removed from the court. He was replaced by Brigadier General J.D. Slough, the Military Governor of Alexandria.

Porter's friends tried to warn him that the court was deliberately stacked against him, but he was so convinced of his innocence that he declined to object to any of its members, as he could have done legally.

It was not until 1 December, three days after the proceedings opened, that Porter finally saw the charges being leveled against him. They consisted of six counts, three concerning alleged mishandling of his orders to advance to Bristoe on 29 August, one concerning his conduct during the attack on Jackson's line on 30 August, and two lesser charges concerning improper march times and routes.

The primary witnesses against Porter were Pope himself and McDowell. Neither could be called unbiased by any means. McDowell was being investigated down the hall, and Pope was seeking to cast blame on Porter for the loss of the battle. A number of minor witnesses were also called, including Captain Douglas Pope, son of the general. Porter was then allowed to open his defense. His lawyers called in several of his subordinates at the battle, including Generals George Sykes, George Morell, Dan Butterfield and Charles Griffin. The most helpful evidence came from Colonel Frederick Locke, Porter's chief of staff, who contradicted some key points of McDowell's testimony. Locke and other witnesses supported Porter's case so well that Advocate Holt took the unusual step of calling one of the court's own officers, General King, as a prosecution witness! Porter's attorney, Reverdy Johnson, countered this move by calling upon two equally splashy witnesses, Generals McClellan and Burnside.

The administration began to grow apprehensive as the case dragged on and Porter's defense continued to pile up points. This situation prompted Secretary of War Stanton to take the unusual step on 6 January 1863 of directing the investigation to be "brought to a close without any necessary delay" because of pressing military needs. The demand was clearly unfounded since the court had only been sitting for four weeks and nobody was conducting any campaigns in the dead of winter following Burnside's disaster at Fredericksburg and Rosecrans' indecisive fight at Stones River. Porter's attorneys were given three days to prepare their final statement, which they then took three and one-half hours to read to the court. The investigation then closed without Porter having taken the stand in his own defense, though he did issue a long statement on 26 December and then a short concluding statement denying that he had ever been a traitor to his country. This tactical decision was taken on the advice of his lawyers, and in retrospect was probably not in his best interest.

Quite astonishingly, the court issued its verdict just three hours after Porter's lawyers finished their summation. They found Porter guilty of all the charges except two minor points, and sentenced him "to be cashiered and forever disqualified from holding any office of trust or profit under the government of the United States." The sentence had to be approved by the President before becoming final. Lincoln had been following the case but did not know all its particulars, so he asked Judge Holt to prepare him a summation. Holt's review, of course, was grossly slanted in favor of the prosecution. After reading Holt's brief, Lincoln naturally let the verdict stand, so making Porter the highest ranking Union officer to be removed by court martial during the war. He was formally cashiered as of 21 January 1863.

Porter was understandably crushed by the verdict, and spent the rest of his life trying to get his good name restored. After Lincoln's death, he unsuccessfully appealed to General William T. Sherman and then to President U.S. Grant for help. He endured considerable financial hardship until 1875, when a family friend won him an appointment to be assistant receiver of the Central Railroad of New Jersey.

Porter's rejuvenated financial condition permitted him to renew his quest for reinstatement. His perseverance finally paid off, and in April 1878 his friend Senator Theodore Randolph persuaded President Rutherford B. Hayes to reexamine the case. Hayes appointed a court of three commissioners, Major General J.M. Schofield, Brigadier General A.H. Terry, and Colonel G.W. Getty, with Major Asa B. Gardner as judge advocate. The court met at West Point, and took the unusual step of calling former Confederate officers James Longstreet and T.T. Rosser to testify. Their evidence showed how much Pope had misunderstood the situation on his left during the entire battle, and, more importantly, demonstrated how Porter could not

have physically carried out most of Pope's orders as issued. Other witnesses included a now quite testy Irvin McDowell, and Robert Todd Lincoln, son of the slain President.

Altogether, the Schofield commission heard some 142 witnesses before it adjourned in January 1879. It met for six months, and then needed two more months to deliberate; in comparison, the original commission had met for 45 days and only used three hours to deliberate. Their decision was to exonerate Porter on every count and to recommend that the findings and sentence of the previous court martial be set aside, with Porter to be restored to his rank.

It was one thing, though, to attain a favorable verdict, and quite another to see it enacted. James Garfield, then Speaker of the House of Representatives, took the reversal as an affront to himself because he had been on the original commission. He worked hard to prevent the decision of the Schofield board from being carried out, in spite of a pro-Porter bill that was endorsed by the House's Committee on Military Affairs on 21 January 1880. Garfield's clout became even stronger when he was elected President that Fall. As a result, Congress adjourned in March 1881 without having passed the legislation needed to restored Porter's rank and authorize payment of his back pay.

Now fate suddenly intervened on Porter's side. Garfield was shot by an assassin in July 1881 and died in October. Porter, who managed to survive a serious illness himself, at length managed to win former President Grant to his side. Grant then approached Garfield's successor,

Chester A. Arthur, on Porter's behalf. Porter's only remaining obstacle was now Attorney General Robert Lincoln, to whom Arthur referred the case. He at length recommended that the 1863 decision should not be reversed, but that the President might issue a pardon to Porter. Porter agreed to the terms of this partial victory, and President Arthur on 4 May 1882 remitted him from his "remaining penalty."

Porter, though, did not rest with this victory, and continued to press to have the court martial's verdict totally reversed and his rank restored. The issue was debated inside and outside Washington for four more years, with powerful figures on each side. Weight at length began to shift in Porter's favor when Grant renewed his support, and both houses of Congress passed a bill in his favor in early 1884. President Arthur, though, was now concerned about the constitutional issue and the legal precedent of Congress overturning the results of a military tribunal. As a result, he acted upon the advice of Robert Lincoln, now the Secretary of War, and Attorney General Benjamin Brewster, and vetoed the Porter bill on 2 July 1884.

Porter was discouraged but still did not give up. Arthur was replaced in 1885 by Grover Cleveland, the first Democratic president since Buchanan. With Robert Lincoln and Porter's other political opponents now out of office, his friends now succeeded at pushing another bill for his support through Congress in early 1886. Porter's twenty-three year drive for reinstatement finally succeeded on 1 July 1886, when President Cleveland signed a bill reinstating him as an officer in the Army of the United States. After the necessary paperwork was completed, Porter was named a colonel of Regular infantry on 5 August 1886, to rank from 14 May 1861. Porter was, of course, delighted by the victory, even though he still won no back pay. Having exonerated himself, he requested to be placed on the army's retired list two days later.

Porter later supplemented his army pension with stints as a police commissioner and then service as a fire commissioner in New York City. After an unsuccessful attempt at running a roofing and paving company, he worked from 1893 to 1897 as a cashier at the New York Post Office. He then moved to Morristown, New Jersey, where he died of kidney disease on 21 May 1901. He was buried with full military honors at Greenwood Cemetery in Brooklyn.

Debate still continues today as to whether or not Porter was guilty as charged in 1862. Historian Kenneth P. Williams argues strongly against him in Volume 2 of *Lincoln Finds a General*, while Otto Eisenschiml presented a quite sympathetic view of the general in his 1950 book, *The Celebrated Case of Fitz John Porter*. Most historians today hold the view that Porter was not treasonous as Pope charged, and that his mistakes on the battlefield were no more heinous than those made by McDowell at the same time, or those committed by other generals at other battles. Porter's greatest faults may well have been his close allegiance to McClellan, and his unfortunate practice of expressing his dislike of Pope much too strongly and much too openly. This set Porter up as an ideal scapegoat for Pope. As a result, the Republican administration supported Pope's charges even though Pope, too, had been discredited, because they felt it was necessary to keep McClellan and his supporters in check. If Porter had learned to hold his tongue, as McClellan supporters Hancock, Sedgwick and Meade did, he might never have been charged or convicted in the first place.

CHAPTER IX

Day of Decision

The heavy fighting on Jackson's front on 29 August and the confused movements along the Warrenton Turnpike that night boded still more fighting for the next morning. The commanding generals on both sides had planned attacks for dawn, but neither side did so, despite the fact that the contending armies were in such close proximity. Instead, tense pickets and skirmishers began exchanging shots even before daylight on 30 August, and would continue to do so, with only sporadic localized flare ups, until well after noon.

Lee's original plan for 30 August was to have Longstreet's left wing (Hood's, Wilcox's and Evans' commands) strike Pope's left, and it was for that reason that he had allowed those troops to advance late on the 29th. However, the unexpected resistance by Hatch's division to the east of Groveton persuaded Hood and his supports to pull back to the west, thereby forfeiting their jump off positions on western Chinn Ridge.

Lee had also planned to use R.H. Anderson's division and S.D. Lee's artillery as supports for Hood's attack, as soon as they reached the field. Anderson had a veteran command of 6000 men, but they were pretty much played out from a 17 hour long march when they reached the field at 0300. For some reason, Longstreet had neglected to tell Anderson where to form, so Anderson kept marching eastward along the Warrenton Turnpike until he came across the debris of the previous day's battle, whereupon he went into camp. It was not until an hour or so later that Hood found out about Anderson's arrival - and the disconcerting fact that Anderson had accidentally marched past Hood's position and was encamped within easy cannon shot of all the Union artillery massed on Dogan Ridge. Hood promptly warned Anderson of his danger, so enabling the latter to withdraw to the safety of Stuart's Hill before the Yankee gunners could see his vulnerable column and open fire on it.

The weary condition of Anderson's troops, along with a continuing concern for Porter's intentions south of Young's Branch, persuaded Lee to postpone his planned dawn attack. Instead, he would hold his men in their positions and wait for Pope to make the first move of the day. A letter that he wrote to Jefferson Davis during the morning shows that Lee was not eager to attack Pope's concentrated army. He was pleased to have "drawn the enemy from the Rappahannock frontier and caused him to concentrate his troops between Manassas and Centreville." Lee continued, "My desire has been to avoid a general engagement, being the weaker force." If he could not secure a victory by forcing the enemy to attack and be defeated, he would follow a campaign of maneuver in order "to relieve other portions of the country." He could risk an offensive attack only when he received enough reinforcements (D.H. Hill's division and other troops were being forwarded from Richmond) in order to have the "larger force."

This strategy indeed presented a marked change from Lee's aggressive attitude of the previous evening. It was probably heavily influenced by Longstreet, who did not want to attack unless he clearly held the advantage. Lee instead hoped that Pope would wreck his army in still more frontal assaults, but when the Yankees made no effort to attack by 0800, Lee called his senior commanders (Jackson, Longstreet and Stuart) to his headquarters for a conference. The four officers discussed the possibility of attacking Pope's left if the enemy commander began assaulting Jackson's line again. But if the enemy remained in position, Longstreet would strive to attact Pope's attention while Jackson began marching around the Union right in a bold effort to reach Germantown or Fairfax and so cut the Federal withdrawal route. This maneuver would in turn allow Longstreet a chance to strike the Yankees' rear as they withdrew past Centreville. Alternatively, if Pope chose to withdraw to

Colonel Stephen D. Lee (no relation to Robert E.) commanded a battalion of Longstreet's artillery that formed a critical link between Lee's right and left wings at 2nd Bull Run. He became a lieutenant general in the Army of Tennessee late in the war.

Washington during the day, Lee could move towards the lower Shenandoah in an effort to draw the Federals out again.

With these plans in mind, Lee's lieutenants shifted their troops around as best they could in order to strengthen their lines. Jackson rotated his brigades so that those which had been most heavily engaged the day before could get some rest and fresh supplies. His divisions still held the same relative positions as the day before: Hill's on the left, Lawton's in the center, and Starke's on the right. Longstreet still had Hood on his left, astride the Warrenton Turnpike, with Kemper on Hood's right. Jones was still farther to the right watching Porter's position. Longstreet's only major positional shift was to put Wilcox on Hood's left. Lee held Anderson's division in reserve just west of the Brawner farm, and posted Stuart's brigades to guard the army's flanks, with Fitz Lee on the left and Robertson on the right. S.D. Lee's reserve artillery battalion was placed on Stony Ridge just northeast of the Brawner house. His 18 guns and Shumaker's large battalion to his left formed a great hinge between the two wings of Lee's army, and dominated all the ground on their immediate front.

During the night of 29-30 August, John Pope remained convinced that his numerous attacks on Jackson's lines had proved successful. Confederate efforts to bring in their wounded gave him more reason to believe that the Southerners were abandoning the field, and the confusing enemy movements along the Warrenton Turnpike after dark were interpreted as a feeble effort to set up a rear guard. This opinion was confirmed in Pope's eyes when he received news an hour before dawn that a large Confederate column was retiring westwards away from the battlefield (this was actually Anderson withdrawing from his exposed forward position). In this state of mind, Pope confidently wrote Halleck at 0500 on the 29th: "We fought a terrific battle here yesterday with the combined forces of the enemy, which lasted with continuous fury from daylight until dark, by which time the enemy was driven from the field, which we now occupy. Our troops are too much exhausted yet to push matters, but I shall do so in the course of the morning, as soon as Fitz John Porter's corps comes up from Manassas. The enemy is still in our front, but badly used up. We have lost not less than 8000 men killed and wounded, but from the appearance of the field the enemy lost at least two to one. He stood strictly on the defensive and every assault was made by ourselves. Our troops behaved splendidly. The battle was fought on the identical battle-field of Bull Run, which greatly increased the enthusiasm of our men. The news just reached me from the front that the enemy is retreating toward the mountains. I go forward at once to see. We have made great captures, but I am not able yet to form an idea of their extent."

Pope's plan for the day, then, was to use Porter's fresh corps to lead the pursuit of the enemy. At 0700 Pope met with most of his corps commanders on Buck Hill to give them their orders for the day. Here he was disconcerted to learn that they did not support his reading of the situation. Instead, his chiefs believed that Jackson's men still held their battle line, despite the strange maneuvers that had been seen along the Warrenton Turnpike. Their meeting lasted for about an hour, and Pope was at last persuaded to order an advance by McDowell, Porter and Heintzelman towards Sudley Mill. If the Confederates were indeed withdrawing, a pursuit could be organized. If not, this large a coordinated attack would surely be able to break Jackson's line, particularly in light of the near success of Kearny's attack in that vicinity the previous evening.

Quite oddly, neither Pope nor his subordinates began to issue orders for their agreed open movement to Sudley Mill. Apparently they wanted to make sure exactly where Jackson's men were before they began organizing their advance. Pope's attention immediately after the meeting concluded was absorbed by Porter, who at that time finally reached the field. Porter did not endorse Pope's plan of attack, and instead spoke long and earnestly about the need to watch the area near Dawkins' Branch that he had just vacated. Porter was certain that there were still strong Confederate forces in that vicinity, but he failed to convince Pope of the danger there. He might have succeeded had he been aggressive enough to capture some prisoners for identification and interrogation, but such had not been the case,

Pope certainly erred greatly by not heeding Porter's advice, at least to the point of sending scouts or a trusted officer to check out the situation south of Young's Branch. Pope had good reason to be wary of Porter because of the latter's failure to carry out the exact letter of his orders to march to Gainesville on the 29th, but he still should have considered the possibility that there was some form of enemy force still lurking southeast of Groveton. If Porter were right, Pope was inviting disaster by stripping the area of all Union troops. A large Confederate force in that area would have a clear route to attack Pope's command from the Union left and rear, particularly if Jackson's men were still on the field in Pope's front.

As the morning progressed, reports started to come in from Heintzelman's and McDowell's pickets that Jackson was indeed still in position. This news must have placed Pope in a quandary, since he no longer knew what to make of the reported Confederate withdrawal down the Warrenton Turnpike. For this reason, Pope held his entire army stationary in anticipation of the arrival of Porter's corps. Porter had marched from Dawkins' Branch well before dawn, in obedience to Pope's injunction to reach the battle area promptly. His march had gone fairly well, except for the fact that Griffin's brigade, which pulled out last, somehow lost its way and ended up heading towards Centreville along with two attached regiments and a battery. Griffin was apparently not too concerned about his error, and went into camp after reaching the Centreville area, but not before requisitioning some new shoes for his men!

Meanwhile, the bulk of Porter's corps began reaching the battle area at about 0830. Porter was instructed to form on Dogan Ridge. He drew up his men astride the Warrenton Turnpike about a mile east of Groveton, with Morell's division in front and Sykes' to Morell's right rear. The guns of two batteries stiffened Morell's line, and three full regiments were sent out as skirmishers from Groveton northeast to McDowell's line. The arrival of Porter's advance permitted Patrick's brigade to withdraw and rejoin the rest of Hatch's division, which Patrick's men were delighted to do after all the tense skirmishing they had endured all night. By the time Porter finished his dispositions at 0930, he had considerable support from the *Pennsylvania Reserves* division, which Reynolds on his own authority had advanced from Bald Hill to the western slopes of Chinn Ridge at about 0900. Reynolds' skirmishers chased Hood's advanced troops out of Groveton after a short, sharp fight, and extended Porter's skirmish line to the south side of the Turnpike.

The largest action on this tense morning arose after 0900 when Ricketts, under orders from Pope, moved two of his brigades to relieve Kearny's worn out troops on the far right of the Union line. A.P. Hill's cannoneers opened fire as soon as they saw Ricketts' infantry approach, as did Early's skirmishers. Hill then became concerned that the Yankees were going to start attacking again, so he sent Archer's and Gregg's brigades to support Early. Their skirmishers soon added weight to Early's, to which Brigadier General Abram Duryee responded in kind. Ricketts then sent to McDowell for help, only to be refused. Faced with this lack of support, Duryee (who had been wounded in the hand) had no choice but to pull back from the position that he had tried to occupy.

Pope was not as much concerned by Duryee's problems as he was by a report from Kearny of a strong Confederate artillery position near Sudley Church. Pope had learned to trust Kearny's sagacity and fighting qualities, so he sent Colonel David Strother of his staff to investigate the situation on the army's right. At the same time, Ricketts was directed to move forward and "feel the enemy cautiously" in order to see what sort of Confederate forces were still on the field.

Strother rode forward to Ricketts' headquarters and delivered Pope's instructions for a probing attack. Ricketts pointed out that he had just conducted an unsuccessful advance that clearly showed that the enemy was present in force. Both he and Duryee, who was present at the interview, refused to accept Pope's belief that the enemy was in retreat. It made no sense to them to attack again, since their troops were "used up," but they would do so if ordered.

Strother allowed Ricketts and Duryee to stand down, and hurried back to Pope in order to report the situation. Pope reportedly "hesitated a moment" and then told Strothers to let Ricketts stay back. Strother felt that Pope was greatly preoccupied, as he "spent the morning under a tree waiting for the enemy to retreat."

At about 1000 Brigadier General Isaac Stevens of Reno's corps grew impatient with the impasse on the field, and rode to Pope's headquarters to report that there were too many Confederate troops on his front for the enemy to be in retreat. Pope refused to believe him, and directed that he send out a reinforced skirmish line to "try the enemy." Accordingly, Stevens sent out 100 men of the *79th New York* at about 1100. The detachment ran squarely into Early's troops along the abandoned railroad line, and got decidedly the worst of the affair. Their commander was wounded and captured, and the survivors came streaming back to the rear.

Kearny notified Pope at once of the results of his probe, but Pope still refused to see the situation clearly. He set too much stock in reports from captured prisoners that Lee was withdrawing. This belief was strengthened at 1100 when a wounded Union soldier was found on Porter's front who had escaped after spending the night within the Confederate lines. He claimed to have "heard the rebel officers say their army was retiring to unite with Longstreet." This news was enough for

Pope, and at 1130 he sent verbal orders for Porter and Hatch to attack what he was certain was only the rearguard of Lee's army. Pope had finally decided to take action, but not the right sort. Interestingly, his decision was promptly supported by two of his chief lieutenants, McDowell and Heintzelman, who had just conducted a personal reconnaissance of the area where Jackson's far left flank had been located the previous evening. They saw no enemies in sight, and promptly reported to Pope that they supported his notion that the Confederates were retreating. McDowell and Heintzelman did not know that Jackson's troops on that front were concealed in the protective shadows of the woods near Sudley Ford, as any of the Union skirmishers in the area could have told them.

After conferring with McDowell and Heintzelman, Pope decided to issue a revised and more detailed pursuit order, which was sent out at 1200. Porter was now directed to advance on the Warrenton Turnpike, supported by Hatch and Reynolds. At the same time, Ricketts and Heintzelman were to proceed on the road from Sudley to Haymarket. The entire advance, consisting of over half of the army, would be led by McDowell, who was to push the pursuit of Lee's command and "press him vigorously during the whole day."

For some reason, Pope did not at once send directions for Porter to redirect the attack that he ordered at 1130. As a result, Porter had his troops in motion to the northwest for some time before he received Pope's revised orders of 1200. He first used the *25th New York* and *1st U.S. Sharpshooters* to secure the Groveton Woods, and then moved his entire command up the Groveton-Sudley Road. Butterfield's division was to go first, supported by Sykes; the only significant body of troops left behind was Colonel G.K. Warren's small brigade of two regiments, which was assigned to support the corps' artillery line deployed on the ridge southeast of Groveton.

Thus, Porter was poised to launch his attack when he received Pope's new orders. The revised directive placed him in an awkward situation, since he could not safely move diagonally across Jackson's front in order to reach the Warrenton Turnpike. His situation was complicated by the fact that his moving columns were undergoing severe fire from S.D. Lee's cannons on Stony Ridge. Rather than pull back to Dogan Ridge, Porter decided to resolve his dilemma by sending Butterfield's division to drive the Confederates away from the railroad line and then chase away S.D. Lee's cannons by striking their exposed left flank. Porter reasoned that this advance should succeed because the Confederates were supposed to be only a rearguard. Once the railroad embankment was cleared and the Confederate guns were driven off, Porter could readily reach the Warrenton Turnpike and from there conduct the pursuit that Pope had ordered at 1200.

While Porter was moving into position for his sidewise pursuit, Ricketts initiated his prong of the army's advance as ordered. His troops hardly advanced a hundred yards before they met such heavy Confederate artillery fire from Jackson's cannons posted near Sudley Church that they were halted in their tracks. McDowell, who witnessed the scene, at once understood that Ricketts faced more than just a small Confederate rearguard, and authorized him to "abandon the pursuit" and pull back to his original position. Thus ended what historian John J. Hennessy aptly calls "the briefest pursuit in American history."

The resistance met by Ricketts' division finally convinced Pope that Jackson was still on the field in force. This revelation, though, did not necessitate a major change in plans. Pope simply turned his previously ordered pursuit into an assault on Jackson's line, to be spearheaded by Porter's troops.

Pope's decision to launch a major assault on Jackson's prepared position was certainly bullheaded, particularly because of his misevaluation of Longstreet's location. He knew by then that Longstreet had to be at or near the field, since Longstreet's column was known to have passed through Thoroughfare Gap the previous morning. Even so, Pope persisted in believing that Longstreet had come up to reinforce Jackson. This makes it all the more unbelievable that Pope was now insisting on assaulting Stonewall's line, which was then, as Pope believed, heavily reinforced by Longstreet.

What Pope refused to consider was the possibility that Longstreet had come up and formed on Jackson's right. He misinterpreted the Confederate movements near the Warrenton

Brigadier General John F. Reynolds' personal warning about the dangerous situation on the army's left flank was not believed by Pope at 1300 on 30 August. Reynolds led the famed **Pennsylvania Reserves** *division at 2nd Bull Run, and later commanded the army's left wing at Gettysburg, where he was killed on the morning of 1 July 1863.*

Turnpike the previous evening, when Hood and Anderson were moving back and forth, and dismissed Porter's reports of the Confederate forces near Dawkins' Branch the previous day. The situation on the Union left could have been clarified by proper use of cavalry or a reconnaissance by a trusted officer, but Pope declined to do either. His vision was too focused on Jackson's front line, like a dog that was worrying a bone and would not let go.

The only Union commander to have a clear picture of what was going on opposite the Union left was Brigadier General John F. Reynolds, commander of the unattached *Pennsylvania Reserves* division. Reynolds had been facing Longstreet's skirmishers along Lewis Lane since the previous evening. Late in the morning, he decided to develop the Confederate position by pushing his skirmishers forward. He was astonished to find "a line of skirmishers of the enemy nearly parallel to the line of skirmishers covering my left flank, with cavalry formed behind them, perfectly stationary, evidently masking a column of the enemy formed for an attack on my left flank."

Reynolds deemed this intelligence so important that he decided to ride hastily to Pope in order to report it in person. He had to dodge Confederate shells all the way, and excitedly rode

During the climax of the fighting on the afternoon of 30 August, Pope was forced to shift troops to his left to meet Longstreet's counterattack. Here Ricketts' division and part of Sigel's corps are seen marching towards Bald Hill, while Porter and Heintzelman attack Jackson's position in the background.

into Pope's headquarters at 1300 gasping, "The enemy is turning our left." Pope, however, nonchalantly dismissed the report with the words, "Oh, I guess not." He did though, reconsider enough to send John Buford's cavalry to the left to see what was happening there. The army commander then continued to focus his attention on Porter's attack.

McDowell, to whose wing Reynolds' division was temporarily attached, took the news slightly more seriously than Pope. He rode in person to Reynolds' front to investigate the situation for himself. What he saw was enough to convince him to withdraw Reynolds' command to Chinn Ridge. Oddly, McDowell chose not to press the case with Pope, who was clearly intent on trying to defeat Jackson by direct assault. Reynolds' withdrawal left Warren's small brigade of Sykes' division as the only Union infantry still deployed on the southern side of the Warrenton Turnpike near Groveton.

By 1400 Pope received still more reports that something ominous was lurking to his left. It seems that Sigel had become anxious about the number of Confederate troops reported to be south of the Warrenton Turnpike, and at around 1200 he had sent the *4th New York Cavalry* to scout the Confederate right flank. When this probe reported back that the enemy "were moving against our left," Sigel at once conveyed the news to Pope. This time Pope reacted to the possible threat to his left wing by directing Sigel to send a brigade to support Reynolds. Sigel assigned McLean's brigade to the task, but was uncertain exactly where to send him. Pope's orders were for him to occupy "that bald hill," but they did not specify which one. McLean ended up joining Reynolds' force on Chinn Ridge, which was a quite reasonable interpretation of his instructions. It turns out, though, that Pope had wanted McLean's brigade to form on Henry House Hill, one-quarter mile east of Chinn Ridge. The effects of this miscommunication will be seen shortly.

Porter spent the early afternoon preparing for his attack, which would be the last major Union assault of the battle. His initial concern was that his right was unsupported. Pope's initial plans had been for Hatch to move up on Porter's right, but at noon he substituted Ricketts' division. When McDowell canceled Ricketts' advance by 1230, Hatch was again directed to take Porter's right. Porter, though, was apparently unaware of this change, and did not tell Hatch to form until about 1400. It would have taken Hatch an hour to come up and take his position on the eastern side of the Groveton Woods. Meanwhile, Porter massed his troops in the central portion of Groveton Woods, where they rested tensely in regimental battle lines that were stacked up only thirty yards apart. Porter's left at the time was only weakly protected by Hazlett's battery, which was drawn up near Groveton, and Warren's small brigade, which moved from Dogan Ridge to support Hazlett in the woods southeast of Groveton.

Porter advanced his skirmishers at 1430, and then launched his attack at 1500. The sight of 10,000 fresh Yankees advancing with their flags flying spurred the Confederates to admiration as they tightened up their formations to receive the attack. S.D. Lee's cannons near the Brawner farm, which were drawn up almost wheel to wheel, at once opened fire at the Federal lines only one-half mile away, and their smoke soon covered the field.

Due to the angle at which Porter's line advanced, the first Union troops to strike Jackson's line were the lead elements of

Sketch of Porter's attack on Jackson's lines on the afternoon of 30 August, as seen from Henry House Hill. The Stone House and Warrenton Turnpike are in the foreground.

Hatch's division, on Porter's right. Here the *24th* and *30th New York* regiments of Sullivan's brigade led the way. They exited Groveton Woods only 300 yards from the line of Stafford's Louisiana brigade, which was posted along the unfinished railroad line. The two New York regiments endured heavy casualties as they boldly rushed forward and seized the southern edge of the railroad embankment, in the process pushing Stafford's men to the rear of the escarpment. The opposing lines then blasted away at each other only fifteen yards apart, with the railroad line as a deadly no man's land in between them.

Roberts' brigade of Butterfield's division advanced quickly on Sullivan's left and endured equally heavy casualties from S.D. Lee's raking artillery fire as well as the Confederate infantry to their front. This fire was in fact so intense that Roberts' men, unlike Sullivan's, were unable to reach the railroad embankment where Johnson's Confederate brigade was posted. Instead, their attack stalled some 20 to 50 yards short of its goal, and Roberts' men had to lie down and seek what shelter they could find in order to try to escape the deadly hail of shells and bullets being rained upon them.

Weeks' brigade on Roberts' left had an even more difficult advance. Colonel Henry Weeks was a novice brigade commander, since he had just that day succeeded to the command of

Butterfield's brigade after Butterfield moved up to lead Morell's division because Morell had gone to Centreville with Griffin. For some reason, Weeks had not formed his five regiments into battle line before the attack, but instead advanced with them still in column formation. This was certainly a more efficient manner of advancing, but was quite ineffective for giving or receiving fire. During Weeks' advance, just one of his regiments, the *17th New York* on the brigade's far right, managed to keep up with Roberts' men. The rest of Weeks' regiments were mauled by S.D. Lee's artillery before they could change their dense column formation into proper battle line.

Once they were more properly formed for fighting, Weeks' veteran regiments rushed the railroad line and managed to dislodge Johnson's right regiment, the 48th Virginia, which was deployed in a flat area just west of the "Deep Cut" (the deepest excavated section on the line of the unfinished railroad). Johnson tried to mount a counterattack with his reserve line, only to see it driven back as the gap in his line widened.

It was now time for the Stonewall Brigade to advance to enter the fight. This famous command had by now been whittled down to a skeleton strength of only 500 men. It was posted in Jackson's second line, 200 yards behind the railroad line. The brigade's commander, Colonel William Baylor, boldly grabbed the flag of the 33rd Virginia and shouted, "Boys, follow me!" He was instantly felled by a hail of Yankee gunfire, and the brigade's attack faltered before it was fairly begun. Colonel Andrew Grigsby of the 27th Virginia rallied the command and led them back to the charge. Despite heavy casualties, they managed this time to cross an open field and plug the hole in Johnson's line. Grigsby, though, knew that he could not hold on for long, so he sent to Jackson for reinforcements.

Jackson was well aware that a crisis was at hand. His troops were largely played out from the previous day's combat, and they faced an entire corps of fresh Union troops. He at once directed Hill to send help from his unthreatened end of the line. At the same time he sent one of his most trusted aides, Major Henry Kyd Douglas, to request Longstreet to send a division as reinforcements.

Longstreet had realized that Jackson might be in trouble as

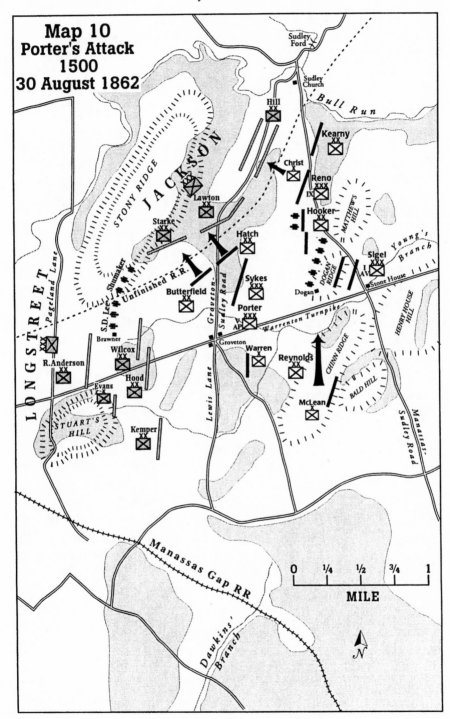

Map 10
Porter's Attack
1500
30 August 1862

soon as he saw Porter begin his "well organized attack, thoroughly concentrated and operating cleverly." He felt that it would take too long to move any infantry to Jackson's line, so he instead chose to rely on his artillery to break up the Union attack by firing on the Federal left flank and rear. S.D. Lee's guns were already sweeping the fields west of the Groveton-Sudley Road, so rendering it difficult for Porter to bring up Sykes' division, which formed his second line of attack. Longstreet effectively added the four guns of Chapman's Dixie Artillery to the fray by posting them north of the Warrenton turnpike, where they were on Hill's front just 400 yards from the left rear of Weeks' brigade. The fire from Chapman's guns helped pin down Butterfield's troops, who chose to hold their advanced position near the railroad line and engage Jackson's infantry rather than retreat and face S.D. Lee's and Chapman's guns again. Much to the discredit of Pope and his commanders, no Union officers were able to organize an effective counter battery fire to try to silence or check this massed Confederate battery. The Union batteries were too spread out and lacked central control, a command problem that had severely plagued the Union armies in Virginia since the beginning of the war.

Porter's first wave, most of whom were now pinned down along the railroad line, desperately needed reinforcements in order to expand their foothold or at least help turn back the inevitable Confederate counterattack. Porter at first had every intention of sending Sykes' two brigades of U.S. *Regulars* to support Butterfield, but the ferocity of the Confederate artillery fire persuaded him for the moment to hold Sykes back rather than expose his men to the 700 yard gauntlet of open ground between Groveton Woods and Butterfield's advance lines. This decision was to cause the loss of all the Union momentum on the Federal left.

Although he held Sykes' two brigades back for the moment, Porter continued to push his attack on the right of his line, where Hatch's men were less exposed to the heavy Confederate artillery fire. Here Hatch had decided to draw up his four brigades into six lines, with the apparent intention of sending them forward in waves at 50 yard intervals. His first wave, Sullivan's *24th* and *30th New York*, succeeded at reaching the

Confederate line but could not breach it. The second wave, composed of Sullivan's *14th Brooklyn* and *22nd New York*, got off to a late start and was greatly disorganized by S.D. Lee's artillery during its advance, so much so that its men provided but little aid to Hatch's first wave.

Hatch's third wave, the *21st* and *35th New York* of Patrick's brigade, met equal difficulty when its turn came to charge. The New Yorkers were hit by a violent blast of Confederate musketry as soon as they emerged from the Groveton Woods, and most of them hit the ground for cover. Some of their return fire then struck Sullivan's men in the back. Then, when Patrick's front line recovered enough to resume their attack, they ran into the disordered troops of Sullivan's second line and also began to lose their cohesion. By now there was so large a mass of Union troops milling about behind the railroad embankment that the Confederate shots could hardly miss. As one soldier of Trimble's old brigade put it, "They were so thick it was impossible to miss. What a slaughter!"

Patrick saw what was happening, and sent in Colonel George Pratt's *20th New York State Militia* on Sullivan's right in order to meet the Confederate flank fire that was raking the blue clad mass that was caught between the railroad line and School House Run. Pratt, however, lost his bearings and struck the Confederate line some 200 yards east of his intended target. This error subjected his regiment to a concentrated fire from half of Lawton's division. Pratt fell mortally wounded along with seven of his color bearers. Even so, the brave regiment pushed forward to within 25 yards of the Confederate line. The New Yorkers found the fire there too intense to bear, and had to withdraw because they had no support of any kind. In just fifteen minutes of fighting, the *20th* had lost 279 of its men.

Pratt's attack would be the last initiated by Porter. He now fully understood how senseless it was to continue trying to batter Jackson's position, especially since he had no reserves on hand. He sent word for his remaining troops to cancel their attack, and so kept about half of his command out of the action. This decision was a wise one tactically, but was clearly contrary to his orders from Pope, a situation for which Porter would pay dearly later.

Major General Fitz John Porter, commander of the Federal V Corps, was blamed by Pope for the loss at 2nd Bull Run. As a result, he was court-martialled and dismissed from the army, a conviction he had to fight for 23 years to overturn.

Porter's decision to hold back his second line of attackers also abandoned his first line to their own fate. As previously noted, Butterfield's regiments and Sullivan's first wave had succeeded at reaching the Confederate lines, where many of the Yankees sought shelter from the Confederate fire by clinging to the embankment of the unfinished railroad line. They were unable to advance farther because of the heavy Confederate fire on their front, but also refused to retreat. As a result, the two sides banged away at each other for over half an hour at almost point blank range. Colonel Bradley Johnson of Taliaferro's division reported, "I saw a Federal flag hold its position for half an hour within 10 yards of a flag of one of the regiments in the cut and go down six or eight times, and after the fight 100 dead were lying 20 yards from the cut, some of them within 2 feet of it."

By this time, many Confederates in Stafford's and Johnson's brigades, which had already been engaged in the previous day's fighting, began to run out of ammunition. Rather than stand idly by, a number of these troops began throwing stones at the Union units massed only a few yards away. Some threw the rocks as hard as they could, while others simply lobbed them like hand

Starke's Louisiana troops threw stones near the "Deep Cut" on the afternoon of 30 August. The importance of this noted incident has been much exaggerated.

grenades. These missiles probably did more to hurt Union morale than they did to cause casualties, but even so, the episode was to become one of the most memorable of the war. It at times became exaggerated in the retelling. The Confederate line at this point was not in danger of being breeched, since Porter's attack had already spent its force. The thrown rocks were actually more of a nuisance than a real danger to the Unionists, some of whom reportedly picked up a few of the missiles and threw them back at the Confederates.

This stalemate along the unfinished railroad line was finally broken when Hill's reinforcements, previously summoned by Jackson from his left, at last arrived to give aid to Stonewall's pressured right wing. Brockenbrough's Virginia brigade calmly formed and pushed forward to support Johnson and Stafford. The fire of all these fresh muskets so discouraged Porter's surviving front line officers that they began ordering their exhausted (and unsupported) regiments to fall back. Their withdrawal quickly became a rout when S.D. Lee's cannoneers redoubled their fire in what became a large scale turkey shoot. Captain Amos Judson of the *83rd Pennsylvania* remembered that, "The whole brigade went back, pell mell... The rebels kept up a heavy fire upon them as they retired, and it is probable that as many men were lost in the retreat as in the advance."

Most of the retiring Union troops could not be stopped by the officers in Porter's uncommitted second line, and continued retreating through and past the Groveton Woods. Quite a number of Confederate units spontaneously began a counterattack, but they were quickly turned back by fire from Sykes' Regular infantry and a number of Union batteries on Dogan Ridge. Their withdrawal in turn enabled all of Porter's men to pull back in reasonably good order to Dogan Ridge, where the line of Sigel's corps formed a strong rallying point.

McDowell, who was then on Chinn Ridge, a mile or so south of Sigel's position, saw Porter's retreat and overestimated the danger of a Confederate counterattack. On his own authority, he sent Reynolds' entire division to support Sigel and Porter. This order proved to be most ill advised, for Reynolds' troops were not needed on Dogan Ridge, and their departure from Chinn Ridge left only two small separated infantry commands to face Longstreet's entire wing on the south side of the Warrenton Turnpike: Warren's brigade of two regiments, still posted in the woods southeast of Groveton, and McLean's brigade, stationed one half-mile behind Warren on Chinn Ridge.

Longstreet Turns the Tide

Longstreet noted with pleasure the defeat of Porter's attack, and at once began executing his long delayed counterattack against Pope's immensely depleted left flank. As a matter of fact, this attack, which Lee and Jackson had unsuccessfully pressed Longstreet to make the previous day, had already been canceled by Lee in favor of a different strategy. As previously noted, Lee had held his troops stationary all morning on the 30th in hopes that Pope would renew his disjointed attacks on

Jackson's line. When the Yankees made no movement by 1430, Lee decided to activate his alternate strategy of sending Jackson on another flank march around the enemy's right, in order to cut off Pope's line of communications near Fairfax. In accordance with this plan, Lee sent orders just before 1500 for Longstreet to advance his troops to Chinn Ridge at 1700 in order to distract Pope's attention and so help Jackson to slip away at dusk.

Porter's attack at 1500 forced the suspension of this plan, and the Confederate commanders reverted to their original strategy. At the proper moment, Longstreet would launch a massive counterattack that would not just relieve Jackson's hard pressed line, but would attempt to drive the Yankees from the field. Longstreet was forming for just such an assault even before he received his attack orders from Lee. His plan was to push forward and seize Henry House Hill, located one-half mile east of Chinn Ridge at the heart of the old First Bull Run battlefield. Seizure of this goal would hopefully isolate most of Pope's command on Dogan Ridge, where the Yankee army could be destroyed.

Longstreet began moving his 25,000 men forward at about 1600 towards their goal, which was some 1½ to 2 miles to the east. Hood's Texas brigade, posted just to the south of the Warrenton Turnpike, was directed to lead the attack. The Texans' first goal was to assault Warren's New Yorkers, who were the only Union troops that Longstreet could see at the moment on the south side of the Turnpike. Beyond them, Longstreet did not know what to expect. Little did he know how weak the Union left had been since Porter had been withdrawn from this area the previous night and Reynolds had been called away by McDowell just a few minutes earlier.

The situation south of the Warrenton Turnpike had been relatively peaceful all day despite the intense fighting a mile to the north. Hazlett's battery had offered what support it could to Porter's attack, and Warren's skirmish line, composed of six companies of the 10th New York posted along Lewis Lane, had exchanged only occasional shots with Hood's skirmishers. The bulk of Warren's line was composed of the 560 men of the 5th New York, who were relaxing on a small rise some 200 yards southeast of Hazlett's battery. This regiment had been raised by

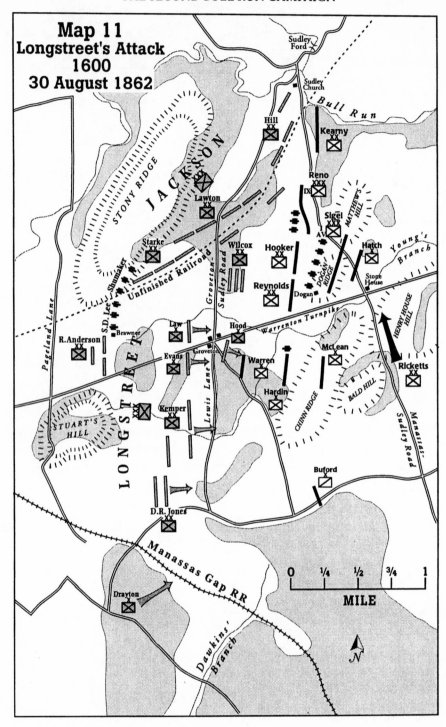

Map 11
Longstreet's Attack
1600
30 August 1862

Abram Duryee and was nattily attired in splashing Zouave uniforms that consisted of red fezes, short blue jackets, baggy red pants, and white leggings. *"Duryee's Zouaves"* were veterans of the Peninsula, and their unit was one of the crack regiments in the Union army.

Hood's brigade, less the 1st Texas (which had lagged behind), easily brushed back the *10th New York's* skirmishers and was upon the *5th New York* before the Zouaves could form their ranks properly. Confederate fire was heavy from the start, and caused numerous casualties while the red legged New Yorkers attempted to draw up their firing line. Just when the Zouaves were ready to unleash their first volley, a large body of skirmishers from the *10th New York* fell back across their front and forced them to hold their fire.

The delay was deadly. Hood's advancing line blasted away at the *10th New York*, whose overwhelmed survivors began fleeing from the field. Once they were gone and the Zouaves of the *5th New York* finally had a clear field of fire, Hood's troops were only forty yards away, and overlapped Warren's line at both ends. The situation was a hopeless one for the Zouaves, all the more so because they stood in the open ground with no cover. The regiment reportedly lost 100 men in just two minutes before it simply disintegrated. The *5th's* historian later described the desperate scene as follows: "It now became apparent that the only hope of saving a man was to fly and run the gauntlet, for in three minutes more there would not have been a man standing. The only alternative was to fly or surrender. But the men of the Fifth did not understand the latter movement; they had never been taught it by their officers. All hope having vanished, and being without officers [due to casualties], the remnant of the once proud regiment broke and ran for their lines. They were nearly annihilated, but not conquered or disgraced, and bore with them all their flags."

The *5th's* retreat was almost as costly as its brief stand had been. The Zouaves were simply mowed down as they fell back to Chinn Ridge. After the battle, one of Hood's men claimed that he could have walked from the *5th's* original position all the way to Young's Branch just on Zouave bodies without touching the ground. Another Texan thought that the sight of all the fallen

Henry House, which burned during the battle of 1st Bull Run, was in ruins at the time of 2nd Bull Run. This is how the ruins appeared in March 1862.

Zouaves with their fancy blue and red uniforms looked like a springtime hillside covered with wild flowers back home.

The pitiful remains of *Duryea's Zouaves* were rallied on Henry House Hill at about 1700. They numbered only 60 men of the 560 who had been in its ranks just an hour before. Nearly 300 had been lost in the brief ten minute fight with Hood's Texans, of whom 120 had been killed—the greatest loss of any Union volunteer infantry regiment in one battle in the entire war.

Ironically, the sacrifice of the *5th New York* and its sister regiment did not slow down Longstreet's advance any more than a few minutes. The crashing of Hood's muskets, though, did serve to alert Pope and McDowell that something was terribly wrong on their left. This new enemy attack would need to be blunted before the Confederates seized the intersection of the Warrenton Turnpike and the Manassas-Sudley Road and effectively cut off the retreat of all the troops on Dogan Ridge. The best way to prevent this was to occupy Henry House Hill in force, which was exactly where Longstreet was headed. Henry House Hill was at the moment unoccupied, and the only Union force between there and Longstreet's 25,000 men was McLean's brigade. As previously noted, Pope had originally wanted

McLean to be posted on Henry House Hill, but a miscommunication caused McLean to move to Chinn Ridge. This was to be
one of the few Union mistakes in the battle that would turn to
their own benefit.

McDowell at once understood that he needed to try to delay
Longstreet's advance by rushing all the troops he could to aid
McLean on Chinn Ridge. His first reaction was to try to recall
Reynolds' division, which had been ordered to move north from
Chinn Ridge just over an hour earlier. Most of Reynolds'
command was by then already north of the Turnpike. McDow-
ell, however, did manage to intercept Reynolds' rear brigade
(led now by Colonel Martin Hardin after Brigadier General
Conrad Jackson had become sick and left the field) and Kerns'
Pennsylvania battery and turn them back to Chinn Ridge.
Hardin managed to form on a rise on just west of Chinn Ridge
just before the survivors of *Duryee's Zouaves* came rushing up.
He declined to open fire on the Confederates for fear of hitting
his own men, so he directed Kerns' battery to shoot over their
heads. The ploy served its purpose and alerted Hood's veterans
to the arrival of a fresh Yankee line. The Confederates who had
been on Warren's front pulled back to the cover of Young's
Branch and paused to regroup.

Hood's flank regiments, however, did not halt when the
brigade's center pulled back. The 4th Texas on the left of the line
had not yet been seriously engaged, and rushed Hardin's line as
soon as they saw it. Their impetuosity encouraged Hood's
center regiments to resume their attack, and Hardin's men were
soon engaged all along their line. The Confederates soon gained
the advantage when the 5th Texas got into position to deliver a
flanking fire on Hardin's left. Hardin himself fell wounded, and
his brigade began to unravel. Its withdrawal left Kerns' battery
unsupported. The soldiers of the 4th Texas saw this and spontaneously rushed the battery in order to seize its prized guns.
Their fire felled thirty of the battery's horses, rendering the unit
immobile. As the Texans closed, the Union cannoneers fled for
safety. Artillerists had no weapons but their implements and a
few pistols, and so were relatively helpless at close range
fighting. The only Yankee who remained behind was Captain
Mark Kerns himself. The Confederates were astonished to see

him calmly load and fire each gun by himself, a task that usually required a full crew of ten men. In acknowledgment of his gallantry, some of the Texans shouted down their line to hold fire and spare him, but he was felled just before the Confederates made their final rush to seize his guns.

Hood would have done well to stop and reform his men at this point, particularly since they were by now somewhat disordered and had outstripped the units assigned to support them on their left and right. Since there was no cover on the rise where Hardin had been defeated, Hood pushed his command forward to the ravine at the western base of Chinn Ridge. Here he encountered some enfilading fire from the Union guns on Dogan Ridge, so he slid to the woods on his right for shelter. During this movement, the 4th Texas misunderstood its orders and headed in the wrong direction, leaving Hood with only three regiments on western Chinn Ridge. These were too few men to attack McLean's line, so Hood sent for Evans' brigade to come up and support him.

Longstreet was by now aware of three major problems facing his attack: the Union artillery on Dogan Ridge that was poised to bombard his left; the fact that Pope could shift troops from Jackson's front to face him; and the difficulty of coordinating a two mile wide advance by five separate divisions. The third difficulty would have to take care of itself as Longstreet's various commands headed towards Chinn Ridge and Bald Hill on their way to Henry House Hill. Solution of the first two problems would require help from Jackson. Lee had already ordered Jackson to "look out for and protect" Longstreet's attack once it began, but stronger measures were now needed. Soon after Hood moved forward, Lee directed Jackson to "advance and drive off the batteries" on Dogan's Ridge in order to relieve Longstreet's troops and so create a diversion in his favor.

Most of Jackson's troops, however, were in no shape to mount an attack. Six of his eleven brigades had been heavily engaged in the sharp fight with Porter, and every one of them had fought the previous day. He had only three brigades in any shape to mount a counterattack (Early's of Lawton's division, and Archer's and Pender's of Hill's division), and these were not

View of Jackson's position (in the background) as seen from Groveton Village.

enough for the task. What Jackson really needed was an infusion of troops from Longstreet's wing. Wilcox's and Anderson's divisions were nearby, posted on Starke's right, but Anderson was being held in reserve and Jackson never attained full communication with Wilcox's. As a result, Jackson did not move for two key hours, from 1600 to 1800. This inactivity allowed Pope to shift his troops at will to Longstreet's front. Results might well have been quite different if Lee had sent just one of Longstreet's several divisions to Jackson's direct support anytime in the previous 24 hours. Jackson then would have had these or equivalent troops available to conduct the diversionary attack that Lee and Longstreet longed for late on the afternoon of the 30th.

Faced with this disagreeable situation, Longstreet determined to deal with the Federal cannons on Dogan Ridge by advancing all the batteries he could to the best available position. Before long, Major Bushrod Frobel, Hood's chief of artillery, had five batteries drawn up in the open ground northeast of Groveton, supported by Law's brigade of Hood's division. Frobel's twenty guns underwent quite a pounding as they drew much, but not all, of the attention of the stronger Union artillery force on Dogan Ridge.

The dominant Federal artillery on Dogan Ridge now unwittingly gave a favor to Longstreet's attack. When Evans' Brigade moved forward to support Hood's right, its advance covered open ground that was extremely vulnerable to a raking fire from the Union cannons. This fire disordered several of Evans' regiments, but it also compelled them to drift to a woods on their right. As a result, Evans did not attack McLean head on, but was now in a position to strike McLean's vulnerable left flank.

The Confederates, however, were unable to exploit their advantage in numbers to drive back McLean as they had just done Warren and Hardin. Instead of making a unified assault, their regiments attacked one at a time, a common problem in the war when units became detached from their brigades (as occurred in Hood's command) or brigade commanders did not keep control of their troops (Evans' problem this day). McLean's four Ohio regiments, on the other hand, were well drawn up and had a good field of fire as well as the able support of Wiedrich's New York battery.

This unevenly matched contest continued until two of Evans' regiments, the 18th and then the 27th South Carolina, emerged from the woods on McLean's left and turned his line just north of the Chinn house. This maneuver forced the 25th and 73rd Ohio to fall back, so exposing Wiedrich's battery. Wiedrich panicked and mounted up to withdraw in haste, leaving McLean's right wing (55th and 75th Ohio) to hold the hill alone.

McLean chose not to withdraw his two units, but instead fronted left to halt the 17th and 18th South Carolina. He then looked to his left and saw a large body of dark clad troops advancing through the fields south of the Chinn house. He thought that they were Confederates, and commandeered Wiedrich's last two cannons to halt and fire on them. Just then. a staff officer rode up to inform McLean that the body of troops was reinforcements coming to help. This news greatly reassured McLean, who sent orders for Wiedrich's guns to hold their fire. He then "rested easily, thinking reinforcements were coming to take position on my left."

In this McLean could not have been more wrong. The mass of troops approaching the Chinn house was not reinforcements, but was actually Kemper's Confederate division of three fresh brigades. Colonel Eppa Hunton, commander of Kemper's left brigade, determined to wheel his command to the left and strike McLean's left rear. His purpose, though, was thwarted when one of his regimental commanders, Colonel R.C. Allen of the 56th Virginia, refused to alter his line of advance without written orders. By the time that Hunton cleared up the situation, his command had marched over Chinn Ridge and past McLean's position. The honor of driving McLean away would not fall to Hunton, but to Corse's brigade, which was advancing in Kemper's second line.

Colonel M.D. Corse saw the same opportunity to turn McLean's line that Hunton had noted. He was better able to change his line of march, and swung his regiments into position on a line perpendicular to the ridge and to McLean's troops. Corse's 600 yard wide command then moved forward to within 50 yards of the Chinn house, where they were surprised by a volley from the 55th Ohio, which had shifted to face them along the line of a fence in the Chinns' front yard. A sharp fire fight followed, during which McLean's division commander, Brigadier General Robert Schenck, received a wound in his lower right arm that would knock him out of the war.

McLean's outnumbered troops fought on gallantly until they were overwhelmed by Corse's men, who were by then supported by reinforcements from Hood's and Evans' commands. The 55th Ohio "quivered and went to pieces," followed by the rest of the brigade. Feisty Colonel McLean withdrew to the northeast towards Buck Hill, having done a noble job of delaying the Confederate advance. His brief stand had cost his brigade over 400 casualties.

McLean's stand permitted McDowell to rush forward two more brigades to try to block the Confederate advance over Chinn Ridge. By 1700, he had Stiles' and Tower's brigades of Ricketts' division moving to aid McLean. They were joined by the 41st New York of Stahel's brigade and all of Koltes' brigade, which were all the troops that Sigel felt he could spare at the moment. He was too preoccupied with Wilcox's troops in the Groveton Woods on his front to be properly concerned with the crisis developing on his left.

As these 7000 Union troops moved belatedly to McLean's

relief, McDowell rode to nearby Henry House Hill to confer with Pope. Quite astonishingly, Pope queried McDowell whether he thought that he was weakening his line too much by sending so many troops to Chinn Ridge. McDowell replied in quite clear terms that Chinn Ridge was where the battle would be decided. Pope now at last understood the gravity of the situation on his left. He now took on the task of forming a defensive line on Henry House Hill while McDowell endeavored to delay the enemy as long as he could on Chinn Ridge.

McDowell was moving the equivalent of a full division to Chinn Ridge, but these reinforcements went in piecemeal, just like the three previous Union brigades that had been defeated by Longstreet's attack. Tower's brigade arrived first, just when McLean's command was collapsing. The confusion on Chinn Ridge was so great that Tower was uncertain on what line to form his men, facing Corse's attack from the south or Evans' from the west. John Vautier of the *88th Pennsylvania* noted that the enemy fire "came from so many directions that our men were at a loss how to return it effectively."

Tower lacked enough troops to face all the Confederates who were assaulting his position, and his line was soon turned by Corse's men on the eastern slope of the ridge. Lieutenant Colonel Joseph McLean of the *88th Pennsylvania* was mortally wounded, and his regiment and the neighboring *90th Pennsylvania* were pushed back. Their withdrawal exposed Leppien's *5th Maine Battery*, which now became the goal of Corse's attackers.

The fighting now intensified as McDowell sent Stiles' brigade to Tower's support. Stiles arrived just as Tower's line was collapsing, and his units lost most of their cohesion as Towers' troops pulled back through their lines. Stiles might have held against the Confederate troops already on the field, but it was his misfortune to run into a fresh attack by Hunton's and Jenkins' brigades of Kemper's division. The firing by both sides became so intense that neither could see the other's lines through all the smoke. They could only tell where the enemy was by judging the direction of the hostile fire and from occasional glimpses of battleflags rising above the firing lines.

It was at this point that the battle took its most noted casualty, Colonel Fletcher Webster of Stiles' *12th Massachusetts*. Webster

One of the most distinguished casualties at 2nd Bull Run was Colonel Fletcher Webster, son of the noted politician, Daniel Webster. He was mortally wounded during the fighting on Bald Hill on 30 August while in command of the 12th Massachusetts of Ricketts' division.

was the eldest son of the noted politician, Senator Daniel Webster, and owed his commission to this connection much more than to any military experience he possessed. He felt that it was his duty to ride along the line of his regiment and encourage his men by shouting and waving his sword. This he bravely did, in the process offering a clear target to the Confederates; both sides learned early in the war the value of shooting any enemy officer on horseback. It was not long before Webster was struck in the chest by a bullet and knocked from his horse. Two of his aides tried to bear him from the field, only to be forced to leave him between the contending battle lines. Webster ended up being captured after his troops withdrew, and he died just an hour later.

The telling blow against Stiles' brigade came when Jenkins' right advanced over Bald Hill to turn the left of the Union line on Chinn Ridge. McDowell saw the maneuver coming and sent Stiles' *83rd New York* to block it. This regiment, though, was unable to hold its position due to some heavy fire from Stribling's Virginia battery, which had just come into position on Bald Hill. The *83rd* withdrew quickly to Henry House Hill, leaving McDowell's left open to Jenkins' fire. At the same time,

McDowell's left flank was about to be struck by D.R. Jones' fresh Confederate division, which was finally coming up to the fight after a mile long march from the far right of Longstreet's line.

The force of Jones' attack was too much for McDowell's troops to endure. Stiles' *11th Pennsylvania* suffered 240 losses, and Towers' regiments each lost more than fifty per cent. These brave troops eventually had no choice but to fall back as best they could, stopping occasionally to turn and fire.

Ricketts' withdrawal left the fight for Chinn Ridge to a handful of Sigel's regiments. Sigel's first unit to arrive had been the *41st New York* of Stahel's brigade. Colonel Leopold von Gilsa of the *41st* wisely chose to delay attacking until he had some support, which soon appeared in the form of Colonel John Koltes' brigade. Von Gilsa then advanced through the smoke to McDowell's line, from where he saw Leppien's guns standing unmanned some 200 yards distant. He bravely ordered a charge to reach them, and almost made it there. The opposing Confederate fire was simply too strong for one unsupported regiment to face, not to mention the friendly fire he was receiving from some Union troops in his rear. He soon had no choice but to withdraw his now shattered command out of the action.

Von Gilsa's charge and subsequent retreat sparked a Confederate counterattack that struck at Koltes' right flank. The Rebel attack was supported by Richardson's Louisiana battery of the famed Washington Artillery, which boldly dashed past the Chinn house and began forming only 200 yards from Koltes' line. Koltes responded by ordering his *68th New York* to charge the battery. It was the last command he would give, for he was then killed by a Confederate shell that exploded next to his head. None of the men in the *68th* managed to reach Richardson's guns in their charge; many of those who were not shot were simply swallowed up by the converging Confederate lines and taken prisoner.

Koltes' brigade was staggering when Krzyzanowski's brigade of Schurz's division started coming up, the last Union troops to enter the fight on Chinn Ridge. Krzyzanowski was well aware that the best he could do would be to cover the retreat of Koltes' brigade and any other stray Union squads remaining on the ridge. He then withdrew to the northeastern base of the ridge.

Krzyzanowski's withdrawal left the Confederates in command of Chinn Ridge, a position they needed as a base for their intended assault on Henry House Hill. All things considered, the seven Union brigades that were sacrificed on Chinn Ridge had not done a bad job, particularly in view of the fact that they were committed piecemeal, and in most cases were overwhelmed one by one. Their efforts had disorganized Hood's and Kemper's Confederate divisions, but more importantly had succeeded at delaying Longstreet's attack for ninety minutes, leaving just one hour of precious daylight before dark. This ninety minutes' delay also gave Pope time to draw up a new defensive line on Henry House Hill. One can only wonder how the battle might have gone had Reynolds' entire division been left on Chinn Ridge earlier in the afternoon. His veteran troops, supported by Warren's and McLean's brigades and later by Ricketts' division and whatever troops Sigel could spare, might well have succeeded at holding Chinn Ridge until close to dark. Such a stand might well have enabled Pope to hold the field after dark, or at least to withdraw under less pressure.

By 1800, it was clear to Pope that the battle was lost. His every effort for two days had failed to dislodge Jackson's line, and now his left was utterly defeated. The best he could do now would be to save his army from total destruction. To accomplish this, he would need to hold on to Henry House Hill, which dominated the Warrenton Turnpike and his withdrawal route to Centreville, and keep the victorious Confederates at bay until dark.

Pope had been hard at work establishing his last ditch line on Henry House Hill since his meeting with McDowell at 1630. For the next ninety minutes, he labored furiously to gather all the available troops he could on Henry House Hill, which initially had just one regiment for its defense. The only troops available for this job had to be stripped from Jackson's front, and few could be spared even there if Jackson began a counterattack. This was a risk that Pope had to take. It was to his good fortune that Stonewall did not initiate a counterattack at this critical hour.

The first troops that Pope called to Henry House Hill were the two brigades of Ricketts' division that had remained on his right

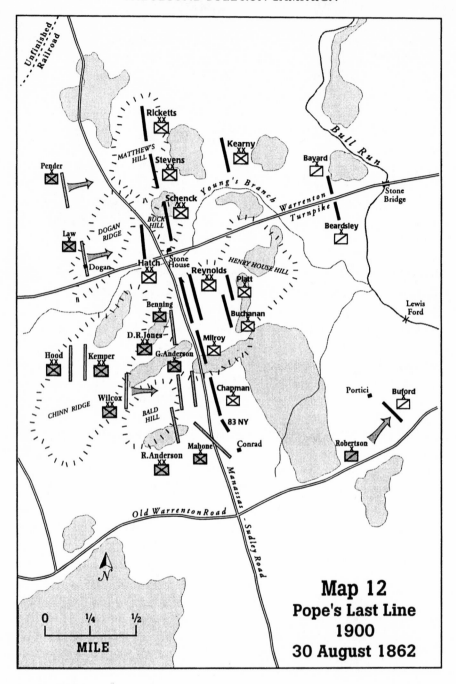

Map 12
Pope's Last Line
1900
30 August 1862

wing behind Dogan Ridge. Colonel Strother of Pope's staff carried the order to Heintzelman, commander on the right, but Heintzelman refused to release the two brigades due to fear of an attack by Jackson. He instead suggested that Strother take Reynolds' two remaining brigades, which had been sitting idly by since they had been called forward from Chinn Ridge two hours earlier. Strother rode quickly to Reynolds, who gladly agreed to go. His march south was a difficult one due to all the battered Union troops that were falling back from Chinn Ridge. It was an ironic situation, since McDowell should never have withdrawn Reynolds' division from Chinn Ridge in the first place, as already discussed.

Pope formed Reynolds' men along the Manassas-Sudley Road, facing west in the direction of the Warrenton Turnpike. Shortly after 1700, he located another stray brigade and placed it a slight distance to Reynolds' left. This unit was Chapman's brigade of *United States Regulars* from Sykes' division. As previously described, Sykes' men had not been committed to Porter's grand assault on Jackson's lines. Consequently, they spent all day standing by on the Union right. Late in the afternoon, Chapman decided that it was time for supper, and pulled his brigade out of position in order to head for the rear and cook some food. Pope saw the command marching rearward near the Robinson house, and was furious to find out where they were headed. He promptly sent them back to the field to his critical new line on the edge of Henry House Hill.

By 1730 Pope had also located a couple other stray units to help buttress his line. When the *83rd New York* drifted back from its unsuccessful effort to block the advance of Jenkins' brigade, it was placed on Chapman's left. Pope then filled a gap in the center of his line with Milroy's brigade of Sigel's corps, which had been doing provost duty along the Warrenton Turnpike because of its heavy casualties the previous day. Pope's half mile long line was supported by Buchanan's brigade of *United States Regulars*, which Pope at length managed to pry loose from his right wing, and also by Piatt's small brigade from Sturgis' *Reserve Division*. Three batteries helped buttress the line, and more reinforcements, notably Ferrero's brigade of Reno's division, were on the way.

Some of McClellan's troops awaiting transport near the railroad roundhouse at Alexandria. Limited trains and operational snafus critically delayed reinforcements from reaching Pope.

Pope now felt strong enough about the rear guard he had established on Henry House Hill, to turn command of the position over to McDowell and arrange for the withdrawal of the army to Centreville. At 1750 he directed his commanders on the right wing to begin pulling back to Matthew's and Buck Hills, on a line with the forces gathered on the edge of Henry House Hill. He then ordered Banks, who had spent the entire battle at Bristoe Station guarding the army's new supply base that had been set up there after Jackson burned the one at Manassas Junction, to "destroy all public property at Bristoe and fall back upon Centreville at once." Ironically, Franklin's *VI Corps* was finally arriving at that moment from Alexandria. Had Franklin arrived even 24 hours earlier, Pope would have been able to use his men to support Porter's assault on the 30th, or possibly to try to turn Jackson's left near Sudley Springs, either of which would surely have changed the course of the battle. But such was not to be. All that Pope could do for the moment was

238

to direct Franklin to occupy the strong points at Centreville and "hold them to the last extremity."

Lee was not content to rest on the victory his troops had won so far, but was determined to drive Pope's army from the field and destroy it if he could. He did not know that Pope was planning to abandon the field, and there was always the possibility that the enemy might receive heavy reinforcements from McClellan and renew the battle on the morrow. Lee also felt that he needed to push his advantage while he held it, in order to cause all the damage that he could to Pope's army and thereby maintain the strategic initiative in the theater in the weeks following the battle.

Lee still had three divisions that had not yet been engaged heavily in the fighting, and relied on them to complete the day's success. D.R. Jones' command of three brigades had helped mop up the victory on Chinn Ridge and would spearhead the attack on Henry House Hill since he was already in position nearby. Jones' right would be supported by Anderson's division of three brigades, which had been held in reserve until this point. Anderson, though, had two miles to cover in order to get into position to attack, and he did not begin moving forward until 1650. Jones' left was to be supported by Wilcox's division of three brigades, which had spent most of the day in Groveton Woods. However, Wilcox misunderstood his orders, and as a result sent only his old brigade, not his entire division, to aid Jones. These factors meant that Jones would have to begin the attack on Henry House Hill all by himself.

Jones initially directed his attack not at Henry House Hill, but at the important crossroads near the Stone House, which he hoped to capture in order to cut off the retreat of Pope's right wing. He sent Benning's Georgia brigade northeastward from Chinn Ridge towards this goal, only to see it stopped in its tracks by a sudden counterattack by Meade's brigade of Reynolds' division. Meade had seen Benning's advance, and decided to seize a momentary tactical advantage by striking at Benning's exposed right flank as the Georgians moved by his position. His plan worked excellently. Benning had to give up on his push for the crossroads, and had all that he could do just to swing his line 45 degrees to the right in order to meet Meade's

The Stone House, located just northeast of the intersection of the War-
renton Turnpike and Sudley Road, served as a hospital during both
battles of Bull Run.

attack. This was a difficult enough maneuver on a flat parade
ground. When executed on uneven wooded ground under
heavy enemy fire, gaps quickly began to develop. As a result,
Benning's regiments turned and met Meade's line one by one.
and so suffered badly as they individually received the concentrated fire of much of McDowell's line. Milroy, who was posted
on Meade's left, noted, "The way the reble [sic] column tumbled
and melted away was most beautiful and cheering." Jones'
attack was definitely not off to a good start.

A few minutes later, G.T. Anderson's brigade entered the fight
and began to take some of the pressure off Benning. Anderson
had been following Benning's diagonal march towards the
Stone House crossroads, and then swung to the right in order to
meet the Union line when Meade opened fire. His approach
brought him face to face with Milroy's and Chapman's troops on
McDowell's center and left. Anderson realized that he did not

have enough strength to enable him to assault the Union line, so he allowed his men to take cover some 50 yards short of the Manassas-Sudley Road that marked the enemy's front line. His arrival encouraged Benning's men to renew their attack, and they advanced again to within 80 yards of Meade's line.

While Jones kept McDowell's front occupied, fresh Confederate forces were moving against the weakest point in the Union line, its unanchored left flank. The first Southern unit to arrive there was Captain B.F. Eshleman's battery of the Washington (Louisiana) Artillery. Eshleman had been unengaged on Longstreet's far right, and was anxious to get his moment of glory. This he did by moving forward to the Conrad house, some 300 yards directly to the left rear of McDowell's far left regiment, the *83rd New York*. Eshleman's unexpected fire raked the New Yorkers' line and most of Chapman's, unsteadying them for the blow that was to follow.

Longstreet's coup de grace was now delivered by R.H. Anderson's division, which at length had passed over Bald Hill and was now ready to enter the action. R.H. Anderson sent his lead brigade, Wright's, to support G.T. Anderson's hard pressed command. This left his primary blow to Mahone's Virginia brigade, which was following Wright. Mahone formed on the right of Wright and G.T. Anderson, and outflanked McDowell's line so much that he was able to swing most of his line to a position squarely on the left flank of the *83rd New York*. The New Yorkers promptly withdrew in confusion after hardly firing a shot, and their retreat threw the left of Chapman's line into considerable disorder.

Chapman retracted his left in order to meet this threat, and held Mahone's troops back for about ten minutes before a new crisis developed to his right. Here the 15th Georgia of Benning's brigade managed to cross the Manassas-Sudley Road and break into Milroy's line. The 15th's success encouraged the rest of Benning's command to press their attack even more. Milroy was beside himself, and yelled what encouragement he could while standing atop a dead horse. He then ran to McDowell for help, crying out, "For God's sake, general, send a few regiments into these woods; my poor men are being cut to pieces." For some reason, McDowell did not respond to Milroy's urgent plea until he received a confirming report from Meade. He then directed Buchanan to send three regiments from Reynolds' second line to help Milroy.

McDowell's delay in sending Milroy aid had been critical. Buchanan's three regiments reached Milroy's line just when Chapman was being forced to yield to Mahone's flanking fire. Buchanan saw how desperate the situation was, and made only a brief effort to support Milroy. He felt that the best he could do would be to fall back to the area of the Henry House.

The Confederates now held the upper hand on Henry House Hill, but they did not understand the situation fully and failed to press their advantage. Even though McDowell's left was in shambles, Reynolds refused to pull back on the right. Instead, his line was reinforced by the *3rd* and *4th United States* of Buchanan's brigade and the *86th New York* from Piatt's command. These fresh troops drove Benning's 15th Georgia back from its foothold in Milroy's line, and then forced Benning's entire brigade to fall back. Benning's withdrawal put more pressure on G.T. Anderson's men, who were almost worn out by their hour of heavy fighting. G.T. Anderson had all that he could do just to hold his position, and could not consider resuming his attack. This is where the absence of Wilcox's full division played a key factor. Had Wilcox's three brigades been present to support Benning, Jones might have been able to break McDowell's right. As affairs developed, Wilcox's old brigade was wandering about in Jones' rear, and his other two brigades remained unengaged to the north of the Warrenton Turnpike.

Despite the repulse of Jones' attack, R.H. Anderson still had sufficient troops to be able to continue to press the Confederate advantage. Mahone's brigade, supported now by Armistead's, was squarely on Milroy's right flank, and was well positioned to drive the Yankees off of the hill and even cause trouble for Pope's remaining troops on the north side of the Warrenton Turnpike. Anderson, though, did not push his attack vigorously. He was probably hesitant to do so because he had no reserves (here again, Wilcox's absence was key), and because it was beginning to get dark. He was not eager to push forward unsupported into the midst of the Union army, and neither he nor Longstreet were nearby to give him instructions on what to do.

As a result, R.H. Anderson contented himself with clearing McDowell's remaining troops from Henry House Hill. The fighting there lasted another half-hour, and would have gone on still longer if Reynolds had not misunderstood one of McDowell's orders and left the field at 1900. His departure astonished Buchanan and Milroy, who were luckily reinforced at the same time by Ferrero's small brigade from Reno's division. Ferrero formed his three regiments and a battery on the crest of the hill, and served as a covering force in order to assist Milroy and Buchanan to disengage and fall back.

It was by now dark. Ferrero ordered his men to lie down and hold their fire so as not to reveal their position, and the Confederates crept forward slowly for fear of an ambush. This is where the time gained by McDowell's stand on Chinn Ridge proved so critical. The Confederates had still more fresh troops to commit to the fight: Drayton's brigade of Jones' division was now up, and Wilcox's brigade finally found its way to the front. But it was simply too late and too dark for them to be put to good use.

Longstreet, who now finally came forward to take charge of the situation, decided now to launch one last attack. It was to be directed by Brigadier General Robert Toombs, who had been under arrest since 18 August for his failure to hold Raccoon Ford during the opening stage of the campaign. Toombs' arrival delighted the Georgians of Drayton's brigade, whom he promptly led straight up Henry House Hill. Their advance ran squarely into Ferrero's concealed line. The Federals blasted Toombs' charge to pieces in only a few minutes. One of the Yankees later complained, "The men had hardly got well warmed up before the firing was stopped." Drayton's men recoiled, and then attempted to flank Ferrero's left. Their attack caused heavy casualties in the *51st New York*, but the Yankees held and forced Drayton back.

The fighting on Henry House Hill was now over. Jeb Stuart, who just then arrived on the front, was eager to conduct a pursuit, just as he had done after the victory of First Bull Run a year earlier on these same fields, but he was prevented by the darkness and a lack of available troops.

Cavalry Action

While this drama was being played out on Chinn Ridge and Henry House Hill, another significant confrontation was occurring on the far southern edge of the battlefield. As already discussed, Pope at 1300 had sent Buford to the south to investigate Reynolds' claim that the Confederates were turning the Union left. Buford dutifully took his four regiments (his *5th New York* was on detached duty at army headquarters, but he had Beardsley's *4th New York* with him in its stead) to the left and began patrolling the old Warrenton and Alexandria Road. What he discovered or reported to Pope is not recorded, since Buford did not file a report on this stage of the campaign. We do know that Buford remained to patrol this flank, and that he withdrew at the start of Longstreet's attack to the Francis Lewis house, "Portici," located about one mile southeast of Henry House Hill, where he could guard the approaches to Lewis Ford on Bull Run.

Buford reached Portici just minutes ahead of Robertson's Confederate cavalry brigade. Robertson had been sent out by Stuart to cover Longstreet's right during the latter's advance, and afterwards to attempt to intercept the Yankees' retreat to Centreville "if possible." Robertson avoided direct contact with Buford until the height of Longstreet's attack, when he decided to take advantage of Buford's withdrawal to rush forward and seize Lewis' Ford. Little did he know that this was exactly the position that Buford had pulled back to defend.

Buford barely had time to draw up his troops before Robertson's men came up. He was ready for a fight, and formed his units in column by regiment, with the *1st Michigan* in front, backed by the *4th New York*, *1st West Virginia*, and then the *1st Vermont*. Robertson did not expect the Yankees to put up much of a fight, especially since the Confederate horsemen disdained their Yankee counterparts at this stage of the war. He directed Colonel T.T. Munford to charge and disperse Buford's troops, and Munford sent forward the lead squadron of his 2nd Virginia, under the command of Lieutenant Colonel J.W. Watts. Watts rode forward confidently and was astonished to see Buford's entire brigade drawn up and ready to fight.

Watts was forced to halt his advance, and sent for the rest of his regiment to come up and support him in a hurry. Buford saw the Confederates hesitate and boldly sent his front two regiments forward to the charge. Munford accepted the challenge and ordered the entire 2nd Virginia to meet the 1st Michigan at full gallop. When the opposing line collided, "men and horses went down and rolled over in the dust." The fight quickly turned in Buford's favor when the 5th New York joined the fray. The 2nd Virginia was forced to retire, the first time in the war that Stuart's vaunted cavalry were defeated in mounted combat.

Robertson now brought up the rest of his brigade and prepared to make a massive counter charge. For some reason, Buford hesitated to reinforce his front two regiments, and Robertson's fresh 12th and 7th Virginia regiments easily overran Buford's winded and slightly disorganized 1st Michigan and 4th New York. The retreating Union troopers then rushed Buford's rear two regiments, which were still holding their original position. They were soon overwhelmed, and Buford had no choice but to retire across Lewis Ford.

Robertson's success left him an open route to the Warrenton Turnpike, which was the lifeline of the defeated Union army. Had he pushed forward with all five of his regiments, he surely would have caused significant distress to Pope's command. This was the classic opportunity that all cavalrymen dreamed of exploiting. But Buford's aggressiveness at Portici had made Robertson cautious. He did not bring his last two fresh regiments into action, but instead continued to pursue Buford with his 7th and 12th Virginia regiments, which were by now winded and more than slightly disorganized from their clash with Buford's front line. For some reason, the 7th went only a short distance, leaving the 12th to carry on the pursuit alone. The 12th advanced cautiously, probably out of fear of another surprise encounter like Munford had just experienced. The regiment managed to reach the vicinity of the Warrenton Turnpike, but was turned back by the remnants of Buford's brigade and the coming of darkness. Thus the Confederates lost a golden opportunity to cut off Pope's retreat route and make their victory even more complete.

The Union Withdrawal

The battle on the Union right concluded with much less drama. As already noted, Jackson had hesitated to support Longstreet's attack as Lee instructed, and so allowed Pope time to shift troops from his right to his now imperiled left. It was not until about 1730 that Pope realized that his right was in danger of being cut off. For this reason he sent orders at 1750 for Heintzelman and Porter to begin withdrawing to Centreville.

Most of the pressure on Pope's right before its withdrawal came not from Jackson's troops, but from Law's brigade of Hood's division. As previously described, Law was supposed to have advanced on Hood's left when Longstreet's attack began at 1600. Law, though, at once lost contact with Hood and spent the next 90 minutes working his way forward on the north side of the Warrenton Turnpike towards the Union troops deployed near the Dogan house. By 1730 Law had reached the course of Young's Branch at the base of Dogan Ridge, and was ready to rush some batteries on Sigel's left that had been causing him trouble throughout his advance.

As Law's troops moved to the attack, the commander of his 11th Mississippi misunderstood his orders and began heading towards Chinn Ridge instead. Lieutenant Colonel Edward Wratislaw of Stahel's *45th New York*, who was supporting Sigel's guns, saw the confusion in Law's advance and elected to conduct a local counterattack in order to spoil the Confederate attack. This proved to be a terrible mistake. Wratislaw had not seen half of Law's brigade because it was concealed in a pine grove, and the Confederate fire decimated the *45th* in only a few moments. The Yankee force promptly "retreated faster than they came."

Law's troops followed up their success by pursuing the *45th New York* to the Dogan orchard, where they unexpectedly ran into a counterattack by the remnants of the *2nd* and *7th Wisconsin* regiments of Gibbon's brigade. Gibbon had seen the Confederates coming, and was still full of fight despite the heavy losses that his units had sustained at Groveton two days earlier. His bold attack persuaded Law to pull back and disengage. Sigel used the respite to pull his troops back to Buck Hill, as ordered by Pope. The movement was covered by Doubleday's brigade and Dilger's Ohio battery.

The Union line on the northern end of Dogan Ridge had a much more difficult time pulling back. Here Stevens and Ricketts received their orders to withdraw at about 1800, the exact moment that Jackson began the belated advance that had been ordered by Lee some two hours earlier. Jackson led his attack with two of Hill's brigades (Archer's and Pender's) on the left and two of Longstreet's (Pryor's and Featherston's orphaned brigades of Wilcox's division) on the right. Stonewall's entire line was to follow behind, with Hill on the left, Starke on the right, and Lawton in the center.

Ricketts' division was already pulling back when Archer's brigade struck Duryee's exposed right flank at the far northern end of Dogan Ridge. Duryee's *104th* and *105th New York* broke up and retreated, exposing a long row of now unsupported Yankee batteries to the Confederate attack. Featherston's Mississippians grabbed three guns of Thompson's battery, and Pender's Tarheels got two of McGilvery's. Archer's brigade captured four of Matthews' guns, and Durell's battery had to leave one of its pieces behind. The loss of these ten guns was embarrassing, but ultimately not significant to the outcome of the battle beyond the fact that they distracted Jackson's advancing troops long enough to enable most of Pope's right wing to withdraw without further opposition to the hill where the Carter mansion ("Pittsylvania") was located. The only pressure felt during this stage of the withdrawal came from some of Fitz Lee's cavalry, who closely pursued Poe's brigade on the far Union right until Poe chased them off with his *2nd Michigan*. By 1900 the Union right was solidly formed from Henry House Hill north to Poplar Ford on Bull Run. The Yankee troops were mostly demoralized and their higher command structure was in shambles, but there were enough of them to deter any further attack by Jackson's men in the growing darkness.

The battle, then, was over by 2000 except for occasional flareups on the skirmish lines. Pope's line was stabilized along a one mile front, its flanks protected by Bull Run and the cover of darkness. Most significantly, his withdrawal route to Centreville was secure. Pope certainly had the choice of holding the field and bringing up Franklin's troops to renew the fight. In fact, this option was strongly supported by Sigel and several other of his lieutenants. But Pope was by now a defeated man, and at 2000 he ordered a general retreat. It was the same order that he could have given 24 hours earlier at much less cost.

Pope's dispirited troops withdrew wearily over the next three hours. Overturned wagons and discarded gear littered the way, and the men "marched in silence on each side of the road, without order." Some called out to try to find their commands or get food, but most just trudged resignedly on, disgusted to have undergone yet another defeat near the banks of Bull Run. The situation certainly could have been much worse, especially if Robertson's Confederate cavalry had succeeded at breaking through and holding a section of the Warrenton Turnpike. The Confederates only challenged the Union retreat at two points, against Ferrero's rearguard on Henry House Hill, and near Pittsylvania, where Archer briefly encountered Thoburn's brigade of Ricketts' division.

Pope's army was safely across Bull Run by 2300, and then stumbled into Franklin's lines near Centreville in the early hours of 31 August. Pope, who had reached Centreville ahead of his troops, had to face the inevitable, and at 2145 wrote to Halleck to explain the situation. He claimed to have met a superior force of the enemy, who forced him to withdraw to Centreville. His army, he stated, was not lost, and he had inflicted crippling losses on the enemy. The withdrawal had been made "in perfect order and without loss." His troops, he claimed, were "in good heart," and he would endeavor to hold his own at Centreville. His accomplishments that day, he thought, entitled the army "to the gratitude of the country." Lee, on the other hand, saw the situation more clearly than Pope. He telegraphed Jefferson Davis at 1100 to report, "The army achieved today on the plains of Manassas a signal victory over the combined forces of McClellan and Pope."

The battle's casualties cost Pope almost 15,000 of his 70,000 men engaged, a little over twenty per cent of his force. This was

Pope's retreat across the Stone Bridge over Bull Run was dispirited but not as frantic as the Union retreat across the same span following their defeat at 1st Bull Run a year earlier.

some fifty per cent higher than Lee's loss of around 9500 men out of 55,000 engaged (seventeen per cent losses). The higher number of Union casualties, of course, was due to Pope's numerous disjointed attacks on Jackson's line for two days, and his unorganized effort to defend Chinn Ridge on the afternoon of the 30th. Lee would have been able to inflict many more Union casualties had darkness not prohibited him from exploiting his victory at the end of the fight. Curiously, there was only one general officer among the casualty lists on each side Confederate Brigadier General Charles W. Field was wounded, as was Union General Robert C. Schenck), despite the high number of losses in what was until then the bloodiest battle of the war.

The Last Surviving Union Combat Soldier

The last surviving Union soldier of the nearly 3,000,000 who served in blue from 1861-1865 was Albert Woolson of Minnesota, who died in 1956 at the age of 109. Woolson had served as a musician in the closing months of the war, and probably never fired a shot in combat. The last surviving Union combat soldier was James Albert Hard, who died in 1953 at the age of 111. Hard was a foot soldier in the *32nd New York* and fought at both battles of First and Second Bull Run.

Hard was born on 15 July 1841 and was 19 years old when he enlisted as a private in the *32nd New York* on 16 April 1861 in the rush of patriotic fervor that followed the firing on First Sumter a few days earlier. He was mustered for two years service on 31 May, and spent his entire military career in the Virginia theater.

Hard's regiment went to Virginia in June, and was drilled for a month at Alexandria before it took the field in Davies' brigade to fight at First Bull Run under McDowell. Miles' division, to which Davies' brigade was attached, received the task of guarding Centreville while the rest of the army proceeded to engage the enemy. Hard's *32nd New York* was only briefly engaged late in the day, when it helped repulse Jones' Confederate brigade at about 1600 when the latter crossed Bull Run at McLean's Ford. Jones' sharp repulse was one of the few unqualified Union successes of the day.

Hard fought through McClellan's Peninsula Campaign the next spring as a member of Newton's brigade of Franklin's *VI Corps*. Franklin's command was transferred to Alexandria too late to contribute much to Pope's Second Bull Run campaign, but it did arrive in time to help stabilize the Union lines on the evening of the second day of the battle. Slocum's division, including the *32nd New York*, passed through Centreville and deployed on the high ground west of Cub Run in order to help settle the fugitives of Pope's retiring command and direct them to Centreville.

Hard then marched with his regiment to Antietam, where he was not harmed in the war's bloodiest day of combat. He later became ill and was absent from his unit from 29 October 1862 until the end of the year, thereby missing the bloody battle of Fredericksburg. His last fights were at Second Fredericksburg and Salem Church during the Chancellorsville campaign, where he was again unscathed.

Private James A. Hard was mustered out of service on 9 June 1863 upon the completion of his two year enlistment. Afterwards he worked variously as a civilian construction boss for the army, a railroader, a contractor, and a veterans' pension attorney. It is amazing that he lived for 98 years after his muster out before he died on 12 March 1953 as the last surviving Union combat soldier.

Oldest Surviving Soldiers

War	Soldier	Died	Age
Revolution	Daniel F. Bakerman	1869	109 yrs. 2 mos.
War of 1812	Hiram Crook	1905	105 yrs.
Mexican War	Owen T. Edgar	1929	98 yrs. 2 mos.
Civil War (US)	Albert H. Woolson	2 Aug 1956	109 yrs. 5 mos. 22 d.
Civil War (CS)	Walter W. Williams	19 Dec 1959	117 yrs. 1 mo. 5 d.

CHAPTER X

Chantilly and After

Sunday, 31 August, dawned gray and rainy, a perfect day to match the dreary mood of Pope's defeated troops, who had slept where they dropped when they reached Centreville during the night. Pope's first task was to try to get his jumbled commands consolidated again, since most had become dispersed by the previous twelve hours' unfortunate events "like a deck of dropped cards." To aid the troops in returning to their units, directional placards were set up, which helped accomplish the task surprisingly well.

Pope himself was justifiably despondent, even to the point of doubting his troops' ability to resist any further enemy attacks. He was not even sure what step to take next, whether to attack with McClellan's reinforcements, to stay where he was and wait for Lee to attack him, or to pull back to Washington. To help resolve his dilemma, he called in several of his senior officers for a conference. The list of those invited (Reynolds, Heintzelman, Franklin, Porter, Sumner) is as significant for those who came as for those who were not summoned (Sigel, Banks, McDowell, Reno). When asked, each commander gave the same response: an offensive was unthinkable, and the army's position was too strong for Lee to attack. Because of the strong possibility that Lee might try to move around the army's right again, all the officers consulted recommended a withdrawal to Washington.

Pope, however, declined to heed their advice. He had appealed to Halleck for instructions, and during the meeting received the following encouraging note which his superior had

Centreville in 1862. Pope formed his army here briefly for two days before withdrawing to Washington late on 2 September.

sent at 1100 that day: "My Dear General: You have done nobly. Don't yield another inch if you can avoid it. All reserves are being sent forward...Can't you renew the attack?...I am doing all in my power for you and your noble army. God bless you and it."

Halleck's telegram buoyed Pope's spirits so much that he resolved to remain at Centreville after all. He announced to his gathered commanders that Halleck had "ordered" him to stay, and that he "was glad of it." All in attendance were astounded, and felt that Halleck must have been misinformed about the army's situation and condition. In fact, Halleck's decision may have been motivated primarily by political considerations, out of the belief that the campaign could not be considered a failure if Pope remained in the field to continue it.

A lesser commander than Lee might have been content to hold the battlefield and bask in what indeed had been a brilliant

The town of Fairfax Court House was thrown into confusion by Pope's retreat and the nearby fight at Chantilly on 1 September. It was occupied by J.E.B. Stuart's troopers late the next day after the last Yankees passed through.

victory. Lee's army had suffered a serious number of casualties, and its battered units could certainly have used a day to rest and reorganize. But Lee was not to be content to let the defeated Union army slip away without further interference. He knew that a direct assault on Centreville was out of the question, as Pope's council of war had already opined. More promising was a flank march around Pope's right to the Fairfax area, the exact maneuver that Lee had been on the verge of beginning when Porter attacked at 1500 the previous afternoon. If the plan worked well, Pope might be made to panic, so exposing the Union army to defeat in detail. If it failed or miscarried, Lee still had the option of falling back to Loudoun County or the protective barrier of the Bull Run Mountains.

Jackson agreed to carry out Lee's flanking march as planned, and put his divisions in motion at about 1200. The rain was coming down even harder when Jackson's column crossed Bull Run and began heading north to Old Gum Springs, five miles distant. At that point, A.P. Hill, who led the column, turned right and marched another three miles (some of it after dark) before encamping near Pleasant Valley Church on the Little River Turnpike. Meanwhile, Stuart's two cavalry brigades moved ahead of Hill's infantry and rode all the way to Germantown, less than two miles northwest of Fairfax. There they engaged some of Franklin's *VI Corps* troops before withdrawing for the night.

Pope, of course, was totally ignorant of Jackson's march, even though Stuart's probe at Germantown should have suggested to him that something untoward was in progress. The arrival of Sumner's corps raised his strength to 62,000, and he promised Halleck that he would resume the offensive in a day or two. Many of Pope's officers and line troops, however, quietly preferred not to fight another battle under the command of John Pope. Porter wrote McClellan that he expected "to hear hourly of our rear being cut and our supplies and trains at Fairfax Station being destroyed." Pope in return felt this lack of confidence personally, and began to send notes to Halleck that questioned the allegiance of some of his subordinates, who had "no heart" and "every disposition to hang back." He was clearly looking for scapegoats for his defeat, even while his army was still in the field facing the enemy.

Jackson's march on the next day (1 September) brought him to Chantilly Crossroads, where he decided to wait for Longstreet, whose column was ten miles behind, to come up. Lee had instructed Stonewall not to engage the enemy unless he was certain that he could secure a victory. Contact with various Union probes during the morning persuaded Jackson that he probably did not have the element of surprise on his side any longer, so he decided to await Longstreet's arrival at Chantilly, which was four miles short of Germantown and about six miles from Fairfax.

By 1100 Pope had received sufficient intelligence reports to convince him that Jackson was again on the move around the

Federal right. He had already discussed this possible scenario with Halleck, and was under orders to respond by pulling back and attacking the enemy flanking column vigorously. If a "decisive victory" could not be attained, Pope was to pull back gradually all the way to Annandale or Alexandria. Pope accordingly determined to send about half his command to Germantown in order to shield Fairfax while he developed the situation on his immediate right.

In order to give his troops more time to reach Germantown and form there, Pope at 1300 sent Stevens' IX Corps (Reno was sick and temporarily replaced by Stevens) to occupy the Little River Turnpike northwest of Germantown. From there he was to locate and then delay Jackson's advance. Pope then sent about one third of his army eastward on the Warrenton Turnpike at 1500. He kept the remainder of his force (about half of his army) at Centreville for the moment, either out of respect for Halleck's orders to hold the place, or for the purpose of falling on Jackson's flank and rear once the Confederate advance was halted near Germantown.

Shortly after 1200 Jackson learned that Longstreet's advance guard was only two hours' march distant, so he began reforming his men and had them on the road by 1400. It took him about two hours of fitful marching to reach Ox Hill, an otherwise insignificant crossroads where West Ox Road met the Little River Turnpike about two miles from Germantown. Jackson's advance was so slow because one of Stuart's brigade commanders, Beverly Robertson, had misunderstood his orders from Stuart and had remained at Chantilly Crossroads, thereby depriving Jackson's column of a guard to its right flank. As a result, Jackson had to march "at a very slow pace with skirmishers 200 yards to the right."

Jackson was aware that Federal forces of unknown size were east of Ox Hill, where they were being held in check by Fitz Lee's cavalry, which had withdrawn from Germantown at about 0930 in order to await Jackson's advance near Ox Hill. What concerned Jackson more, though, was the newly detected presence of another Union force approaching Ox Hill from the south. In response, Jackson ordered Hill to send two brigades to face

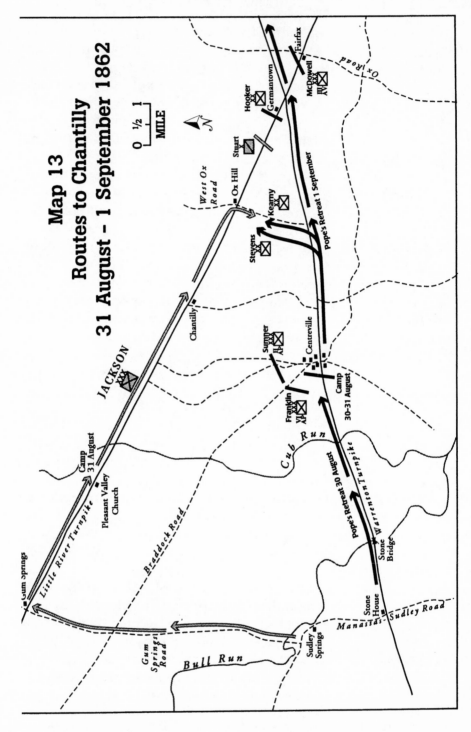

Map 13
Routes to Chantilly
31 August – 1 September 1862

0 ½ 1
MILE

this new threat, while he held the rest of his wing back to await Longstreet's arrival.

The Union troops on Jackson's southern flank were the lead elements of Stevens' corps. As already noted, Stevens had marched out of Centreville at 1300 with the goal of intercepting Jackson somewhere west of Germantown. At 1500 Pope sent Heintzelman's corps to follow and assist Stevens, but apparently neglected to let Stevens know this. Meanwhile, Stevens managed to get lost, and ended up approaching Ox Hill from the southwest. Heintzelman was uncertain where Stevens had disappeared to, and pushed his men eastward on the Warrenton Turnpike in search of the *IX Corps*.

Stevens approached Ox Hill by advancing eastward along a section of the same unfinished railroad line that Jackson's men had just defended for two days near Sudley Ford, some nine miles to the west. Stevens turned northward just before reaching the Ox Road at 1600 and formed his brigades into line near the southern edge of the Reid cornfield, an open area about one-quarter mile south of the Little River Turnpike that would serve as the main stage for the coming fight. His intention was to pitch into Jackson's column and deflect Stonewall's advance, as ordered by Pope. Reno, though, did not much care for this plan when he arrived at about 1630 with Ferrero's brigade. However, he was unable to assume active command because he was still sick, and so left tactical command of the field to Stevens. Reno then moved with Ferrero's brigade into a woods east of the Reid cornfield for the purpose of supporting Stevens' attack.

It was Stevens' command that Jackson saw when he directed Hill to send two brigades at the right at about 1600. Hill dutifully deployed Branch's and Field's brigades as ordered, and by 1630 it was clear that the Federals intended to attack in spite of a darkening cloud that threatened a thunder storm. In response Jackson began to deploy his entire command. Hill's entire division was sent to join Branch and Field in the woods at the northern end of the Reid cornfield. Lawton's brigades were drawn up on Hill's left, astride the Ox Road, and Starke was positioned on an arc from Lawton's left to the Little River Turnpike.

Stevens had little idea about the size of the Confederate force

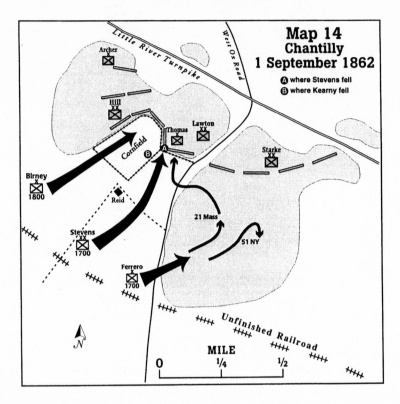

Map 14
Chantilly
1 September 1862
Ⓐ where Stevens fell
Ⓑ where Kearny fell

he was engaging when he led off his attack at about 1430. He sent the *28th Massachusetts* and *79th New York* into action first, and they were soon stalled by the unexpected severity of the Confederates' fire. To make matters worse, several of Stevens' other regiments managed to get entangled or lose their way as they were being brought up to the battle line. In order to spur his men on, Stevens bravely went to the front line and grabbed the flag of the *79th New York*, which he had once commanded. This was not a wise move, since the unit had already lost five color bearers. Stevens waved the flag in front of the unit and called its men forward to the attack. The *79th's* Highlanders responded to his call and charged behind Stevens' lead all the way to the fence at the northern edge of the Reid cornfield. There Stevens fell dead, struck by a bullet to the brain.

At the height of Stevens' attack, lightning began to flash and sheets of rain began pouring from the heavens. The downpour cut visibility to just 20 yards, enabling the *79th* to penetrate and

Isaac Stevens of the **IX Corps** *was one of two Union major generals killed in the short fight at Chantilly on 1 September 1862.*

break through the line of Hays' Louisiana brigade. This same rain storm, however, caused such confusion in the New Yorkers' ranks that they were unable to exploit their success, particularly since Stevens was no longer alive to lead them.

Meanwhile, the rest of Stevens' division pushed forward with moderate success through the heavy rain. On the left, Christ's brigade drove Branch back, and in the center Farnsworth's *28th Massachusetts*, supported by Leasure's brigade, managed to catch Gregg's and Thomas' Confederate brigades in the awkward position of exchanging places. This Union advantage would also be only a temporary one. By 1720 the Confederates were beginning to use their superior numbers to good advantage. Ten minutes later Stevens' soaked regiments were in retreat. The situation was even worse to the east of the Ox Road, where Ferraro's *21st Massachusetts* stumbled through the woods and rain until it literally ran into Trimble's entire Confederate brigade. The ensuing sharp conflict cost the *21st* 100 killed and wounded plus another 20 captured, including the unit's commander.

The battle took on a new phase shortly after 1730 when the lead elements of Kearny's division of Heintzelman's corps began to reach the field and deploy. It seems that Stevens had sent a staff officer to get help from some Union troops he had heard were advancing eastwards on the Warrenton Turnpike. The officer had to plead his case to several generals before he came upon Brigadier General Phil Kearny, commander of Heintzelman's *1st Division*. Kearny quickly agreed to support Stevens, and pulled his command off the Pike in order to march to his date with destiny.

The arrival of Kearny's lead brigade, commanded by Brigadier General David Birney, permitted Stevens' battered units to pull back and try to reorganize. Birney put his seven regiments into action on the western side of the Reid cornfield and started heading for Hill's right flank, held by Branch. The ensuing fight proved to be a strange one as both sides had trouble seeing each other because of the darkness of the storm and often could make out the enemy's position only by the flash of their guns. In addition, a fair number of troops could not fire their weapons because the rain soaked their cartridges.

At the peak of his attack, Birney became concerned that he had no support on his right and went to Kearny to request help. Kearny, who had just reached the field a few minutes before, decided to scout Birney's right in order to see what the problem was, before committing any troops there. He rode into the open field east of the Reid farm, passing on the way the broken battalions of the *79th New York*. He next rode to the position held by the shattered *21st Massachusetts*, whose commander, Captain Charles Walcott, declined to reenter the fight until he had a chance to reorganize first. A few stern words from Kearny (including a threat to turn a nearby battery on the Bay Staters) persuaded Walcott to move forward.

Major General Philip Kearny was killed at Chantilly on 1 September when he rode too close to the Confederate lines during a rainstorm. His death was lamented by fellow officers on both sides.

Walcott's advance, though, was not fast enough to suit Kearny, and he rode forward to rebuke the *21st's* commander for a second time. Walcott now asserted that there were too many Confederates on his front and right to allow an advance. Kearny reportedly uttered a few expletives and then rode forward to show Walcott that there was nothing to fear.

Kearny proceeded to a position about 100 yards from the northern edge of the field, where he ran into a line of troops drawn up in the dim light. "What troops are these?" he called out. "49th Georgia" was the reply. Kearny replied, "All right," and turned to return to his own lines. He did not show fear or rush to safety, since either action would have revealed his Union allegiance. Instead, he just rode quietly off, hoping to escape to safety in this manner.

Kearny had escaped a similar close encounter with Confederate troops during the Peninsula campaign, but was not to be so lucky this time. One of the Georgians shouted, "That's a Yankee officer!" and cried out for him to halt. Kearny responded by spurring his horse to a gallop as he leaned forward Indian style in order to give less of a target to his foes. The technique did not work. A Confederate bullet struck him in the buttocks and passed through all of his vital organs before lodging inside his chest. Kearny fell from his horse and expired. His riderless mount then wandered into the Confederate lines and was taken captive.

Kearny's body was not initially recognized after the battle, largly because its emblems of rank had been picked over by the battlefield thieves who plied their trade after every fight, win or lose. He was at last identified by a captured Union officer. When Jackson was told, he reportedly exclaimed, "You have shot the most gallant officer in the United States army. This is Phil Kearny, who lost his arm in the Mexican War!" A.P. Hill was aghast at the location of the wound and commented, "Poor Kearny, he deserved a much better death than that!" Lee returned the body the next day, along with a brief note for Kearny's widow; many of the general's missing personal effects, along with his horse, were located and returned by Lee a month later at Mrs. Kearny's request. Kearny was first buried at Trinity Church in New York City before being transferred to his present resting place in Arlington National Cemetery.

Kearny's death, which occurred at about 1815, marked the turning point of the battle. Thomas' brigade, to which the 49th Georgia belonged, began a counterattack that drove most of Birney's right back through the cornfield. At around 1830 the two sides began to disengage, even though the rain had begun to stop. By then the sun was setting and it was increasingly difficult to see anything because of the heavy cloud cover.

Both sides received substantial reinforcements after 1830, but neither chose to renew the fight. The remainder of Kearny's division came up, followed by Hooker's, to strengthen the Union forces already on the field. On the Confederate side, Longstreet's command started arriving at 1840. Jackson politely refused their help, and Longstreet turned back, bivouacking most of his troops near Chantilly Crossroads. At about 2300 Jackson withdrew all his troops except for Branch's and Pender's brigades. The Yankees withdrew at about 0230 to a new position that had been prepared on the high ground near Difficult Run, a mile to the east of the battlefield.

Each side ended up claiming a victory the next day. The Confederate claim was based on the fact that they had repulsed all the Yankee attacks and had held possession of the field after the fight. In addition, they had also lost fewer casualties (516 to the Yankees' 679), not to mention the felling of the two Union generals. The Federals, on the other hand, claimed victory because they had succeeded at stopping Jackson's progress and so ensured the safe withdrawal of Pope's command from Centreville to Fairfax. Perhaps the battle is best called a draw. The only thing certain about the battle's immediate outcome was that it would have been longer and bloodier had not the rain and darkness intervened. Neither side directed their troops very well in the engagement: Stevens and Kearny had attacked impetuously against adverse odds (for which they paid with their own lives), and Jackson and Hill did not manage their defense well.

Pope ably used the time gained by the fight at Chantilly (more properly called Ox Hill) to establish a defensive line near Germantown, thereby relieving the Confederate pressure on Fairfax and turning aside Lee's latest attempt to outflank his army. That evening he withdrew the last of his troops from Centreville. At 0730 the next morning (2 September) he was at Fairfax and wrote Halleck a whining letter that made it clear he was now powerless to take the initiative any longer. He complained strongly of the broken down condition of his troops, particularly those from McClellan's command, and stated that he did not anticipate being able to thwart Lee's next flanking move, which he expected to begin at any moment. Halleck and his superiors felt that they now had no choice but to humbly ask McClellan to take command of all the Union troops then in front

Map of the defenses of Washington, to which the Union troops retired after 2nd Bull Run.

of Washington. Lincoln and Halleck went to McClellan in person that morning and begged him to actively assume the command that he had been longing to hold ever since he was recalled from Richmond. McClellan, of course, accepted joyously.

McClellan's appointment, of course, would leave Pope without a command. Late on the morning of 2 September Halleck directed Pope to bring his troops back to Washington and turn them over to McClellan. Lincoln, however, hinted to Pope the next day that McClellan's tenure might only be temporary. This support reinvigorated Pope to offer a proposal on 4 September for the reorganization of a new army under his command, to consist of four corps led by Banks, McDowell, Reno and Hooker. Halleck by now had experienced quite enough of Pope, and on 5 September formally ordered the merger or the *Army of Virginia* into McClellan's *Army of the Potomac*. Pope was to report to headquarters in Washington for "further orders." His term as army commander was over in just ten weeks.

Some would argue that Pope's mission had been essentially an unwinable one: that he had been hamstrung by Halleck to hold the upper Rappahannock line longer than he wanted, and that the lack of cooperation, even treachery, of McClellan and his allies doomed the *Army of Virginia* to failure. The fact remains, however, that Pope had plenty of men to accomplish his mission. However well he conducted the first two-thirds of his campaign, he fell apart at the critical moment when Jackson reached Manassas, and then could not keep track of Longstreet's whereabouts. One bad decision then followed another on 28-30 August, and Pope simply did not manage his men well on the field. The defeat he suffered at Second Bull Run was fully deserved, however much his partisans claim that he won a moral victory by distracting Lee's army and causing the Confederates so large a number of irreplaceable casualties on the eve of their invasion of Maryland. In the last analysis, Pope would have done better to have withdrawn and not fought the battle of Second Bull Run at all. This might have necessitated a bit of explaining to Halleck, but it at least might have kept him in command of his army.

Lee's victory at Second Bull Run, following immediately after his defeat of McClellan's army in the Peninsula campaign, confirmed his position as a master strategist. He used effective strategy to push Pope back from his strong position on the upper Rappahannock and then boldly split up his command in order to send Jackson to Manassas, a move that befuddled Pope more than anyone expected. Lee and his senior lieutenants managed their troops well tactically on the field of Second Bull Run, and came within a hair's breadth of crushing Pope's entire

Monument near the unfinished railroad, dedicated to the Union sol-
diers who fell at 2nd Bull Run. It was erected in 1865 along with a
similar monument on Henry House Hill dedicated to the Union casu-
alties at 1st Bull Run.

army at the end of the battle's second day, the closest that Lee
would come to such a complete success in any battle. In the
process he improved the army's organization measurably and
also used his cavalry and artillery more effectively than in any
other of his battles except possibly Chancellorsville. Most importantly, Lee's victory at Second Bull Run opened the door for
his invasion of Maryland, a maneuver that Lee felt was necessary for political and strategic reasons, even if his command was
already worn out from ten weeks of marching and fighting in
two separate and highly successful major campaigns.

The Battlefields Today

Manassas Battlefield Park today embraces some 5500 acres commemorating the battles of First and Second Bull Run. The Park traces its origins to the 1922 purchase of 128 acres on Henry House Hill by Manassas Battlefield Confederate Park, Inc., and the Sons of Confederate Veterans. This tract was deeded to the United States government in 1938, and was designated as Manassas National Battlefield Park in 1940. The Park was enlarged significantly in 1949 with the purchase of the Stone House and Dogan House properties. The battlefield today includes all the key areas of the Second Bull Run battle from Sudley Springs Ford south to Bald Hill, and from Stuart's Hill and the Brawner Farm east to Henry House Hill. Significant inholdings exist in the Stonewall Memory gardens northeast of Groveton, and in private holdings southeast of Groveton and southeast of Henry House Hill. The two lane Warrenton Turnpike (U.S. 29) remains a busy thoroughfare through the Park, despite the fact that much traffic has been diverted to Interstate 66, which passes over Chinn Ridge and Stuart's Hill on the southern edge of the battle area. In the early 1990s, a major entertainment center was planned by the Disney Corporation for the fields just west of the battleground, but this was defeated by local and national opposition.

The original Stone House and Dogan House are still standing, as is Sudley Church. The original Henry House was destroyed during the war. The unfinished railroad line held by Jackson's troops is still basically in its wartime condition, though the tree lines and fields have changed considerably over the years. There are only a few monuments on the battlefield relating to Second Bull Run, most notably a plaque where Colonel Fletcher Webster fell on Chinn Ridge, and monuments to the 5th and 10th New York regiments on the ground where Warren's brigade was decimated. There are also a few Union regimental markers near the unfinished railroad line. In 1864-1865 the units of Gamble's cavalry brigade erected two memorials to the Union dead at the two battles of Bull Run. These were set up on Henry House Hill and near the Deep Cut, and consisted of a number of artillery shells set on a base supporting a 27 foot tall shaft. They survive today, though the shells have been removed, and are examples of some of the earliest Civil War monuments.

Chantilly battlefield was never preserved as an organized park. In 1915 the veterans of Kearny's New Jersey Brigade erected two monuments to honor the deaths of generals Kearny and Stevens. The battle area was gradually built over through the years until a 1986 housing development consumed almost every remaining portion. It took a massive effort just to preserve the monuments to the two fallen generals on their original site. Today all that remains of the Chantilly battlefield are two acres immediately surrounding the Kearny and Stevens monuments. Hopefully Cedar Mountain battlefield will escape a similar fate. It is unmarked except for a few roadside markers and is in almost as pristine a condition as it was during the war. Perhaps its distance from the urban sprawl of metropolitan Washington will save it until preservationists can arrange the creation of a historic park there.

The Hill We Held for Hooker (Anonymous)

We'd formed out guns for action. for they'd started on the
    right,
Where Sykes had bumped on Jackson and their lines had
    clinched at sight,
While we waited there for Longstreet, who never missed a
    Fight.

An aide-de-camp in short sleeves came lopin' up the hill;-
"You hold this hill for Hooker!" he yells at Captain Bill;
"And mind you hold it longer than you did at Gaines's
    Mill!"

Old Captain Bill made answer; "You boys must have your
    fun,
But we didn't break at Gaines's till all the staff had run;
And we'll hold this hill for Hooker while we've men to
    work a gun."

Across the field below us ripped out the rebel yell
As Longstreet's line of battle came streakin' up the swell,
And we whipped the limbers closer and opened out with
    shell.

But shell was meat for Longstreet; he ate it with his bread,
And so we changed the menu to canister, instead;
And when that didn't stop 'em we let the grapeshot spread.

We pounded 'em to jelly, - but the jelly wouldn't jell;
The powder scorched their faces but they took it like the
    shell,

And they reached our muzzles and tumbled through, pell-
    mell.

It seemed we'd best be goin', with bayonets so near,
When through the woods behind us there rolled a roarin'
    cheer,
And Captain Bill yelled; "Hold 'em; That's Hooker, almost
    here!"

We fought between the sections just like a game of tag;
A Johnny jumped my field-gun and waved a battle-flag;
Bur I lammed him with the gun-swab and dropped him like
    a rag.

They had forced us to the limbers, where the teams were
    tangled thick,
and were pivoting our pieces to teach us our own trick,
When Hooker's boys came through us, deploying double-
    quick.

The Johnnies hung like bulldogs and faced us breast to
    breast,
But Longstreet's men were winded, while Hooker'd had a
    rest,
And when the smoke had lifted we Yankees held the crest.

And Hooker stopped to thank us, and then said Captain Bill;
"They thought we couldn't hold 'em, but General here's
    your hill;-
And I'd like to ask Jim Longstreet if we're quits for Gaines's
    Mill!"

Orders of Battle

CEDAR MOUNTAIN

UNION ARMY	Strength	Losses
ARMY OF VIRGINIA		
II CORPS		
Maj. Gen. N.P. Banks		
FIRST DIVISION	7,650	2,222
Brig. Gen. A.S. Willliams		
First Brigade		867
Brig. Gen Samuel Crawford		
5th Conn., 10th Me., 28th N.Y., 46th Pa.		
Second Brigade		344
Brig. Gen. George H. Gordon		
27th Ind., 2nd Mass., Pa. Zouaves, 3rd Wis.		
SECOND DIVISION	3,150	943
Brig. Gen C.C. Augur (w)		
First Brigade		465
Brig. Gen. John W. Geary (w)		
5th Ohio, 7th Ohio, 29th Ohio, 66th Ohio, 28th Pa.		
Second Brigade,		452
Brig. Gen. Henry Price (c)		
3rd Md., 102nd N.Y., 109th Pa., 111th Pa., 8th & 12th U.S.		
Third Brigade		26
Brig. Gen. George S. Greene		
1st D.C., 78th N.Y.		
Artillery	800	67
Capt. C.L. Best		
4th Me., 6th Me., K 1st N.Y., L 1st N.Y., M 2nd N.Y., 10th N.Y., E Pa., F 4th U.S.		
ARMY OF THE POTOMAC		
III Corps		102
Maj. Gen. Irvin McDowell		
SECOND DIVISION		100
Brig. Gen. James B. Ricketts		
First Brigade		13
Brig. Gen. Abram Duryee		
97th N.Y., 104th N.Y., 105th N.Y., 107th Pa.		

Second Brigade 1
Brig. Gen Zealous B. Tower
    26th N.Y., 94th N.Y., 88th Pa., 90th Pa.
Third Brigade 17
Brig. Gen. George L. Hartsuff
    12th Mass., 13th Mass., 83rd N.Y., 11th Pa.
Fourth Brigade 69
Col. Samuel S. Carroll
    7th Ind., 84th Pa., 110th Pa., 1st W. Va.
Artillery 2
Maj. Davis Tillson
    2nd Me., 5th Me., F 1st Pa., C Pa.
Unattached
    16th Ind. Bat., 13th Pa. Res.
CAVALRY 1,150 79
Brig. Gen. George D. Bayard
    1st Me., 1st N.J., 1st Pa., 1st R.I.
OTAL UNION FORCES 17,900 2,403

	Strength	Losses
ONFEDERATE ARMY		
Iaj. Gen. Thomas J. Jackson		
FIRST DIVISION	5,200	725
Brig. Gen. Charles Winder (k)		
First Brigade		62
Col. Charles A. Ronald		
2nd Va., 4th Va., 5th Va., 27th Va., 33rd Va.		
Second Brigade		331
Lt. Col. Thomas S. Garnett		
21st Va., 42nd Va., 48th Va., 1st Va. Battn.		
Third Brigade		323
Brig. Gen. William B. Taliaferro		
10th Va., 23rd Va., 37th Va., 47th Ala., 48th		
Ala.		
Fourth Brigade		24
Col. Leroy A. Stafford		
2nd La., 9th La., 10th La., 15th La.		
Lawton's Brigade		4
Brig. Gen A.R. Lawton		
13th Ga., 26th Ga., 31st Ga., 38th Ga., 60th		
Ga., 61st Ga.		
Artillery		4
Maj. Snowden Andrews (w)		
Carpenter's Va., Poague's Va., Caskie's		
Va.		
Cavalry	1,200	21
Brig. Gen. Beverly H. Robertson		
7th Va., 17th Va.		

Orders of Battle

LIGHT DIVISION	12,000	448
Maj. Gen. A.P. Hill		
Branch's Brigade		99
Brig. Gen. L. O'B. Branch		
7th N.C., 18th N.C., 28th N.C., 33rd N.C., 37th N.C.		
Archer's Brigade		132
Brig. Gen. James J. Archer		
5th Ala. Battn., 19th Ga., 1st Tenn., 7th Tenn., 14th Tenn.		
Thomas' Brigade		152
Col. Edward L. Thomas		
14th Ga., 35th Ga., 45th Ga., 49th Ga.		
Field's Brigade		13
Brig. Gen. Charles Field		
22 Va. Battn., 40 Va., 47th Va., 5th Va.		
Gregg's Brigade		0
Brig. Gen. Maxcy Gregg		
1st S.C., 12th S.C., 13th S.C., 14th S.C., 1st S.C. Rifles		
Pender's Brigade		15
Brig. Gen. William D. Pender		
16th N.C., 22nd N.C., 34th N.C., 38th N.C.		
Artillery		1
Lt. Col. R.L. Walker		
Pegram's Va. Hardy's Va., Braxton's Va., Latham's N.C.		
THIRD DIVISION	7,200	224
Maj. Gen. Richard S. Ewell		
Fourth Brigade	167	
Brig. Gen. Jubal A. Early		
12th Ga., 13th Va., 25th Va., 31st Va., 44th Va., 52nd Va., 58th Va.		
Seventh Brigade		16
Brig. Gen. Isaac R. Trimble		
15th Ala., 21st Ga., 21st N.C.		
Eighth Brigade		16
Col. Henry Forno		
5th La., 6th La., 7th La., 8th La., 14th La.		
Artillery		25
Maj. A.R. Courtney		
Dement's Md., Brown's Md., D'Aquin's La., Latimer's Va., Terry's Va.		
TOTAL CONFEDERATE FORCES	24,400	1,418

Sources: Krick, *Stonewall Jackson at Cedar Mountain*; Stackpole, *From Cedar Mountain to Antietam*; *Battles and Leaders of the Civil War, Volume II*

SECOND BULL RUN

	Strength	Losses
UNION ARMY **Commander, Maj. Gen. John Pope**		

ARMY OF VIRGINIA

	Strength	Losses
I CORPS	12,500	208
Maj. Gen. Franz Sigel		
FIRST DIVISION	3,800	604
Brig. Gen. Robert Schenck		
First Brigade		169
Brig. Gen. Julius Stahel		
8th N.Y., 41st N.Y., 45th N.Y., 27th Pa., 2nd N.Y Bat.		
Second Brigade		434
Col. Nathaniel C. McLean		
25th Ohio, 55th Ohio, 73rd Ohio, 75th Ohio Bat., K 1st Ohio		
SECOND DIVISION	2,500	401
Brig. Gen. Adolph Von Steinwehr		
First Brigade		401
Col. John A. Koltes (k)		
29th N.Y., 68th N.Y., 73rd Pa.		
THIRD DIVISION	2,800	534
Brig. Gen. Carl Schurz		
First Brigade		158
Brig. Gen. Henry Bohlen (k)		
61st Ohio, 74th Pa., 8th W.Va., Bat. F Pa.		
Second Brigade		372
Col. Wladimir Krzyzanowski		
54th N.Y., 58th N.Y., 75th Pa., Bat. L 2 N.Y.		
Unattached		
Bat. I 1st Ohio		4
INDEPENDENT BRIGADE	2,000	247
Brig. Gen. Robert Milroy		
2nd W.Va., 3rd W.Va., 82nd Ohio, 3 cos. 1st W.VA. Cav., 12th Ohio Bat.		
CAVALRY BRIGADE	1,500	83
Col. John Beardsley		
1st Conn., 1st Md., 4th N.Y., 9th N.Y., 6th Ohio		
RESERVE ARTILLERY	200	26
Capt. Frank Buell (k)		
Bat. I 1st N.Y., 13th N.Y. Bat., Bat. C W.Va.		
II CORPS		
Maj. Gen. Nathaniel P. Banks		

CAVALRY BRIGADE	1,500	200
Brig. Gen. John Buford		
1st Mich., 5th N.Y., 1st W.Va		
III CORPS	20,000	4,840
Maj. Gen. Irvin McDowell		
FIRST DIVISION	9,000	2,728
Brig. Gen. Rufus King		
First Brigade		772
Brig. Gen. John P. Hatch		
22nd N.Y., 24th N.Y., 30th N.Y., 84th N.Y.,		
2nd U.S. S.S.		
Second Brigade		447
Brig. Gen. Abner Doubleday		
56th Pa., 76th N.Y., 95th N.Y.		
Third Brigade		
Brig. Gen. Abner Doubleday		
56th Pa., 76th N.Y., 95th N.Y.		
Third Brigade		568
Brig. Gen. Marsena R. Patrick		
21st N.Y., 23rd N.Y., 35th N.Y., 80th N.Y.		
Fourth Brigade		894
Brig. Gen. John Gibbon		
2nd Wis., 6th Wis., 7th Wis., 19th Ind.		
Artillery		
1st N.H., D 1st R.I., L 1st N.Y. B 4th U.S.		46
SECOND DIVISION	9,000	1,912
Brig. Gen. James Ricketts		
First Brigade		391
Brig. Gen Abram Duryee		
97th N.Y., 104th N.Y., 105th N.Y., 107th Pa.		
Second Brigade		696
Brig. Gen. Zealous B. Tower		
26th N.Y., 94th N.Y., 88th Pa., 90th Pa.		
Third Brigade		657
Brig. Gen. George L. Hartsuff		
12th Mass., 13th Mass., 83rd N.Y., 11th Pa.		
Fourth Brigade		114
Col. Joseph Thoburn (w)		
7th Ind., 84th Pa., 110th Pa., 1st W.Va.		
Artillery		
2nd Me., 5th Me., F 1st Pa., C Pa.		
CAVALRY BRIGADE	1,500	127
Brig. Gen. George D. Bayard		
1st Me., 2nd N.Y., 1st N.J., 1st Pa., 1st R.I.		
REYNOLDS' DIVISION	4,700	676
Brig. Gen. John F. Reynolds		
First Brigade		186
Brig. Gen. George G. Meade		

3rd Pa. Res., 4th Pa. Res., 7th Pa. Res., 8th
Pa. Res., 13th Pa. Res.

Second Brigade   138
Brig. Gen. Truman Seymour
  1st Pa. Res., 2nd Pa. Res., 5th Pa. Res., 6th
Pa. Res.

Third Brigade   287
Brig. Gen. Conrad F. Jackson
  9th Pa. Res., 10th Pa. Res., 11th Pa. Res., 12th
Pa. Res.

Artillery   66
Capt. Dunbar R. Ransom
  A 1st Pa., B 1st Pa., G 1st Pa., C 5th U.S.

UNATTACHED   26
  3rd Me. Bat., 16th Ind. Bat., Bat. E 4th U.S.,
Det. 13th Pa. Res.

RESERVE CORPS   800   222

Brig. Gen. Samuel D. Sturgis
Piatt's Brigade   145
Brig. Gen. A. Sanders Piatt
  63rd Ind., 86th N.Y.

Unattached   77
  2nd N.Y. Heavy Art., 11th N.Y. Bat., Bat. C
1st N.Y.

ARMY OF THE POTOMAC
II CORPS   10,000   2,256

Maj. Gen. Samuel P. Heintzelman
FIRST DIVISION   4,500   1,029

Maj. Gen. Philip Kearny (k)
First Brigade   217
Brig. Gen. John B. Robinson
  20th Ind., 63rd Pa., 105th Pa.

Second Brigade   629
Brig. Gen. David B. Birney
  3rd Me., 4th Me., 1st N.Y., 38th N.Y., 40th
N.Y.

Third Brigade   178
Col. Orlando M. Poe
  37th N.Y., 99th Pa., 2nd Mich., 3rd Mich.,
5th Mich.

Artillery   3
  E 1st R.I., K 1st U.S.

SECOND DIVISION   5,500   1,227

Maj. Gen Joseph Hooker
First Brigade   487
Brig. Gen. Cuvier Grover

2nd N.H., 1st Mass., 11th Mass., 16th Mass.,

26th Pa.

Second Brigade 329

Col. Nelson Taylor

70th N.Y., 71st N.Y., 72nd N.Y., 73rd N.Y.,

74th N.Y.

Third Brigade 393

Col. Nelson B. Carr

2nd N.Y., 5th N.J., 6th N.J., 8th N.J., 115th

Pa.

Artillery 18

6th Me.

V CORPS   10,100   2,151

Maj. Gen. Fitz John Porter

FIRST DIVISION 6,000 1,233

Maj. Gen George W. Morell

First Brigade 576

Col. Charles W. Roberts

2nd Me., 18th Mass., 22nd Mass., 13th N.Y.

25th N.Y., 1st Mich.

Second Brigade 0

Brig. Gen Charles Griffin

9th Mass., 32nd Mass., 4th Mich., 14th N.Y.,

62nd Pa.

Third Brigade 590

Brig. Gen. Daniel Butterfield

12th N.Y., 17th N.Y., 44th N.Y., 83rd Pa.,

16th Mich.

Sharpshooters 61

Col. Hiram Berdan

1st U.S.S.S.

Artillery 400 6

C 1 R.I., D 5 U. S.

SECOND DIVISION 4,100 918

Brig. Gen George Sykes

First Brigade 285

Lt. Col. Robert Buchanan

3rd U.S., 4th U.S., 12th U.S., 14th U.S.

Second Brigade 218

Lt. Col William Chapman

1st U.S., 2nd U.S., 6th U.S., 11th U.S., 17th

U.S.

Third Brigade 412

Col. G.K. Warren

5th N.Y., 10th N.Y.

Artillery 700 3

Capt. Stephen H. Weed

EG 1st U.S., I 5th U.S., K 5th U.S.

	Strengths	Losses
I CORPS		
FIRST DIVISION		
1st Brigade	600	339
Brig. Gen George W. Taylor (k)		
1st N.J., 2nd N.J., 3rd N.J., 4th N.J.		
X CORPS	8,000	1,522
Maj. Gen. Jesse L. Reno		
FIRST DIVISION	4,000	746
Maj. Gen. Isaac I. Stevens (k)		
First Brigade		231
Col. Benjamin C. Christ		
50th Pa., 8th Mich.		
Second Brigade		163
Col. Daniel Leasure		
46th N.Y., 100th Pa.		
Third Brigade		339
Col. Addison Farnsworth (w)		
28th Mass., 79th N.Y.		
Artillery		13
8th Mass., E 2nd U.S.		
SECOND DIVISION	4,000	776
Maj. Gen. Jesse L. Reno		
First Brigade		518
Col. James Nagle		
6th N.H., 48th Pa., 2nd Md.		
Second Brigade		258
Col. Edward Ferrero		
21st Mass., 51st N.Y., 51st Pa.		
KANAWHA DIVISION	1,800	106
First Provisional Brigade		106
Col. E. Parker Scammon		
11th Ohio, 12th Ohio		
Unattached		
30th Ohio, 36th Ohio		
UNION TOTAL	77,000	14,449

	Strengths	Losses
CONFEDERATE ARMY		
ARMY OF NORTHERN VIRGINIA		
Commander, Gen. Robert E. Lee		
RIGHT WING	27,800	4,668
Maj. Gen. James Longstreet		

ANDERSON'S DIVISION	7,000	344
Maj. Gen. R.H. Anderson		
Armistead's Brigade		20
Brig. Gen. Lewis A. Armistead		
9th Va., 14th Va., 38th Va., 53rd Va., 57th Va., 5th Va. Batn		
Mahone's Brigade		234
Brig. Gen. William Mahone		
6th Va., 12th Va., 16th Va., 41st Va.		
Wright's Brigade		190
Brig. Gen. Ambrose R. Wright		
44th Ala., 3rd Ga., 22nd Ga., 48th Ga.		
JONES' DIVISION	5,200	1,270
Brig Gen. David R. Jones		
Toombs' Brigade		367
Col. Henry L. Benning		
2nd Ga., 15th Ga., 17th Ga., 20th Ga.		
Drayton's Brigade		93
Brig. Gen. Thomas F. Drayton		
50th Ga., 51st Ga., 15th S.C., Phillips' Ga. Legion		
G.T. Anderson's Brigade		809
Col. George T. Anderson		
1st Ga., 7th Ga., 8th Ga., 9th. Ga., 11th Ga.		
WILCOX'S DIVISION	4,000	333
Brig. Gen Cadmus M. Wilcox		
Wilcox's Brigade		70
Brig. Gen. Cadmus M. Wilcox		
8th Ala., 9th Ala., 10th Ala., 11th Ala., E.J. Anderson's Va. Bat.		
Pryor's Brigade		95
Brig. Gen. Roger A. Pryor		
14th Ala., 5th Fla., 8th Fla., 3rd Va.		
Featherston's Brigade		168
Brig. Gen. W.S. Featherston		
12th Miss., 16th Miss., 19th Miss., 2nd Miss. Batn., Chapman's Va. Bat.		
HOOD'S DIVISION	3,800	972
Brig. Gen. John B. Hood		
Hood's Brigade		638
Brig. Gen. John B. Hood		
18th Ga., Hampton S.C. Legion, 1st Tex., 4th Tex., 5th Tex.		

Law's Brigade   324
Col. E.M. Law

    4th Ala., 2nd Miss., 11th Miss., 6th N.C.

Artillery   10
Maj. B.W. Frobel

    Bachman's S.C. Bat., Garden's S.C. Battery,
    Reilly's N.C. Battery

KEMPER'S DIVISION   4,000   977
Brig. Gen. James L. Kemper

Corse's Brigade   274
Col. Montgomery D. Corse (w)

    1st Va., 7th Va., 11th Va., 17th Va., 24th Va.

Jenkins' Brigade   469
Brig. Gen. Micah Jenkins (w)

    1st S.C., 2nd S.C. Rifles, 5th S.C., 6th S.C.,
    4th S.C. Batn., Palmetto S.C. Sharpshooters

Pickett's Brigade   434
Col. Eppa Hunton

    8th Va., 18th Va., 19th Va., 28th Va., 56th Va.

EVAN'S INDEPENDENT BRIGADE   2,200   734
Brig. Gen. Nathan G. Evans

    17th S.C., 18th S.C., 22nd S.C., 23rd S.C.,
    Holcombe S.C. Legion, Boyce's S.C. Bat.

ARTILLERY   2,500   38

Washington (La.) Artillery   32
Col. John B. Walton

    Squires' Bat., Richardson's Bat., Miller's
    Bat., Eshleman's Bat.

S.D. Lee's Battalion   6
Col. Stephen D. Lee

    Eubank's Va. Bat., Grimes' Va. Bat., Jordan's
    Va. Bat., Parker's Va. Bat., Taylor's Va. Bat.

Miscellaneous

    Huger's Va. Bat., Leake's Va. Bat.,
    Donaldsonville La. Art., Moorman's Va.
    Bat., Rogers' Va. Bat., Stribling's Va. Bat.

EFT WING   24,200   4,518

1aj. Gen. Thomas J. Jackson

JACKSON'S DIVISION   5,000   1,106
Brig Gen. William B. Taliaferro (w)

First Brigade   411
Col. W.S.H. Baylor (k)

2nd Va., 4th Va., 5th Va., 27th Ba., 33rd Va.

Second Brigade   120
Col. Bradley T. Johnson
    21st Va., 42nd Va., 48th Va., 1st Va. Batn.

Third Brigade   169
Col. Alexander G. Taliaferro
    47th Ala., 48th Ala., 10th Va., 23rd Va., 37th
    Va.

Fourth Brigade   385
Brig. Gen. W.E. Starke
    1st La., 2nd La., 9th La., 10th La., 15th La.,
    Coppens' La. Batn.

Artillery   21
Maj. L.M. Shumaker
    Brockenbrough's Md. Bat., Carpenter's Va.
    Bat., Caskie's Va. Bat., Cutshaw's Va. Bat.,
    Poague's Va. Bat., Raine's Va. Bat., Rice's
    Va. Bat., Woodring's Va. Bat.

LIGHT DIVISION   12,000   1,845
Maj. Gen. A.P. Hill

Branch's Brigade   327
Brig. Gen. L. O'B. Branch
    7th N.C., 18th N.C., 28th N.C., 33rd N.C.,
    37th N.C.

Pender's Brigade   223
Brig. Gen. William D. Pender
    16th N.C., 22nd N.C., 34th N.C., 38th N.C.

Thomas' Brigade ·   232
Col. Edward L. Thomas
    14th Ga., 35th Ga., 45th Ga., 49th Ga.

Gregg's Brigade, Brig. Gen. Maxcy Gregg   722
    1st S.C., 1st S.C. Rifles, 12th S.C., 13th S.C.,
    14th S.C.

Archer's Brigade   234
Brig. Gen. James J. Archer
    5th Ala. Batn., 19th Ga., 1st Tenn., 7th Tenn.,
    14th Tenn.

Field's Brigade   95
Brig. Gen. Charles Field (w)
    40th Va., 47th Va., 55th Va., 22nd Va. Batn.

Artillery   12
Lt. Col. R.L. Walker

Braxton's Va. Bat., Crenshaw's Va. Bat., Davidson's Va. Bat., Hardy's Va. Bat., Potts' N.C. Bat., McIntosh's S.C. Bat., Pegram's Va. Bat.

EWELL'S DIVISION   7,200   1,567
Maj. Gen Richard S. Ewell (w)

Lawton's Brigade   512
Brig. Gen. A.R. Lawton
13th Ga., 26th Ga., 31st Ga., 38th Ga., 60th Ga., 61st Ga.

Trimble's Brigade   447
Brig. Gen. Isaac R. Trimble (w)
15th Ala., 12th Ga., 21st Ga., 21st N.C., 1st N.C. Batn.

Early's Brigade   220
Brig. Gen. Jubal A. Early
13th Va., 25th Va., 31st Va., 44th Va., 49th Va., 52nd Va.

Forno's Brigade   361
Col. Henry Forno (w)
5th La., 6th La., 7th La., 8th La., 14th La.

Artillery   27
Garber's Va. Bat., Brown's Md. Bat., D'Aquin's La. Bat., Dement's La. Bat., Johnson's Va. Bat., Latimer's Va. Bat.

CAVALRY DIVISION   3,000
Maj. Gen. James E.B. Stuart

Robertson's Brigade   114
Brig. Gen Beverly H. Robertson
2nd Va., 6th Va., 7th Va., 12th Va., 17th Va. Batn.

F. Lee's Brigade   no
Brig. Gen. Fitzhugh Lee   report
1st Va., 3rd Va., 4th Va., 9th Va.

Artillery
Pelham's Va. Bat   6

RMY TOTAL   55,000   9,420

rces: Stackpole, *From Cedar Mountain to Antietam; Battles and Leaders of the Civil*; *Volume II*

GREATEST CONFEDERATE LOSSES AT SECOND MANASSAS
(Figures include Groveton and Chantilly)

UNIT	Brigade/Division	Killed	Wounded	Missing	Tot
5th Texas	Wofford/Hood	15	224	1	240
11th Georgia	Anderson/Jones	20	178		198
17th South Carolina	Evans	15	163	1	189
21st Georgia	Trimble/Ewell	38	146		184
13th South Carolina	Gregg/Hill	31	142		173
12th South Carolina	Gregg/Hill	15	131		156
Holcombe Legion	Evans	24	131		155
1st South Carolina	Gregg/Hill	25	126		151
18th Georgia	Wofford/Hood	19	133		152
23rd South Carolina	Evans	27	122		149
1st South Carolina Rifles	Gregg/Hill	24	122		146
20th Georgia	Toombs/Jones	19	113		132
9th Georgia	Anderson/Jones	12	116		128
26th Georgia	Lawton/Ewell	37	87		124
60th Georgia	Lawton/Ewell	22	101		123
6th South Carolina	Jenkins/Pickett	13	102		115
15th Alabama	Trimble/Ewell	21	91		112
2nd Louisiana	Starke/Jackson	25	86		111

GREATEST CONFEDERATE LOSSES AT CEDAR MOUNTAIN

UNIT	Brigade/Division	Killed	Wounded	Missing	Tot
21st Virginia	Jones/Jackson	37	85		122
42nd Virginia	Jones/Jackson	36	71		107
37th Virginia	Taliaferro/Jackson	12	76		88
47th Alabama	Taliaferro/Jackson	12	76		88
48th Alabama	Taliaferro/Jackson	12	61		7?

GREATEST CONFEDERATE PERCENTAGE LOSSES AT SECOND MANASS

UNIT	Division	Engaged	Killed	Wounded	Missing	%
21st Georgia	Ewell	242	38	146		76.
17th South Carolina	Evans	284	25	164	1	66.
23rd South Carolina	Evans	225	27	122		66.
12th South Carolina	Hill	270	23	121	2	54.
4th Virginia	Jackson	180	16	84	12	53.
1st South Carolina	Hill	283	25	126		53.
17th Georgia	Hood	200	10	91		50.

GREATEST UNION LOSSES AT SECOND MANASSAS
(Includes Groveton and Chantilly)

UNITS	Division/Corps	Killed	Wounded	Missing	Total
d Wisconsin	Hatch/I	53	213	32	298
ì New York	Sykes/V	79	170	48	297
th New York	Hatch/I	32	165	82	279
th Indiana	Hatch/I	47	168	44	259
th Pennsylvania	Ricketts/I	44	114	88	246
th New York	Hatch/I	36	115	86	237
th Massachusetts	Stevens/IX	33	188	13	234
ì Wisconsin	Hatch/I	31	153	33	217
ì New Hampshire	Reno/IX	30	117	70	217
t Michigan	Morell/V	33	114	31	178
th Massachusetts	Morell/V	34	106	29	169
th New York	Ricketts/I	26	106	37	169

GREATEST UNION LOSSES AT CEDAR MOUNTAIN

UNIT	Division/Corps	Killed	Wounded	Missing	Total
th Pennsylvania	Williams/II Va.	31	102	111	244
d Massachusetts	Williams/II Va.	40	93	40	172
ì Ohio	Augur/II Va.	31	149	2	182
th Maine	Williams/II Va.	24	145	4	172

GREATEST UNION PERCENTAGE LOSSES AT SECOND MANASSAS
(Includes Groveton and Chantilly)

UNIT	Corp	Engaged	Killed	Wounded	Missing	%
1st New York	III A.P.	168	6	101	17	73.8
ì New York	V	490	79	170	48	60.6
d Wisconsin	I	511	53	213	32	58.3
t Michigan	V	320	33	114	31	55.6

GREATEST LOSS IN KILLED AT SECOND MANASSAS
(Includes Groveton and Chantilly)

UNIT	Division	Corps	Killed	Engage
5th New York	Sykes	V	117**	490
11th Pennsylvania	Ricketts	I	72	
6th New Hampshire	Reno	IX	67	450
30th New York	Hatch	I	66	341
19th Indiana	Hatch	I	62	423
28th Massachusetts	Stevens	IX	56	
21st New York	Hatch	I	54	
18th Massachusetts	Morell	V	54	421
1st Michigan	Morell	V	54	320
80th New York	Hatch	I	51	

**Greatest loss in killed by any single Union infantry regiment in one battle in war.

Source for data on all charts: William Fox, *Regimental Losses in the American Civil Wc*

Guide for the Interested Reader

*T*he Second Bull Run campaign has not been the subject of a detailed scholarly study until relatively recent days. The first two significant accounts of the battle were decidedly pro-Union in outlook, and were affected by the authors' biases as well as by the fact that not all the official battle reports had yet been published, nor had the Porter case yet been retried. George H. Gordon's *History of the Campaign of the Army of Virginia under John Pope* (Cambridge, 1880), is a good narrative by one of the campaign's minor participants (Gordon commanded a brigade at Cedar Mountain), but it is at times marred by the author's dislike for Pope. John C. Ropes' *The Army under Pope* (New York, 1881), is very dry and also slightly opinionated as the author casts as much blame on Halleck as on Pope, and generally supports Porter and McClellan.

The Confederate view of the campaign was not presented in depth until Douglas S. Freeman's excellent narrative *From Cedar Mountain to Chancellorsville*, Volume 2 of his classic study, *Lee's Lieutenants* (New York, 1943). The first balanced account stressing both sides equally did not appear until the Civil War Centennial, when Edward J. Stackpole wrote *From Cedar Mountain to Antietam* (Harrisburg, 1962). This book, which is an operational study at the divisional level, reads very easily and has 38 excellent situation maps by Wilbur Nye. It tends to eulogize Lee, Jackson and Longstreet while being quite critical of Pope.

By far the most balanced, detailed, and analytical study of the campaign is John J. Hennessy's classic study, *Return to Bull Run* (New York, 1993), which completely overshadows all previous accounts of the battle. It is based on solid scholarly research into the battle's extensive supply of primary sources, and deals with all the principal commanders fairly, treating their strengths as well as their mistakes. It also is well supplied with detailed maps. The book's only weakness is that it does not deal with Cedar Mountain and Chantilly with the same detail as the fighting at Bull Run.

The battle of Cedar Mountain, though, has been the subject of a recent significant monograph by Robert K. Krick, *Stonewall Jackson at Cedar Mountain* (Chapel Hill, 1990). This study is almost overwhelming in its detail, and dovetails nicely with Hennesy's campaign study. The fight at Chantilly is yet to see thorough analysis. Perhaps the best recent account of the battle is a lengthy article by Joseph A. Whitehorne in the May 1987 issue of *Blue & Gray Magazine*.

Due to the complexities of the campaign, it is recommended to refer to a good set of maps that update the action frequently. The best reference maps for the campaign are those in *The West Point Atlas of the Civil War* by Vincent Esposito (New York, 1959), and the situation maps in Stackpole's *From Cedar Mountain to Antietam*, already cited. For the battle itself, nothing can beat the highly detailed set of 13 by 20 inch maps prepared for the National Park Service in 1985 by John J. Hennessy. These have been issued for the general public along with Hennessy's descriptive unit by unit commentary under the title *Second Manassas Battlefield Map Study* (Lynchburg, n.d.).

Much of one's understanding of the campaign depends on how John Pope's activities are interpreted. Pope defended himself in several publications, including his official battle report (submitted on 27 January 1863) and in a much longer report sent to Secretary of War Stanton, which was published among the Excutive Documents of the 37th Congress (1863). He also testified at the Porter court-martial, and wrote a lengthy article entitled "The Second Battle of Bull Run" for the *Century Magazine* in the 1880s.

Pope's view of events, understandably, is always distorted in his favor. It is also regrettable that the only full length biography done on Pope, *Abandoned by Lincoln*, by Wallace J. Schutz and Walter N. Trenery (Chicago, 1990), is quite defensive and apologetic. Most historians through the years have been critical of Pope's handling of the campaign, with comments bearing from sympathetic (John C. Ropes in *The Campaign under Pope*) to caustic (Bruce Catton in *A Centennial History of the Civil War* and Shelby Foote in *The Civil War, A Narrative*). The only other recent historian to be supportive of Pope is Kenneth P. Williams, in *Lincoln Finds a General* (New York, 1949).

Not much has been written about Pope's principal lieutenants, most of whom soon disappeared from the center of the war's action. On Banks, see *Fighting Politician*, by Fred Harrington (Philadelphia, 1948); no modern biographies of McDowell or Sigel have been written. McClellan's complex personality is dealt with in *George B. McClellan, The Young Napoleon*, by Stephen W. Sears (New York, 1988), and Halleck's life can be reviewed in *Halleck, Lincoln's Chief of Staff*, by Stephen Ambrose (Baton Rouge, 1961). For the roles of selected secondary Union figures in the campaign, see the following: *General John Buford*, by Edward G. Longacre (Conshohocken, Pa., 1995); *Personal Recollections of the Civil War*, by John Gibbon (New York, 1928); *Kearny the Magnificent*, by Irving Werstein (New York, 1961), and *Meade of Gettysburg*, by Freeman Cleaves (Norman, Ok., 1960).

Two of the leading Confederate participants in the campaign never wrote an account of their role beyond their official battle reports. Lee chose not to write any military memoirs, and Jackson died a little over eight months after the battle. For a good analysis of Lee's participation, see Douglas S. Freeman's classic biography *R.E. Lee* (New York, 1934), and more recently, *Robert E. Lee, A Biography*, by Emory Thomas (New York, 1995). There are several good biographies of Jackson available, including *Mighty Stonewall*, by Frank Vandiver (New York, 1957). Longstreet was the only top Confederate commander to write extensively on the campaign. He was the author of a *Century Magazine* article, "Our March Against Pope," now in *Battles and*

Leaders of the Civil War, and then wrote a slightly defensive autobiography, *From Manassas to Appomattox* (Philadelphia, 1896). An excellent modern biography of him is *General James Longstreet* by Jeffrey Wert (New York, 1993). Other Confederate biographies of interest include: *General A.P. Hill, The Story of a Confederate Warrior,* by James Robertson (New York, 1987); *The Gallant Hood,* by John Dyer (New York, 1950); *Bold Dragoon, The Life of J.E.B. Stuart,* by Emory Thomas (New York, 1986); and Ewell's biography, *The Road to Glory,* by Samuel Martin (Indianapolis, 1991).

Fitz John Porter's court-martial has generated perhaps more controversy than any other Civil War topic except those connected with Gettysburg. The proceedings of the original 1862-1863 court were published as a 1143 page supplement to Series I, Volume 12, Part II of *The War of the Rebellion, Official Records of the Union and Confederate Armies* (Washington, 1886), and the evidence taken by the Schofield inquiry was published as an Executive Document of the Senate (Washington, 1879). A detailed review of the Porter case, largely sympathetic to the general, can be found in *The Celebrated Case of Fitz John Porter,* by Otto Eisenschiml (New York, 1950).

The battle reports submitted by most of the campaign's leading officers can be found in Volume 12 of *War of the Rebellion, The Official Records of the Union and Confederate Armies* (Washington, 1885). Several good accounts of different aspects of the campaign were written by Pope, Longstreet, W.B. Taliaferro, and others for the *Century Magazine* in the 1880s; these were reissued in Volume 2 of *Battles and Leaders of the Civil War* (New York, 1889). An interesting collection of assorted primary sources on the campaign can be found in *Voices of the Civil War: Second Manassas* (Time Life, 1995).

The role of the Union artillery in the battle is narrated by L. Van Loan Naisawald in *Grape and Canister* (New York, 1960), and that of the Confederate artillery by Jennings Cropper Wise in *The Long Arm of Lee* (Lynchburg, 1915). For the activity of the Union cavalry in the campaign, see *The Union Cavalry in the Civil War,* by Stephen Starr (Baton Rouge, 1979). The following selected unit histories contain interesting accounts of different important commands during the campaign: *Camp and Field Life*

in the Fifth New York Volunteer Infantry (Duryea Zouaves), by
Alfred Davenport (New York, 1879); *History of the 88th Pennsyl-
vania*, by John Vautier (Philadelphia, 1894); *The Iron Brigade*, by
Alan T. Nolan (New York, 1961); *One of Jackson's Foot Cavalry*, by
John Worsham (New York, 1912); *The History of a Brigade of South
Carolinians (Gregg's)*, by J.F.J. Caldwell; and *History of the Doles-
Cook Brigade*, by Henry Thomas (Atlanta, 1903).

Wargames

The Second Bull Run Campaign has been the subject of
several wargames, but not anywhere near as many as Gettysburg and some of the war's other major engagements. Chief
among these is the "monster" regimental level *Road to Washington* by Command Perspectives (1979). *Cedar Mountain: Prelude to
Bull Run* (*Strategy & Tactics*, No. 86, 1981), is an accurate and
much less complicated one map game.

Other Literature

The Second Bull Run Campaign was the setting for a major
modern novel, *Unto this Hour*, by Tom Wicker (New York, 1984).
The battle did not inspire any poetry of note beyond an
anonymous piece entitled "The Hill We Held for Hooker."

Genealogical and Study Groups

Most major urban areas now have study groups called Civil
War Round Tables, which sponsor speakers and interesting
debate on the war. For a list of Round Tables in your area, write
to Civil War Round Table Associates, PO Box 7388, Little Rock,
Arkansas, 72217. The Sons of Confederate Veterans and Sons of
Union Veterans are also active in this area. For the S.C.V., contact
P.O. Box 41818, Houston, Texas, 77241. The S.U.V. can be reached
by contacting the author of this book, care of the publisher.

Index